Shakespeare & the Modern Novel

Shakespeare &

Series Editor:
Graham Holderness, *University of Hertfordshire*

Volume 11
Shakespeare & the Modern Novel
Edited by Graham Holderness

Volume 10
Shakespeare & Social Engagement
Edited by Rowan Mackenzie and Robert Shaughnessy

Volume 9
Shakespeare & the First Hamlet
Edited by Terri Bourus

Volume 8
Shakespeare & Biography
Edited by Katherine Scheil and Graham Holderness

Volume 7
Shakespeare & Money
Edited by Graham Holderness

Volume 6
Shakespeare & His Biographical Afterlives
Edited by Paul Franssen and Paul Edmondson

Volume 5
Shakespeare & the Ethics of War
Edited by Patrick Gray

Volume 4
Shakespeare & Creative Criticism
Edited by Rob Conkie and Scott Maisano

Volume 3
Shakespeare & the Arab World
Edited by Katherine Hennessey and Margaret Litvin

Volume 2
Shakespeare & Commemoration
Edited by Clara Calvo and Ton Hoenselaars

Volume 1
Shakespeare & Stratford
Edited by Katherine Scheil

Shakespeare & the Modern Novel

Edited by
Graham Holderness

berghahn
NEW YORK · OXFORD
www.berghahnbooks.com

First published in 2025 by
Berghahn Books
www.berghahnbooks.com

© 2025 Berghahn Books

Originally published as a special issue of *Critical Survey*:
volume 33, issue 2, unless otherwise noted.

All rights reserved. Except for the quotation of short passages
for the purposes of criticism and review, no part of this book
may be reproduced in any form or by any means, electronic or
mechanical, including photocopying, recording, or any information
storage and retrieval system now known or to be invented,
without written permission of the publisher.

Library of Congress Cataloging-in-Publication Data

Names: Holderness, Graham, editor.
Title: Shakespeare & the modern novel / edited by Graham Holderness.
Other titles: Shakespeare and the modern novel
Description: New York : Berghahn, 2024. | Series: Shakespeare & ; volume 11 | Includes bibliographical references and index.
Identifiers: LCCN 2024013507 (print) | LCCN 2024013508 (ebook) | ISBN 9781805397014 (hardback) | ISBN 9781805397021 (paperback) | ISBN 9781805397038 (epub) | ISBN 9781805397090 (adobe pdf)
Subjects: LCSH: Shakespeare, William, 1564–1616—Adaptations—History and criticism. | Shakespeare, William, 1564–1616—Influence. | Fiction—History and criticism. | LCGFT: Literary criticism.
Classification: LCC PR2880.A1 S46 2024 (print) | LCC PR2880.A1 (ebook) | DDC 822.3/3—dc23/eng/20240604
LC record available at https://lccn.loc.gov/2024013507
LC ebook record available at https://lccn.loc.gov/2024013508

British Library Cataloguing in Publication Data

A catalogue record for this book is available from the British Library

ISBN 978-1-80539-701-4 hardback
ISBN 978-1-80539-702-1 paperback
ISBN 978-1-80539-703-8 epub
ISBN 978-1-80539-709-0 web pdf

https://doi.org/10.3167/9781805397014

Contents

Introduction   1
Graham Holderness

Chapter 1
'All the world's a [post-apocalyptic] stage'   6
The Future of Shakespeare in Emily St. John Mandel's Station Eleven
Charles Conaway

Chapter 2
Ian McEwan Celebrates Shakespeare   27
Hamlet *in a* Nutshell
Elena Bandín and Elisa González

Chapter 3
Modernising Misogyny in Shakespeare's *Shrew*   44
Natalie K. Eschenbaum

Chapter 4
Almost Shakespeare – But Not Quite   58
Keith Jones

Chapter 5
Canon Fodder and Conscripted Genres   68
The Hogarth Project and the Modern Shakespeare Novel
Laurie E. Osborne

Chapter 6
Loving Shakespeare   86
Anne Tyler's Vinegar Girl *and the Hogarth Shakespeare Project*
Elizabeth Rivlin

Chapter 7
Millennial Dark Ladies
Katherine Scheil
104

Chapter 8
Flights of Fancy and the Dissolution of Shakespearean Space-Time in Angela Carter's *Nights at the Circus*
Kate Myers
121

Chapter 9
Hamlet's Displacement as a Recurrent Case in Cather's *A Lost Lady* and Al Halaby's *Once in a Promised Land*
Tareq Zuhair
137

Chapter 10
Susan Abulhawa's Appropriation of Shakespeare's *Romeo and Juliet*
Yousef Abu Amrieh
156

Index
179

Introduction
Shakespeare and the Modern Novel

Graham Holderness

When I first studied the novel, the form was believed to have originated in the eighteenth century with the fiction of Daniel Defoe, Henry Fielding and Samuel Richardson, and was synonymous with literary realism. The novel emerged from the Age of Reason, was closely associated with journalism, satire and conduct literature, and marked a profound break with the supernatural, fantastic and romance narratives of the past. Its perfect embodiment was to be found in the work of Jane Austen, even today an immensely popular writer, and widely regarded as a defining practitioner of the novel form. This kind of novel was/is in every respect different from Shakespeare: new, 'novel', not old; prose, not poetry; narrative, not dramatic; realist, not magical; fictional, not metafictional; and could deal with Shakespeare only as an objective feature of the society and culture being represented.

This restrictive view of the novel, invented by literary historians and critics, is still to be found in the reviewing practices of the quality press, and in the shortlists of prestigious literary prizes. But there is a huge gap between this highbrow conception of the novel, as a kind of ethically-informed social and psychological realism, and the actual practice and popularity of the form. A list of the best-selling novels of all time published in the *Guardian* was easily dominated by thrillers, magic, erotica and the Gothic: by Dan Brown, J. K. Rowling, E. L. James and Stephanie Meyer. The novel encompasses both literary and popular fiction, and as such flourishes in a myriad of different genres: adventure, crime, romance, history, supernatural, Gothic, enchantment, utopian, dystopic, pornographic and so on. In addition, its form allows for the widest possible range of artistic experimentation, and for creative engagement with other media such as film, visual art and digital technologies.

This diversity and flexibility of the novel form suggests that the notion of its history as coterminous with modernity is simply false, since long narratives of fantasy, romance and historical fiction go back some two thousand years, and flourished in the classical, medieval and early-modern worlds. The term 'novel' derives from the Italian *novella*, a form of short story popular in the Renaissance, and which provided the plots for most of Shakespeare's comedies, and some tragedies. If the fictional prose narratives of Boccaccio, Bandello and Cinthio were 'novels', then the first link between Shakespeare and the novel is that many of his plays were initially derivative of the form. The novel is already inside Shakespeare, before we start to consider his subsequent impact on what we now know as the novel.

Shakespeare was able to incorporate plots, characters and themes from Italian novellas because the form of drama he practised was as diverse and varied as is our contemporary popular fiction, and his plays thrived on the imaginative plenitude and aesthetic flexibility of romance, adventure, enchantment, verbal extravagance and metafiction. The early practitioners of what we may call the 'modern novel' in the eighteenth century, basing their stories in the reality of contemporary life, could not adapt Shakespeare's works in the way that Shakespeare appropriated the Italian novel.

In our own twenty-first century, the Shakespearean novel is undergoing a Renaissance. The long prose narrative has been energised by interfaces with different media, especially TV, film and the internet. New methods of publishing and consuming literature have transformed the nature of readership into an interactive participation. The postmodern collapsing of generic restrictions has enabled Shakespeare to migrate much more comprehensively across previously sealed boundaries, into popular genres such as crime fiction, paranormal romance, dystopian fable and supernatural fantasy. In contemporary fiction, Shakespeare himself is as likely to be found killing zombies or vampires as writing poems and plays. Major fiction writers have based whole novels on Shakespeare plays. *Lunar Park* (2005) by American Brett Easton Ellis, *101 Reykjavik* (1996, trans. 2002) by Icelander Hallgrimur Helgason, and *Something Rotten* (2004) by British author Jasper Fforde are all direct and explicit reworkings of *Hamlet*. In a landmark publishing initiative currently in progress, the Hogarth Press has commissioned a pantheon of top fiction authors to write novels based on specific Shakespeare plays, some of them discussed in this issue. This powerful and cosmopolitan team of authors, whose work encompasses a wide range of fictional styles, will undoubtedly consolidate the status of the Shakespearean novel as a global phenomenon for the twenty-first century. Fiction writers now can imitate and adapt Shakespeare's plays as easily as he was able to adapt the novel into drama. Over four centuries, Shakespeare's plays have undergone some remarkable transformations, but none so striking as the gradual evolution of the novel form to a point where Shakespeare, poet and playwright of yesterday, could be so readily and successfully incorporated into the fiction of today.

This book provides space for a number of distinguished Shakespeare critics to reflect on the interactions between Shakespeare and the modern novel. Charles Conaway discusses Emily St. John Mandel's 2014 novel, *Station Eleven*, set in a world without electricity, motorised transportation, modern technology and abundant resources, and focused on a small troupe of actors and musicians who perform concerts and stage Shakespeare's plays in the scattered communities of survivors of an influenza pandemic. The novel dramatises a constant struggle for survival, and probes, from a variety of perspectives, the notion that Beethoven and Shakespeare can enrich our lives in post-apocalyptic times. Elena Bandín and Elisa González analyse Ian McEwan's *Nutshell*, published in September 2016 on the occasion of the fourth centenary of Shakespeare's death, as a modern rewriting of *Hamlet*. The novel attempts to fill an important gap that Shakespeare left unclear and unexplained and that is integral in reconfiguring the meaning of the play: the love triangle of Gertrude, Claudius and King Hamlet. Natalie Eschenbaum considers how Anne Tyler's novel *Vinegar Girl* (Hogarth Press, 2016) adopts and adapts the critical debate concerning misogyny in Shakespeare's *Taming of the Shrew*. She considers Tyler's purposeful use of the powerful term 'girl' to show how the taming plot is modernised, but remains misogynistic. *Vinegar Girl* reveals how *any* tale about taming a woman has an underlying message of male dominance. Keith Jones also considers Emily St. John Mandel's *Station Eleven* together with Gary Schmidt's *Wednesday Wars* as test cases to explore generic considerations in modern novels that employ Shakespeare, but do not retell or recast the plot of any particular work by Shakespeare. Questions to be considered include how the works employ the Shakespearean genres of comedy, tragedy, history, romance and tragicomedy to create their own genres – and, conceivably, to transcend them.

Laurie Osborne shows how the *Hogarth Shakespeare* novels bring into focus several features emerging in the encounter between Shakespeare and fiction writing, and so both contributes to, and emphasises, Shakespeare's participation in the three zones of cultural capital: our individual and collective artistic investment in series, culturally provoked shifts in adaptive choice, and evolving genres that increasingly test former lines between literary and genre fiction. Elizabeth Rivlin also focuses on Anne Tyler's *Vinegar Girl* to explore how both the novel and the Hogarth series seek to create affective 'middlebrow' communities that purport to keep Shakespeare alive through love. This analysis helps to clarify the nature of the Hogarth Shakespeare Project as a middlebrow publishing enterprise, not in any pejorative sense, but in the sense that it uses Shakespeare to cultivate large, expansive communities built on the relationship between the adapting author and her readers. Katherine Scheil shows how the Dark Lady of the Sonnets has become a central figure in millennial novels by women writers, designed primarily for a female reading audience. Meredith Whitford's *Shakespeare's Will* (2010), Alexa Schnee's *Shakespeare's Lady* (2012), Victoria Lamb's *His Dark Lady* (2013), Grace Tiffany's *Paint: A Novel of Shakespeare's Dark Lady* (2013), Sally O'Reilly's *Dark Aemelia* (2014), Andrea Chapin's *The Tutor* (2015) and Mary Sharratt's *The Dark Lady's Mask* (2016) all explore the possible identity and role of a Dark Lady in Shakespeare's artistic and (often intimate) personal life. This article considers what's at stake by placing this imaginary woman at the heart of Shakespeare's artistic inspiration, and what this tells us about the meaning(s) of 'Shakespeare' for contemporary women writers and readers. Kate Myers examines Shakespeare's influence on Angela Carter's earlier novel *Nights at the Circus*, which like *Wise Children* builds a bricolage of Shakespearean allusions, but more subtly reconsiders the ontological issues of legitimacy by returning to Shakespeare's interest in ambiguity, in deniability, in time, and in space. Carter, she argues, reverses time and dismembers space to criticise the masculine-made-legitimate at the expense of the feminine, which Shakespeare's temporal and spatial manipulations ultimately uphold.

Tareq Zuhair explores how displacement in Shakespeare's *Hamlet* is tacitly approached, and how this reaction has become a recurrent case in Willa Cather's *A Lost Lady* (1923) and Laila Al Halaby's *Once in a Promised Land* (2007). Freudian neurosis, despite being a psychological disorder rather than a literary topic, has been used in literature to conceptualise characters' suffering. Freud contends that the suppression of desires due to hidden and unhidden causes leads to neurosis. Being unable to succeed in life, individuals feel neurotic and tend to displace their frustrations onto other persons or objects. This chapter analyses the incentives of neurosis in each work, how these reasons lead to the onset of displacement and how literary works share relatively similar implications about displacement despite being about different issues.

Finally Yousef Abu Amreih shows how Palestinian-American novelist Susan Abulhawa appropriates in her novel *The Blue between Sky and Water* (2015) some of the themes, tropes and motifs that Shakespeare employs in *Romeo and Juliet* (c. 1596) in order to depict how wars and conflicts turn Palestinian people's love stories/marriages into tragedies. In particular, love at first sight, the (negative) impact of families on love stories, exile and banishment, the use of herbs and traditional medicine, humour and parties that practically turn ominous and fateful are among the themes, tropes and motifs that both Shakespeare and Abulhawa employ to represent love stories and marriages that are embroiled in ongoing violent events. Overall, in its depiction of 'love and violence', Abulhawa's novel appropriates Shakespeare's greatest love tragedy and throws light on some of the conditions under which Palestinians live in Gaza.

Chapter 1

'All the world's a [post-apocalyptic] stage'
The Future of Shakespeare in Emily St. John Mandel's *Station Eleven*

Charles Conaway

The Shakespeare apocalypse

The circulation of Shakespeare in modern popular culture continues at a dizzying pace, and our current critical understanding of 'adaptation' as a term that describes both a product and a process as well as Douglas Lanier's theory of Shakespearean rhizomatics broaden our sense of how and in what form Shakespeare circulates.[1] A strict fidelity to the plays, for example, is no longer required of a text to merit our attention to it and analysis of it in order to see how we are conceiving, constructing and mobilising Shakespeare's cultural capital. Texts are subject to such analysis, no matter how faithfully, transgressively or even tangentially they interact with his plays, poems or persona. Recently, Hogarth Press launched a series of novels written by well-known writers, whose revisions of the plays tend to include radically different settings and characterisations. Numerous films continue to be produced and released from around the world in a variety of languages. Shakespeare's words and phrases are frequently abstracted from his plays and poems and can be found on coffee mugs, calendars and t-shirts. They are casually referenced in everything from cookbooks, television shows and websites to political speeches and everyday conversations. Adaptations and theatrical productions of Shakespeare's plays are often set in different eras, from pre-historic times, as when Fred and Barney play Romeorock and Julietstone in the 'Curtain Call at Bedrock' episode of *The Flintstones*, to our own more or less present moment, as in Michael Almereyda's *Hamlet* or Joss Whedon's *Much Ado About Nothing*.[2] Less frequent, however, are stage productions, adaptations and allusions that set or otherwise refer to Shakespeare in the future. Some well-known exceptions to such a claim come rather immediately to mind: Fred Wilcox's *Forbidden Planet*, episodes of *Doctor Who* and *Star Trek*, and Isaac Asimov's short story, 'The Immortal Bard', among others.[3] But only recently, in conjunction with the seeming explosion of post-apocalyptic novels and films at the end of the twentieth century and into the new millennium, has Shakespeare increasingly found his way into futuristic, dystopian and especially post-apocalyptic settings.

The boom in post-apocalyptic fiction itself merits attention. We have, perhaps, always been interested in apocalyptic narratives. In *The Sense of an Ending*, Frank Kermode argues that our interest in such tales derives from our desire to connect the end of times to our origins so that we can make sense of our lives. In apocalyptic narratives, he writes, we imagine or 'project ourselves ... past the End, so as to see the structure whole, a thing we cannot do from our spot of time in the middle'.[4] Nevertheless, as Kermode notes, our efforts to make sense of our lives in such a fashion are frequently frustrated. Predictions about the end of times tend to be disconfirmed as time marches on. Curiously, this near-constant refutation of forecasted endings does not lead to disillusion and disbelief. In response to our thwarted expectations, it seems, most of us simply turn our attention to the next best available narrative about the end. As Kermode contends, we 'need to show a marked respect for things as they are' and acknowledge the failure of our predictions, but at the same time we continue to make 'considerable imaginative investments in coherent patterns' which make satisfying connections between the end, our origins and the middle (17). Ultimately, then, we seem to think of the end as something that is predictable and *imminent*, or about to happen, at the same time that we know the end is something that eludes our grasp, but nevertheless remains somehow *immanent* – pervasive and inescapable. 'Eschatology is stretched over the whole of history', Kermode concludes, 'the End is present at every moment' (26). In such a light, it seems we have always been and always will be interested in apocalyptic narratives.

In *After the End: Representations of Post-Apocalypse*, James Berger modifies these ideas by describing the logic behind the more recent phenomenon of such narratives, focusing on the fact that apocalyptic texts discuss not only the end of days, but what happens after the end: 'the end', he writes, 'is never the end'.[5] 'Something is left over', he adds, 'and that world after the world, the *post-apocalypse*, is usually the true object of the apocalyptic writer's concern' (6). This interest in post-apocalyptic times, Berger contends, does not stem from a desire to connect the end of time to our origins in order to help us make sense of our own time in the middle, but emerges as a symptom of an assumption that some sort of actual apocalypse has already occurred. The creators of post-apocalyptic novels and films assume that we are already living in post-apocalyptic times, and they use their fictional characters and plots to work through the trauma their own supposed apocalypse has wrought (19). Post-apocalyptic narratives, Berger argues, 'are simultaneously symptoms of historical traumas and attempts to work through them' (19).

The identification of a particular historical event as apocalyptic is arbitrary: one person's apocalypse might be another person's cause for celebration, as is evident in Berger's discussion of the late-twentieth-century backlash rhetoric of Ronald Reagan, who identified the civil rights movement of the 1960s as 'the real apocalypse' of recent American history (143). If we attempt to read the boom of post-apocalyptic novels and films in recent decades through Berger's lens, then, we might imagine that it is symptomatic of the psychological trauma resulting from any one or another of a number of apocalyptic-like trends or events of the twentieth and twenty-first centuries, from the state-sponsored development of chemical and nuclear weapons, to terrorist attacks, school shootings and genocides; from *Citizens United*, unfettered capitalism or the rise of the Alt-Right, to global warming and epidemics running the gamut from AIDS to Zika. When various characters in these novels and films attempt to rebuild their lives and communities, we might imagine that they not only attempt to work through the trauma associated with the catastrophes in their fictional worlds, but also represent the hopes and despairs writers and filmmakers have about our ability to work through past, present and future traumas.

Many scholars have examined the ways in which Shakespeare uses apocalyptic references, imagery and rhetoric in his plays and poetry, but 'The Apocalypse in Shakespeare' – that is, Shakespeare's depiction of catastrophic events and his attitude or thoughts on things apocalyptic – is not the central concern of this article; nor will I explore, as other scholars have done, theatrical or cinematic re-settings of the plays in apocalyptic or post-apocalyptic times.[6] Rather, the article stems from my interest in novels that demonstrate concerns about the circulation of Shakespeare's cultural capital and his relevance in after-the-end times.

Some novels have famously imagined future worlds in which Shakespeare, if not all of Western culture, is threatened with destruction. In *Brave New World*, for example, Mustapha Mond, the Resident World Controller for Western Europe, appears to be something of a bardolator when he defends the idea that culture can be beautiful by quoting Caliban's marvellous description of Ariel's music: 'Sometimes a thousand twangling instruments will hum about my ears'.[7] But he then backtracks, reminding everyone that Shakespeare's works are prohibited 'because [they're] old ... [and] we haven't any use for old things here', especially when those old things are beautiful: 'Beauty's attractive, and we don't want people to be attracted by old things. We want them to like the new ones' (186). 'Besides', he adds, 'they couldn't understand it' (187). Likewise, in *Nineteen Eighty-Four*, Winston Smith's co-worker, Syme, who helps develop Newspeak, predicts:

> By 2050 – earlier, probably – all real knowledge of Oldspeak will have disappeared. The whole literature of the past will have been destroyed. Chaucer, Shakespeare, Milton, Byron – they'll exist only in Newspeak versions, not merely changed into something different, but actually changed into something contradictory of what they used to be.[8]

Aldous Huxley and George Orwell dramatise near-worst-case scenarios for the future circulation of Shakespeare in the depictions of these fictional regimes which threaten deliberately to destroy or corrupt his texts.

But even in cases where there is no repressive or ideological state apparatus plotting any such kind of annihilation of the Bard and his works – that is, even when there is no obvious conspiracy to bring about a 'Shakespeare Apocalypse' – concerns about his existence, his relevance and the potential corruption of his texts continue to circulate in a number of science fiction novels that are set in post-apocalyptic times. Emily St. John Mandel's *Station Eleven* presents a post-apocalyptic world in which allusions, quotations, performances and other references to Shakespeare invite us to consider the nature of his continued cultural importance in a world where civilisation as we know it has been devastated. The catastrophic, apocalyptic event in *Station Eleven* has nothing to do with a deliberate, politically organised effort to destroy or corrupt Shakspeare, yet the question of his ability to survive and matter remains central to the novel's concerns.

'Because survival is insufficient': the therapeutic value of Shakespeare

In Mandel's novel, the thematic concerns with Shakespeare are evident from its opening pages. On the same night that an alarming swine flu strain crosses continents, in the first step of a pandemic that spreads with sudden ferocity and leaves few standing in its wake, a young girl who appears in a non-speaking role in a Toronto production of *King Lear* watches in uncertain horror as the actor playing Lear clutches his chest in mid-performance and drops dead of a heart attack. Twenty years later, the so-called Georgia flu pandemic has brought an end to the recognisable world, and Kirsten Raymonde, the young girl from the Toronto production of *Lear*, is an actress with the Traveling Symphony, a small troupe of actors and musicians who venture from one scattered community to another performing orchestral works and staging Shakespeare's plays. Tattooed on Kirsten's arm, and scrawled across one of the Traveling Symphony's caravans, is a phrase borrowed from *Star Trek: Voyager*, 'Because survival is insufficient', a phrase that would seem to explain the motivations of the actors and musicians of the Traveling Symphony, and a phrase that attempts to explain the function of Shakespeare in *Station Eleven*. When asked about the troupe's motto in a June 2015 interview with NPR's Scott Simon, Mandel replied:

I remember being absolutely struck by that line. Survival was never sufficient. Here in the present, we play musical instruments in refugee camps. We put on plays in war zones. Immediately following the Second World War, there was a fashion show in Paris. But there's something about art, I think, that can remind us of our humanity and it can remind us of civilization. So that line became almost the thesis statement to the entire novel.[9]

According to Mandel, art adds something to a life of mere survival in order to make existence sufficient. In her novel, then, 'the Beethoven symphonies, the Shakespeare plays, the things that we think of as the highest and most exalted expressions of our culture' are performed by the Traveling Symphony in order to enrich the lives of the traumatised survivors of the viral apocalypse who comprise the touring group's audiences.

Mandel imagines a world in which Nature plagues us for no discernible reason. There is no backstory to indicate exactly how the swine flu virus emerged, jumped species, went undiagnosed or broke containment. We only learn that 'a story had broken the day before about an alarming new flu in the Republic of Georgia, [and there were] conflicting reports about mortality rates and death tolls'.[10] The next day, the virus is in Toronto, arriving on the night of the fatal production of *Lear*. Mandel then quickly jumps twenty years and turns her attention to the adventures of the Traveling Symphony. She set a good deal of the action so many years after the pandemic because she was less interested in exploring the 'immediate aftermath of horror and mayhem' that it might cause, and more curious about 'the new culture and the new world that begins to emerge' in its wake.[11] Here, Mandel seems rather clearly to be the kind of writer Berger identifies when he speaks of apocalyptic narratives that are not as interested in the end as they are in what happens after the end. Likewise, her focus on the Traveling Symphony's motto suggests, again in line with Berger, that she is thinking about how her characters might work through the psychological trauma brought on by the Georgia flu pandemic.

If we attempt to read Mandel's novel through Berger's theoretical lens, then, we might conclude that the Georgia flu pandemic is imagined symptomatically as a result of the psychological fallout resulting from any one or more of a number of twentieth- and twenty-first-century biological disasters we have already experienced, such as Ebola outbreaks, the Marburg Virus, SARS or the AIDS epidemic.[12] The survivors of such viral attacks are traumatised not only by the loss of loved ones and the seeming collapse of society, but also by the reminder of the fragility of their own existence and the inevitability of death. In effect, such trauma results from the forced recognition of a breakdown between Self and Other, where the self is hubristically defined as the human agent who is supposed to be separate from and, in the biblical tradition, granted dominion over, the othered natural world. In such a light, the trauma experienced by the survivors of such a pandemic might be something very much like the subjective horror that Julia Kristeva identifies as abjection. The viral threats are devastating not only for the loss of life they trigger, but because they so profoundly disturb the 'identity, system, [and] order' on which the concept of humankind, in the Western, Judeo-Christian tradition at least, is based.[13] Likewise, Mandel's reading of the Traveling Symphony's motto and its efforts to nurture others by bringing great orchestral works and the plays of Shakespeare to them can be read as symptomatic of her hope that we might be able to work through the trauma of such abjection when we are reminded of 'our humanity and ... civilization'.[14] We might turn to Shakespeare, Beethoven and others in order to attempt to remind ourselves of our supposed distinction from and supremacy over the natural world which has, for the moment at least, shown no 'respect [for the] borders, positions, rules' that we have set up to identify ourselves as humans.[15]

When reading the novel through Berger's lens, however, it is possible to argue that the fictional events are symptomatic of other imagined apocalypses. Mark West argues, for example, that the novel 'explicitly links the economic collapses of 2007–8 and the collapse occasioned by the Flu'.[16] Pieter Vermeulen and Martin Paul Eve contend that the apocalyptic event at the heart of *Station Eleven* can be thought of as symptomatic of our present fears about global warming.[17] Philip Smith argues that Mandel reworks 'The Apocalypse in Shakespeare', transforming his vision of apocalypse as a return to primitive times to one in which the return to primitivism occasioned by the Georgia flu pandemic heralds a process of 'recovering modernity'.[18] Regardless of how we define any sort of actual apocalypse at the heart of Mandel's novel, however, the Traveling Symphony's motto and mission remain constant. When Kirsten and her fellow actors play the works of Beethoven and perform the plays of Shakespeare, they attempt to brighten the lives of the pandemic's survivors, just as those who played musical instruments in refugee camps, put on plays in war zones and staged a fashion show in Paris immediately after the Second World War enriched the lives of the traumatised survivors of those apocalyptic events.

In such a fashion, the novel attributes to Shakespeare a therapeutic value that helps its characters (and us) work through traumatic experiences. Philip Smith, Andrew Tate and Maximilian Feldner follow such a line of reasoning in their various analyses of the novel, arguing, as Smith puts it: 'the preservation, and continued performance of, Shakespeare's works, then, is central to the theme of survival throughout the text. For as long as the characters continue to perform Shakespeare, ... Mandel suggests, something, perhaps all, of civilization survives'.[19] Such a therapeutic value is evident in the ways in which the novel's two main characters engage with Shakespeare. Kirsten very clearly thrives on performing his plays. She 'never feels more alive than' when she is acting, we're told, and 'when onstage she fears nothing' (57). At the conclusion of a performance of *A Midsummer Night's Dream*, she experiences something very much like the self-transcendent state of ecstasy: 'Kirsten stood in the state of suspension that always came over her at the end of performances, a sense of having flown very high and landed incompletely, her soul pulling upward out of her chest' (59). In such moments, Shakespeare appears to be offering Kirsten something much more than mere survival. She is transported by her experience, as though Shakespeare offers her the opportunity metaphysically to transcend her material body and, presumably, the dystopian, post-apocalyptic world she inhabits. Likewise, Arthur Leander, the actor who plays Lear in the ill-fated Toronto production, gains from his interaction with Shakespeare. He has had a lengthy run as a successful film and stage actor, but his third marriage has just fallen apart. He's been an absent father. He's in the midst of a breakup with a much younger woman, and he decides that he will walk away from his career, give away his fortune and move to Jerusalem, where he will be able to spend every day with his son (323). Perhaps the opportunity to play Shakespeare's aging, addled king – to rehearse, understand and perform the mistakes Lear makes, only to come to his senses moments before it's all too late – inspires Arthur to leave it all behind and spend time with *his son* before it's too late *for him*. If such is the case, then we might conclude that Arthur's engagement with Shakespeare has finally had a profound and wholesome effect on him, offering him the opportunity to reflect on his own life, and work through his own personal, familial apocalypse.

But Mandel's novel does not present any sort of simplistic argument about how Shakespeare can help us. Apart from Kirsten and Arthur, for example, no other characters in the novel seem to be smitten with his works. When we first meet the members of the Traveling Symphony, they are on the road to St. Deborah by the Water – a town located somewhere near the coast of Lake Michigan – and they are running lines from Act IV, Scene VI of *King Lear*. When the actor playing Edgar responds to Lear's entrance with the line, 'Oh ... thou side-piercing sight', another member of the troupe, identified metonymically as the Symphony's third trumpet, interjects, 'You know what's side-piercing? ... Listening to *King Lear* three times in a row' (36). And the Symphony's clarinet finds Shakespeare just as painful as the third trumpet does. 'THE TRUTH WAS, [she] hated Shakespeare' (288): 'twenty years after the collapse, she loved the music of the Symphony, loved being a part of it, but found the Symphony's insistence on performing Shakespeare insufferable. ... Survival might be insufficient, she'd told Dieter in late-night arguments, but on the other hand, so was Shakespeare' (288). Such less than stellar endorsements of Shakespeare demonstrate that rather than uncritically defending what amounts to the novel's stated intention, Mandel and her characters ceaselessly probe it.

Furthermore, in her NPR interview, Mandel indicates that she is also interested in the role that other cultural artefacts might play in a post-apocalyptic world. Specifically, she wonders what it would mean if one of the things that survived is something like 'a self-published comic book', and her interests, here, further complicate our understanding of the therapeutic value of culture.[20] Throughout the novel, she writes flashback scenes depicting incidents in the pre-pandemic lives of Arthur Leander and Kirsten. We learn, for example, that *Station Eleven* is also the title of the first volume of *Dr. Eleven*, an unfinished science-fiction graphic novel, self-published by Arthur's first wife, Miranda. Backstage, before going on for what will be his final curtain, Arthur gives his copy of *Dr. Eleven* to Kirsten, who still cherishes it twenty years later – in part because it reminds her of Arthur. The graphic novel chronicles the lives of the survivors of a planetary apocalypse who have left their home and live aboard a space station, Station Eleven, and hope to find relief from their suffering by returning to their home planet or finding a new one. Given that

Kirsten finds herself in circumstances fairly similar to the characters in the graphic-novel-within-the-novel, we can easily imagine that her emotional attachment to *Dr. Eleven* must also result from her sympathetic identification with the characters in it and the therapeutic value it thus has for her in the way that it enables her to imagine a community that shares her fears and hopes. Mandel thus complicates any ideas we might have about attributing a therapeutic value exclusively to what are supposedly the highest and most exalted expressions of our culture. She collapses conventional distinctions between high and low, an agenda already evident in the fact that the Traveling Symphony's motto, 'Because survival is insufficient', which seems to apply to Shakespeare and Beethoven, comes from a science fiction television show, *Star Trek: Voyager*. Recognising the proverbial notion that one man's trash is another man's treasure, Mandel dramatises not only the fact that some people do not adore Shakespeare, but that they might rightfully prefer to revere, identify with, and find therapeutic value in traditionally less exalted cultural artefacts.

It is one thing to acknowledge in such a fashion that Shakespeare lacks universal appeal, or even that some items of popular culture might be as worthwhile as his texts, but it is another thing altogether to question the idea, as initially proposed, that his plays can help us work through our trauma. Therapists remain divided about the efficacy of prolonged exposure therapy – the guided and gradual recollection of traumatic memories – and a handful of literary scholars have argued that *Station Eleven* demonstrates not how our cultural memories help us work through trauma, but how they serve as a constant reminder of what has been lost and consequently inspire feelings of melancholy.[21] As Diletta De Cristofaro contends, such recollections are the source of the novel's 'lament about the lost "wonders of technology" and "the splendours of the former world" (Mandel, 2014: 288, 231)'.[22] Furthermore, although Kirsten feels ecstatic, alive and fearless while performing Shakespeare, it is not clear that her time on stage does anything for her other than offer a momentary escape from, rather than an opportunity to work through, the trauma she has experienced. Likewise, while performing Shakespeare's Lear might lead to an epiphanic moment for Arthur when he resolves to quit the stage and begin spending time with his son, he might just as easily be read as 'a walking shadow, a poor player / That struts and frets his hour upon the stage, / And then is heard no more'.[23] He is, perhaps, a plaything of the gods, who bring him to such a transformative moment and then literally break his heart before he has the chance to act on his resolve. If such is the case, then whatever help Shakespeare might serve in attempting to work through trauma is trumped by a darkly ironic version of the kind of nihilistic fatalism that overwhelms Macbeth and plagues Jacques to melancholy in *As You Like It*. In *Station Eleven*, if 'All the world's a [post-apocalyptic] stage, / And all the men and women merely players', then Shakespeare seems more likely to instantiate an existential crisis than serve a therapeutic function.[24] In fact, it is not until the final pages of the novel that Mandel returns to the night of the Toronto production of *Lear*, revealing the news of Arthur's new-found resolve to change his life. She thus creates a profound moment of dramatic irony for the reader, who has known of Arthur's on-stage death for some three hundred pages, and in so doing, she seems very deliberately to emphasise a *theatrum mundi*–like fatalism as though this, finally, is the thesis the novel attempts to argue about the therapeutic value of Shakespeare in apocalyptic times.

Post-apocalyptic action adventure and kick-ass heroines; we're back on the grid

Station Eleven not only interrogates, or even contradicts, the idea of Shakespeare's therapeutic value, it also throws into question what seems to be the novel's most basic assertion: 'Because survival is insufficient'. At least some of the members of the Traveling Symphony, for example, are uncertain about their mission:

> SOMETIMES THE TRAVELING SYMPHONY thought that what they were doing was noble. There were moments around campfires when someone would say something invigorating about the importance of art, and everyone would find it easier to sleep that night. At other times it seemed a difficult and dangerous way to survive and hardly worth it, especially at times when they had to camp between towns, when they were turned away at gunpoint from hostile places, when they were traveling in snow or rain through dangerous territory, actors and musicians carrying guns and crossbows, the horses exhaling great clouds of steam, times when they were cold and afraid and their feet were wet. (119)

The Symphony's motto, we are told, is 'painted on the canopy in answer to the question that had dogged the Symphony since they'd set out on the road' (137), but that question continues to hound them: they are unconvinced by their own claim.

Furthermore, even if survival is insufficient in this post-apocalyptic world, it is nothing that can be taken for granted. In a landscape without electricity, motorised transportation, modern technology or abundant resources, encounters with strangers on the road occasionally turn confrontational, even deadly. A considerable portion of *Station Eleven*'s narrative dramatises a fairly constant struggle for survival that complicates the idea that survival is insufficient. After the Symphony's production of *A Midsummer Night's Dream* reaches its conclusion in St. Deborah by the Water, the town's leader – the Prophet – steps onstage and tells the townspeople how 'blessed [they are] to have these musicians and actors in [their] midst' (59). They are just as blessed, he reminds them, to be alive. The Georgia flu pandemic, as he instructs his audience, provided a 'cleansing of the earth' (60) that is comparable to the Old Testament's flood. 'We were saved', he adds, 'because we *are* the light. We are the pure' (60), and he argues that the viral apocalypse was 'just the beginning [...] only an initial culling of the impure [...] and there will be more cullings, far more cullings to come' (61). The town of St. Deborah by the Water has become 'a doomsday cult' (62), led by the mysterious Prophet, whose desiring gaze falls, during the performance of *A Midsummer Night's Dream*, on fifteen-year-old Alexandra, the youngest actress in the Traveling Symphony. When the Prophet tells the Symphony's Conductor he is looking for another bride and would like them to leave Alexandra with him, the troupe of actors and musicians packs up immediately and leaves town, but they soon discover a stowaway, Eleanor, a young girl from St. Deborah by the Water who had hidden under the costumes in one of the caravans. When the Conductor tells her that they can't take children with them, the girl breaks down, crying that she had to leave: '"I didn't have any choice", she said. "I was going to be his next wife"' (123). They take the twelve-year-old girl with them, because none of them 'could imagine delivering a child bride back to the prophet' (124), who, with a handful of followers, soon comes to claim her.

From this point forward, the novel's exploration of the value of Shakespeare is side-lined. Survival itself becomes much more important than the idea that mere survival is insufficient. In an attempt to force a trade for the twelve-year-old stowaway, the Prophet and his men abduct three members of the Symphony, one of whom dies during his captivity. While fleeing the Prophet's pursuit of them, the troupe splits up, and the hunted become the hunters. Kirsten and August, the Symphony's second violin, duel with and kill two of the Prophet's men. In fact, we learn that whereas the Symphony's motto had been tattooed on Kirsten's left forearm when she was fifteen, she 'also had two black knives tattooed on the back of her right wrist' (119), one for each of the lives she had already taken since joining the Symphony. In the lengthy *action* portion of the novel, Kirsten appears less a lover of the arts and considerably more like a late-twentieth- or early-twenty-first-century kick-ass heroine. It's a thrilling though rather conventional read, but there are no more symphonies or any productions of Shakespeare's plays until the threat of the Prophet is eliminated, which doesn't happen until a near-end-of-the-novel shoot-out in which the Prophet is finally killed by one of his own followers (297–303). In such a light, Mandel's novel appears to suggest not that survival is insufficient, but that survival is constantly threatened, and in such circumstances, questions about whether or not Shakespeare can enrich people's lives are rendered irrelevant.

Still, the *action* portion of the novel comes to an end, and the Traveling Symphony resumes its mission. They arrive at the Severn City Airport – a community established twenty years ago by a rare planeload of survivors – where they rest for five weeks and make 'repairs to the caravans, performing Shakespeare and music on alternate evenings' (331). But even in this post-Prophet world, it is not very clear that Shakespeare has much of an impact on the Symphony's audience. One man, we're told, as the Traveling Symphony gets ready to depart, 'hummed a Brandenburg concerto while he worked in the gardens' (331). A woman 'whispered fragments of Shakespeare to herself' while she cleaned, and children engaged imaginatively with Shakespeare – or, perhaps, with the recent heroics of the Symphony on the road to Severn City – when they 'practiced swordplay with sticks' (331). But if these whispered fragments of poetry or the imaginative duels in which children engage are intended to serve as evidence of the ways in which Shakespeare can enrich one's life, the argument is rather tepid: Mandel goes to much greater lengths to set our hearts pounding when the Symphony is threatened by the Prophet than she does when attempting to support a claim about Shakespeare's therapeutic value.

In fact, what seems most relevant to hope and happiness as the novel nears its end is neither the arts in general nor Shakespeare in particular, but the restoration of technology, getting back on the grid.

At the Severn City Airport, Clark Thompson, an old friend of Arthur Leander, tells Kirsten shortly after meeting her that 'there's something I think you'd like to see' (309). He takes her to the airport's air traffic control tower and points her gaze through a telescope where she sees 'on the side of a hill some miles distant: a town, or a village, whose streets were lit up with electricity' (311). The novel ends when the Symphony departs from the airport while Kirsten is 'beside herself with impatience to see the far southern town with the electrical grid' (331). Meanwhile, Clark remains tethered to the airport, where, in the final words of the novel, he ponders his own hopes for the future, knowing that at least one town has managed to restore electric power and wondering 'what else might this awakening world contain?' (332). He doubts he'll ever see an airplane take off again, but he wonders if perhaps there are ships 'setting out even now, traveling toward or away from him, steered by sailors armed with maps and knowledge of the stars, driven by need or perhaps simply by curiosity' (332–333). The novel thus gradually de-emphasises the importance and value of Shakespeare, even countering the claim that Shakespeare might be able to help us, and ultimately, through Kirsten and Clark, suggests that it is the electric light and the possibility of overseas travel and trade that seem to offer the greatest hope for a future in which survival itself will not be sufficient.

Then again, perhaps the novel demonstrates what amounts to a kind of failed vision in Kirsten and Clark. Elsewhere – a settlement called McKinley in the former state of Virginia – we overhear a discussion between three characters who argue about whether or not 'it still make[s] sense to teach kids about the way things were' (269). Apparently, some of the children born after the pandemic find that their lessons about the past are incomprehensible and upsetting. Michael, a former truckdriver, is worried about his daughter who came home from school 'crying that afternoon, because the teacher had let slip that life expectancies were much longer before the Georgia Flu, that once sixty hadn't been considered particularly old, and she was scared, she didn't understand it' (269). The conversation remains inconclusive. Daria is 'not sure' (269) what to do. Michael thinks that 'maybe it's time we let go' (270), and Jeevan, Daria's husband, says that '[he doesn't] want to let go' (270). They are then interrupted by a violent encounter with the Prophet, though the action, here, takes place well before the Symphony meets him in St. Deborah by the Water. In fact, Kirsten and Clark do not meet these characters and therefore get no chance to participate in the discussion. Mandel doesn't answer the question about what the children should learn, nor does she give it a central place in her novel, but she at least introduces the idea that the value of learning about the past might be questioned, especially, perhaps, if that knowledge simply indicates that things were better in the past and simplistically implies that we might want to redeem, recuperate and rebuild it rather than, say, improve upon it. The dominant mood at the end of the novel, as expressed through Clark's dreams of a return to globalisation and Kirsten's hopes for the resurrection of modern technology, seems to be uplifting, but *Station Eleven* has taken at least a brief moment to encourage our own questions about whether or not such hopes and actions are in our collected best interest.[25]

Shakespearean rhizomatics reconsidered

Finally, the gradual de-emphasis on Shakespeare as the novel progresses – from Kirsten's ecstasy on stage through the *action* portion of the novel to the demystification of his therapeutic value and the ultimate emphasis on the resurrection of technology and global trade – might itself be symptomatic of Orwellian and Huxley-like fears that, even in our own time, Shakespeare is becoming less important or that his texts are being changed into something different from what they once were. Perhaps the constant revision of his works on stage, in print, film and other media fuels anxieties that he is disappearing, being replaced by texts that, in Newspeak-like fashion, change his words. In fact, given our sense of adaptation as a process, as Thomas Cartelli and Katherine Rowe argue, 'every copy, edition, display, publication, exhibit, recording, or performance of an artwork is fundamentally an *adaptation*, in that it reframes prior versions of that work in new environments, periods, and material, and for new purposes'.[26] Adaptation, they rightfully conclude, 'is the very mechanism by which culture transmits its classic works: unmaking and remaking them, renegotiating their meaning in specific reception contexts' (28). Perhaps such sensibilities lead to anxieties, outside of academia, that 'the real Shakespeare' is disappearing, or has disappeared, leaving us only with adulterated versions of his works.

For the most part, questions and concerns about adaptation and authenticity have receded to the background of our critical practice. Following the work of Gilles Deleuze and Félix Guattari, Douglas

Lanier encourages us to think of 'our shared object of study not as Shakespeare the text but as the vast web of adaptations, allusions and (re)productions that comprises the ever-changing cultural phenomenon we call "Shakespeare"'.[27] According to this model of Shakespearean rhizomatics, 'the real Shakespeare' is not located in a stable, printed text. In fact, there is no 'real Shakespeare'. There is only our understanding of Shakespeare, which is a function of innumerable possibilities at play in a network of texts – including printed editions of his plays in all their variant forms, stage productions, films, adaptations, allusions, criticism and so on. Lanier argues that 'if we [thus] conceive of "Shakespeare" rhizomatically, our chief responsibility is to the Shakespearean rhizome itself. At its heart, that responsibility is to acknowledge, map, and preserve (in the sense of not disciplining) "Shakespeare's" creative potentialities, not to stand as guardians of authenticity' (33). In such a model of adaptation, Shakespeare does not become less important, though our sense of him is redefined. His meaning is neither fixed in a stable, printed text, nor corrupted in Newspeak-like fashion; rather, his meaning is, as it always has been, ever-changing and proliferating. Furthermore, even though Shakespeare is decentralised in the model of the adaptational rhizome, this, arguably, does not amount to an improper devaluation of his intrinsic merit as much as it offers a palliative limit to the sometimes tyrannical effect his culturally constructed literary authority can have, especially on students who are unfamiliar with the texts.

However, leaving questions of authenticity aside, we should note that in Lanier's model of the rhizome, individual texts tend to disappear. I am not speaking of the erasure of an 'authentic' text, here, but of the gradual disappearance of all texts. Lanier 'purposely avoid[s] offering close readings of individual examples' because they tend 'to focus our critical attention on individual acts of Shakespearean appropriation'.[28] He admits that there is 'value in attending to the dynamics' of close reading, but he prefers to focus on how 'individual works also always participate in collective acts of Shakespearean adaptation' (113). In effect, then, he urges a practice in which analyses of individual adaptations and allusions tend to fade from the critical landscape. Ultimately, it seems that there are no individual texts, but only 'collective acts of Shakespearean adaptation, acts that considered as an aggregate are reshaping our conceptions of Shakespeare' (113). He demonstrates such a critical process when he discusses the ways in which the late-twentieth-century boom in cinematic Shakespeare 'loosen[ed] the equivalence between Shakespeare and text', noting that in the films of Kenneth Branagh, at least, we see 'what is mentioned or reported in the text – we *see* the accoutrements of royal power piled in a cart in Henry V's "Idol ceremony" speech, the supposed seduction of Hero, which is only reported in *Much Ado*, the sexual tryst between Hamlet and Ophelia, only hinted at in *Hamlet*' (106). 'In these and other Shakespeare films of the day', Lanier concludes, Shakespeare is 'firmly resituate[d] ... in the regime of the (moving) image, not that of the word. One consequence of this is that by decade's end, the presence of Shakespeare's language is no longer the essential element it once was in Shakespeare film – witness *10 Things I Hate About You* or *O*' (106). Here, Lanier pools his observations about a handful of scenes and cinematic strategies or practices – collective acts of adaptation. We don't see detailed, close readings of the individual films or of the plays, even though they are named. His conclusion about the ways in which Shakespeare's language is no longer the essential element it once was in Shakespearean films, I think, is right on target insofar as our understanding of the aggregate is concerned. But if we were to consider one of the individual texts that comprise the aggregate, Branagh's so-called 'full-text' *Hamlet*, for example, we might not come to the same conclusion. Likewise, a similar assessment about the less essential nature of Shakespeare's language might also be reached after consideration of, say, the Hogarth Shakespeare novels, but if we were to ask students in an undergraduate Shakespeare class who were grappling for the first time with the plays those novels adapt, they might not come to such a conclusion. If our responsibility to the Shakespearean rhizome means that we remain inattentive to close readings of the texts that comprise it, then we may be engaging in a critical practice that creates an apocalyptic-like effect in which the individual adaptations, allusions and (re)productions of Shakespeare – as well as the Shakespearean text, which is itself a collection of quarto, folio, conflated and otherwise edited versions of a play – tend gradually to disappear. This might very well lead to the sense of a Shakespeare Apocalypse that is signified, perhaps, in the diminishing role and relevance played by Shakespeare over the course of Mandel's novel.

As I have argued elsewhere, a slight modification to the model of the rhizome, derived from Joseph Grigely's discussion of the relationship between individual texts and an aggregate work in *Textualterity: Art, Theory, and Textual Criticism*, can help us work through the potential trauma of such an apocalypse, giving us a framework to discuss, for example, not only Lanier's observations about how Branagh's films 'loosen[ed] the equivalence between Shakespeare and text' (106) but also how his full-text *Hamlet* managed, at the same time, to reaffirm that equivalence.[29] Likewise, such a modification might also stave off any misplaced notions that adaptations, allusions and performances will lead to any sort of Shakespeare Apocalypse where Shakespeare is replaced and erased by an aggregate. Our understanding of the aggregate *Lear, Hamlet, Romeo and Juliet* or any other Shakespeare play is constantly evolving, but our understanding of the aggregate does not need to annihilate or trump the existence or our understanding of any individual text that helps to comprise the aggregate. We can account for the individual texts and the differences between them at the same time that we monitor the aggregate's process.

Charles Conaway is an Associate Professor of English at the University of Southern Indiana, where he has taught since 2007. His research focuses on adaptations of Shakespeare and the circulation of his cultural authority from the time of his death to the present. He has published articles on adaptations of Shakespeare during the Restoration and eighteenth century and in modern popular culture. He is currently working and publishing on late-twentieth- and early-twenty-first-century novels that imagine the circulation of Shakespeare in post-apocalyptic and other post-traumatic stress-inducing times.

Notes

1. A draft of this article was presented at the Conference on 'Shakespeare in Modern Popular Culture' at the Université d'Artois in Arras, France on 15–17 June 2016. For their support and suggestions, I would like to thank all of the conference participants in general, and Julie Assouly, Vincent Roger, Guillaume Winter, Douglas Lanier and Stephen O'Neill in particular. A revised version of the article was circulated in Douglas Trevor's seminar on 'Shakespeare and the Modern Novel' at the 46th Annual Shakespeare Association of America Conference in Los Angeles, California on 29–31 March 2018. Again, I would like to

thank all of the seminar participants in general, and Douglas, Graham Holderness, Keith Jones, Laurie Osborne, Elizabeth Rivlin and Katherine Scheil in particular. Without their encouragement, this article might never have taken wing.

For a discussion of recent adaptation theory, see, for example, Linda Hutcheon, *A Theory of Adaptation* (New York: Routledge, 2006); Margaret Jane Kidnie, *Shakespeare and the Problem of Adaptation* (London: Routledge, 2009); Douglas Lanier, 'Recent Shakespeare Adaptation and the Mutations of Cultural Capital', *Shakespeare Studies* 38 (2010), 104–113; and Douglas Lanier, 'Shakespearean Rhizomatics: Adaptation, Ethics, Value', in *Shakespeare and the Ethics of Appropriation*, ed. Alexa Huang and Elizabeth Rivlin (New York: Palgrave Macmillan, 2014), 21–40.

2. 'Curtain Call at Bedrock', dir. Joseph Barbera and William Hanna; perf. Alan Reed, Jean Vander Pyl, Mel Blanc; Hanna-Barbera Productions, 1966. *Hamlet*, dir. Michael Almereyda; perf. Ethan Hawke, Kyle MacLachlan, Diane Venora; Miramax, 2000. *Much Ado About Nothing*, dir. Joss Whedon; perf. Alexis Denisof, Amy Acker, Nathan Fillion; Lionsgate, 2013.

3. *Forbidden Planet*, dir. Fred M. Wilcox; perf. Walter Pidgeon, Anne Francis, Leslie Nielsen; Metro-Goldwyn-Mayer, 1956. Isaac Asimov, 'The Immortal Bard', *Universe Science Fiction* 5 (May 1954).

4. Frank Kermode, *The Sense of an Ending: Studies in the Theory of Fiction with a New Epilogue* (Oxford: Oxford University Press, 2000 [1967]), 8. Subsequent page numbers from this source are given in parentheses in the text.

5. James Berger, *After the End: Representations of Post-Apocalypse* (Minneapolis: University of Minnesota Press, 1999), 5. Subsequent page numbers from this source are given in parentheses in the text.

6. For discussions of 'The Apocalypse in Shakespeare', see, among many others: R. M. Christofides, *Shakespeare and the Apocalypse* (London: Continuum International Publishing Group, 2012); Gregory Foran, 'Eschatology and Ecclesiology in *Macbeth*', *Religion and Literature* 47, no. 1 (Spring 2015), 1–30; Maurice Hunt, '"Forward Backward" Time and the Apocalypse in *Hamlet*', *Comparative Drama* 38, no. 4 (Winter 2004/2005), 379–99; Joseph Wittreich, '"Image of that Horror": The Apocalypse in *King Lear*', in *The Apocalypse in English Renaissance Thought and Literature: Patterns, Antecedents and Repercussions* (Ithaca, NY: Cornell University Press, 1984), 175–206; David Womersley, *Divinity and State* (Oxford: Oxford University Press, 2010). For analyses of films that set Shakespeare's plays in apocalyptic or post-apocalyptic times, see the collection of essays in Melissa Croteau and Carolyn Jess-Cooke, *Apocalyptic Shakespeare: Essays on Visions of Chaos and Revelation in Recent Film Adaptations* (Jefferson, NC: McFarland & Company, Inc., 2009).

7. Aldous Huxley, *Brave New World* (New York: Alfred A. Knopf, 2013 [1932]), 186. Subsequent page numbers from this source are given in parentheses in the text.

8. George Orwell, *Nineteen Eighty-Four* (New York: Alfred A. Knopf, 1992 [1949]), 56.

9. 'Survival Is Insufficient: "Station Eleven" Preserves Art After the Apocalypse', *National Public Radio*, 20 June 2015, https://www.npr.org/transcripts/415782006, no pagination.

10. Emily St. John Mandel, *Station Eleven* (New York: Alfred A. Knopf, 2014), 17. Subsequent page numbers from this source are given in parentheses in the text.

11. 'Survival Is Insufficient: "Station Eleven" Preserves Art After the Apocalypse', no pagination.
12. Such concerns might also include anxieties associated with the plagues that devastated Europe from the fourteenth to the seventeenth centuries. In fact, the appearance of the Traveling Symphony in the novel seems deliberately to invoke such fears, given that theatrical companies in Shakespeare's day sometimes left London during plague seasons and toured the countryside.
13. Julia Kristeva, *Powers of Horror: An Essay on Abjection*, trans. Leon S. Roudiez (New York: Columbia University Press, 1982), 4.
14. 'Survival Is Insufficient: "Station Eleven" Preserves Art After the Apocalypse', no pagination.
15. Kristeva, *Powers of Horror*, 4.
16. Mark West, 'Apocalypse Without Revelation? Shakespeare, Salvagepunk, and *Station Eleven*', *Open Library of Humanities* 4, no. 1 (2018), https://doi.org/10.16995/olh.235, no pagination.
17. Martin Paul Eve, 'Reading Very Well for Our Age: Hyperobject Metadata and Global Warming in Emily St. John Mandel's *Station Eleven*', *Open Library of Humanities* 4, no. 1 (2018), https://doi.org/10.16995/olh.155, no pagination; Pieter Vermeulen, 'Beauty that Must Die: *Station Eleven*, Climate Change Fiction, and the Life of Form', *Studies in the Novel* 50, no. 1 (2018), 9–25.
18. Philip Smith, 'Shakespeare, Survival, and the Seeds of Civilization in Emily St. John Mandel's *Station Eleven*', *Extrapolation* 57, no. 3 (2016), 289–303, here 289.
19. Ibid., 297; Andrew Tate, *Apocalyptic Fiction* (London: Bloomsbury, 2017); Maximilian Feldner, '"Survival is insufficient": The Postapocalyptic Imagination of Emily St. John Mandel's *Station Eleven*', *Anglica* 27, no. 1 (2018), 165–79.
20. 'Survival Is Insufficient: "Station Eleven" Preserves Art After the Apocalypse', no pagination.
21. See, for example, Marco Caracciolo, 'Negative Strategies and World Disruption in Postapocalyptic Fiction', *Style* 52, no. 3 (2018), 222–241; and Diletta De Cristofaro, 'Critical Temporalities: *Station Eleven* and the Contemporary Post-Apocalyptic Novel', *Open Library of Humanities* 4, no. 2 (2018), https://doi.org/10.16995/olh.206, no pagination.
22. 'Critical Temporalities: *Station Eleven* and the Contemporary Post-Apocalyptic Novel', (no pagination).
23. William Shakespeare, *Macbeth*, *The Norton Shakespeare*, 2nd ed., gen. ed. Stephen Greenblatt (New York: W. W. Norton & Company, 2008 [1997]), 5.5.23–25.
24. William Shakespeare, *As You Like It*, *The Norton Shakespeare*, 2nd ed., gen. ed. Stephen Greenblatt (New York: W. W. Norton & Company, 2008 [1997]), 2.7.138–39.
25. Mark West argues that it is Miranda, the former first wife of Arthur Leander and the author of *Dr. Eleven*, who makes the explicit connection between the Great Recession and 'the collapse occasioned by the Flu' ('Apocalypse Without Revelation', no pagination). But no other character, West notes, makes any sort of connection between the Georgia flu virus and the economic recession. That notion thus dies with Miranda when she succumbs to the pandemic shortly thereafter. In such a light, West contends, Mandel seems to invoke an apocalypse that 'does not lead to revelation' (no pagination). Neither Jeevan, Daria nor Michael make any sort of connection between the pandemic and economic collapse, but they

question the value of returning to the past in a way that Kirsten and Clark, who hope for a resurrection of past technologies and economies, do not.

26. Thomas Cartelli and Katherine Rowe, *New Wave Shakespeare on Screen* (Malden, MA: Polity Press, 2007), 28. Subsequent page numbers from this source are given in parentheses in the text.
27. Lanier, 'Shakespearean Rhizomatics', 29. Subsequent page numbers from this source are given in parentheses in the text.
28. Lanier, 'Recent Shakespeare Adaptation', 112–13. Subsequent page numbers from this source are given in parentheses in the text.
29. Joseph Grigely, *Textualterity: Art, Theory, and Textual Criticism* (Ann Arbor: University of Michigan Press, 1995); Charles Conaway, '"I'll always consider myself mechanical": Cyborg Juliette and the Shakespeare Apocalypse in Hugh Howey's *Silo Saga*', in *Shakespeare/Not Shakespeare*, ed. Christy Desmet, Natalie Loper and Jim Casey (Palgrave Macmillan, 2017), 79–95; Charles Conaway, '"The ... monster, which doth mock / The meat it feeds on": R.E.M.'s *Monst(e)rous Othello*', *Journal of Adaptation in Film and Performance* 5, no. 1 (2012), 5–24.

Chapter 2
Ian McEwan Celebrates Shakespeare
Hamlet in a *Nutshell*

Elena Bandín and Elisa González

In 2016, the culture industry celebrated Shakespeare's life, works and enduring legacy with massive events in the UK and across the world, proving 'that Shakespeare is the swiftest conduit to understanding the great similarities that pull the world together, but also, more importantly, the fundamental differences'.[1] One year earlier, the Hogarth Press, founded by Virginia and Leonard Woolf in 1917, launched the Hogarth Shakespeare Project aimed at offering Shakespearean prose rewritings by acclaimed contemporary authors: Jeanette Winterson's *The Gap of Time* (*The Winter's Tale*) was followed by Howard Jacobson's *Shylock is My Name* (*The Merchant of Venice*), Anne Tyler's *Vinegar Girl* (*The Taming of the Shrew*), Margaret Atwood's *Hag-Seed* (*The Tempest*), Tracy Chevalier's *New Boy* (*Othello*), Gillian Flynn's *Hamlet*, Jo Nesbø's *Macbeth* and Edward St Aubyn's *King Lear*. Hogarth Press commissioned a number of best-loved novelists to take the plays of Shakespeare and use them

Notes for this section begin on page 40.

to create something entirely their own in an attempt to follow in Shakespeare's steps as the greatest re-teller of stories and in order to introduce his works to a new generation of readers. Although the initiative was promising for the media, the project turned out to be rather disappointing. Reviewing Ann Tyler's *Vinegar Girl*, one critic from *The Guardian* pointed out:

> While these might be great authors who write great books – and under their own steam they might well want to write something inspired by an existing work – the process of commissioning these works ramps up the pressure and gives the whole enterprise an artificiality that is hard to overcome. In some ways it's a noble and bold gesture, potentially bringing new readers to the classics. But let's admit that it's also marketing gone mad.[2]

When reading the reviews of any of the works individually, critics seem to agree that all these great novelists' original works are better than these retellings written at the request of a publishing house, Atwood's *Hag-Seed* being the most acclaimed.[3] Ángeles de la Concha even argues that, in fact, all the novels are surpassed by Ian McEwan's rewriting of *Hamlet*, *Nutshell*.[4]

Nutshell is a funny and captivating novel that deals with an unnamed thirty-eight-week-old foetus gifted with the ability of eavesdropping from the womb on everything that goes on around him. Thanks to this secret listening, he relates from his own point of view the adulterous affair that his mother, Trudy (Gertrude), maintains with her brother-in-law, real estate developer Claude (*Hamlet*'s Claudius), and how they plot the murder of her actual husband, John Cairncross, a melancholic hero of literature and noble publisher.[5] John is prevented from taking care of his pregnant wife and is expelled from the decaying Georgian family townhouse in central London. After moving out, John apparently begins life anew with an aspiring 'owl poet', Elodie, who turns out to be his apprentice. Since the betrayed husband refuses to accept the failure of the marriage, Claude persuades Trudy to poison the contents of a bottle of juice in order to get rid of him.

McEwan fleshes out some marginal characters from the original play and he also reduces the number of people in the action, getting rid of important figures, such as Ophelia, whose relationship is essential to comprehend the development of Hamlet's feigned madness. Thus, this appropriation provides the background of the extramarital affair, setting aside that of Claudius's counsellor,

Polonius, and his children, Ophelia and Laertes. However, a female figure, Elodie, is included to cast doubt on John Cairncross's fidelity and purity of sentiments towards Trudy as well as to hinder the attainment of Claude's ultimate goal of killing his brother.

There are not many direct references throughout the novel to Shakespeare's *Hamlet* (apart from the title, *Nutshell*). Not even the baby is bound to be called this way, but anybody familiar with the original play would identify the unborn narrator with Shakespeare's main character. When interviewed by *The Australian*, McEwan denied his intention to rewrite Hamlet, stating: 'I didn't really intend to write a version of Hamlet. It just sort of crept in'.[6] Nonetheless, allusions to the original are everywhere. The novel's title derives from *Hamlet*, Act II, Scene II – 'I could be bounded in a nutshell and count myself king of infinite space' – as does the plot. The confinement of this character in a womb symbolises the state of Denmark in the original play: 'To be bound in a nutshell, see the world in two inches of ivory, in a grain of sand'.[7] *Nutshell* is not located in Denmark, but, unambiguously, in London: 'Instead I'll inherit a less than united kingdom ruled by an esteemed elderly queen'.[8] Not only does the geographical location change, but so does the inhabited dwelling, switching the magnificent castle of Elsinore for the family house of the unborn baby's father: 'A Georgian pile on boastful Hamilton Terrace was my father's childhood home'.[9] In addition, the plot is updated to the contemporary era when neither hunger nor disease are widespread: 'I'll inherit a condition of modernity ... and inhabit a privileged corner of the planet – well-fed, plague-free Western Europe'.[10] Furthermore, thanks to the current affairs mentioned in the podcasts Trudy usually listens to, such as the conflict in the Middle East which it is feared could trigger a world war, the context can be further determined: the story occurs around 2015–2016.

Hamlet has been adapted to every mode and genre and, although the figure of an unborn narrator might seem brand new, there have been other talking unborn babies throughout the history of literature.[11] Appropriations of this Shakespearean story had already been carried out by authors but never from the viewpoint of an unborn Hamlet in his third trimester. Ian McEwan is almost certainly the first writer to combine both: rewriting Hamlet from the point of view of a foetus. Julie Sanders argues that 'what places *Hamlet* at the centre of the twentieth-century literary canon is the influence of Freud and theories of psychoanalysis, as the exploration of a man in crisis'.[12] Modern literary rewritings borrow a wide range of aspects from the source text and reinterpret them to offer a different perspective, a shift in the central character being the most predominant to avoid the constraints of knowing only those facts concerning the traditional main figure, Hamlet. Ophelia has also been the subject of study of many reinterpretations because of her intense relationship with Hamlet, including *Ophelia* (2001) by Jeremy Trafford and 'The Rose of Elsinore' by Mary Cowden Clarke, belonging to the collection *The Girlhood of Shakespeare's Heroines* (1850), among others.

Following Linda Hutcheon,[13] *Nutshell* entails a transition from the showing mode to the telling mode, focused on the problematic love triangle (King Hamlet, Claudius and Gertrude). McEwan is not the first writer to speculate in some way on the triangle of Claudius, King Hamlet and Gertrude. *Gertrude and Claudius* by John Updike intends to figure out the starting point of the incestuous affair and the possible cooperative murder of King Hamlet.[14] The short story 'Gertrude Talks Back' by Margaret Atwood restricts the focus of discussion to the extent of displaying Scene IV of Act III of *Hamlet*, the juncture when Hamlet confronts his mother, reproaching her for the incestuous marriage and dishonesty towards his dead father.[15] Unlike the original play, in this extension of the scene Atwood only gives voice to Gertrude for her to tell Hamlet the truth, rather than being silenced because of her supposed frailty. Consequently, this renewed woman embodies the feminist reactionary power against the untoward misjudgements of men because she decided to marry a second husband, which is rejected in most cases as an offence to loyalty. Atwood's short story differs from the vast majority of rewritings in blaming not only Claudius, but somebody else, for King Hamlet's death: Gertrude herself.[16] While the revelation of King Hamlet's ghost in the Shakespearean version indicts Claudius, Atwood dismisses this idea in favour of the reinforcement of Gertrude's misery in the company of King Hamlet, to the extent that her only way out was to end his life. Surprisingly, she is fearless, and even proud, to admit this homicide, refusing to allow her son to belittle Claudius: 'It wasn't Claudius, darling. It was me'.[17]

McEwan acknowledged during a conference that the idea of bestowing on a foetus the power of narrating a story came out of nowhere, while he was daydreaming at a boring meeting in a foreign language about himself. He also declared that, by that time, he was re-reading random pages from *Hamlet*, 'as Shakespeare is a continuous source of inspiration for all English writers'.[18] The sentence that came to his mind opens the work pointedly, portraying the actual situation of this extremely unusual narrator: 'So here I am, upside down in a woman'.[19]

Interviewed by Sebastian Groes in 2007, McEwan stated that he had lost interest in first-person narrators: 'I want narrative authority. ... I want the authorial presence taking full responsibility for everything. ... Of course there is a way of loading a first-person narrative voice with authorial insight, or brilliant turns of phrase, but most writers don't try for this – it's difficult'.[20] Part of *Nutshell*'s originality resides precisely here; we find a proto-Hamlet first-person narrator loaded with McEwan's authorial insight, although too often the baby's voice is drowned out by its creator. To be a foetus is a very privileged position from the point of view of narrative, allowing McEwan to reflect upon themes and issues that are often the distinctive marks of his narrative: the breaking of social conventions, codes and taboos, incest, sex and murder, family relationships, politics, history, science or identity and gender politics. The foetus' interior monologue and that monologue's encounter with the truth in the outside world show McEwan's ability to replicate consciousness.

Due to his interest in psychoanalysis as a structure for understanding the self and the world, much of McEwan's work is concerned with innocence, particularly about what it means to be a child and what it means to lose one.[21] McEwan has also deeply explored the relationship between childhood and adulthood and the different bonds between fathers and mothers and their offspring. *Nutshell* can be aligned with his anti-Oedipal narratives (such as *The Innocent* and *The Child in Time*), where he depicts a complex and curious figure of the child that 'allows us to open McEwan's work away from the private realm of family relationships to the public realms of politics and history'.[22] According to the author, 'as the influence of Freud in literary and intellectual culture has faded, we have returned to the idea that childhood is a form of innocence ... They come into the world not responsible for it, and they are sometimes acted upon by people with terrible intent'.[23] This perspective is present in *The Child in Time*, a novel about an innocent three-year-old girl, Kate, who gets lost in a supermarket and never returns to the family household. As Claire Colebrook points out, it 'presents the loss of the child and its connection with politics literally – for the central character's search for his abducted daughter is intertwined with an account of a government enquiry into child development'.²⁴ The vision of the child as 'a world closed in upon itself'²⁵ is voiced by one of the members of a sub-committee that Stephen, the girl's father, is taking part in: 'by forcing literacy on to children between the ages of five and seven, we introduce a degree of abstraction which shatters the unity of the child's world view'.²⁶ Furthermore, Stephen's friend, Charles Darke, abandons publishing activity to engage in politics, but after retiring he behaves like a child, despite living in the family household with Thelma, his wife: 'once a businessman and politician, now he was a successful pre-pubescent'.²⁷

McEwan has experimented with the unreliable narrator in previous works – Briony Tallis in *Atonement*, for example – but in *Nutshell* we are confronted with an *over*-reliable narrator who reflects upon his own condition and who possesses a profound knowledge of the world with which he is going to be confronted. After the development of his central nervous system, the unborn baby is aware of the physical changes his body is undergoing: 'Many weeks ago, my neutral groove closed upon itself to become my spine and my many million young neurons'.²⁸ He wonders about the moment when he begins to think and, definitely, *to be* himself as an individual, not just a foetus inside a woman's womb: 'I once drifted in my translucent body bag, floated dreamily in the bubble of my thoughts through my private ocean in slow-motion somersaults'.²⁹ Nevertheless, this narrator does not regard himself as a completely developed human being because he has not completed the last stage of gestation and is still confined to his mother's uterus: 'I'm still a creature of the sea, not a human like the others'.³⁰ It is obvious that this foetus goes beyond the laws of nature because of his innate knowledge of the world he is about to join. Therefore, instead of being an entirely innocent creature, he is 'like Humbert Humbert in Nabokov's *Lolita*; the same grand elegiac tone; the same infinite knowledge of history and English poetry, the same covetous, obsessively physical eye'.³¹ His source of knowledge is apparently the podcasts his mother usually listens to: 'How is it that I, not even young, not even born yesterday, could know so much, or know enough to be wrong about so much? I have my sources, I listen'.³² As Colebrook notes,

> McEwan's writing deconstructs the opposition between knowing and not knowing, between science and art, between adult and child, between sexuality and innocence. The condition for knowing, speaking, narrating or adopting an adult point of view of mature relations is a

recognition that the world is not one's own, that relations to others are mediated and that we are subjected to a system not of our making.[33]

Likewise, the main character in *The Child in Time* functions as an *over*-reliable narrator. Stephen Lewis, a writer of children's books, maintains a fairly distant relationship with his parents because he was sent to boarding school at the age of twelve and had not had the chance to spend his youth with them. At the beginning of the novel, he confesses to having been unaware of his parents' existence before conceiving him and the mystery that surrounded their previous life: 'however familiar, parents are also strangers to their children'.[34] On one occasion, he has an odd flashback and witnesses them as a young, unmarried couple having a conversation in a café about whether to interrupt pregnancy or not: 'whatever it was, he did not want the child. That was what was on his mind. It was abortion'.[35] He realises that the unborn baby they are referring to is himself. Surprisingly, his mother saw his face at the window while Stephen was staring at them, which made her abandon the idea of getting rid of the unborn baby. Thus, in this fragment, Stephen is portrayed as a witness in the same way as the narrator of *Nutshell*: they both overhear, and witness in the case of Stephen, private conversations, becoming aware of their parents' lack of desire for offspring and, consequently, their birth is jeopardised.

This foetus is gifted with a prodigious imagination as well, recalling the inner world of Peter in *The Daydreamer*, who belongs to nowhere and makes up an alternative mental reality. Unlike Peter, the unborn baby has not been in real contact with the outside world and, consequently, his daydreaming is not constrained by his sensory perception. This narrator is conceived as completely trustworthy, because he has not been corrupted by the outside world; thus, the lack of firm convictions and prejudices as well as religious beliefs implies his reliability: 'No one to contradict or reprimand me, no name or previous address, no religion, no debts, no enemies'.[36] However, the lack of experience of the real world leads him to misunderstandings and sometimes to getting things wrong: for instance, the assumption of his father's endless love is at odds with his actual carelessness, not even taking his birth into account. This profoundly disappoints the unborn baby who had conceived his future by his side.

According to Biwu Shang, 'through rewriting Shakespeare's *Hamlet*, McEwan pays tribute to Shakespeare on the one hand, and he projects his own view on the ethics of life on the other hand', reminding us that we are moral beings.[37] McEwan declares himself atheist but respectful: 'my own view of religion is that people must be free to worship all the gods they want. But it's only the secular spirit that will guarantee that freedom'.[38] Religion is the framework through which Hamlet judges what is wrong or right; he complies with the commandments of God and becomes even more pious after the shock suffered because of the incestuous marriage.[39] Hamlet's religious faith is also reflected in his behaviour when refusing to commit suicide. The foetus, like *Hamlet*, is constantly hesitating between waiting patiently in his mother's womb and taking revenge for his father's murder. At one point in *Nutshell*, the narrator tries to interrupt Trudy and Claude's plot by strangling himself with his umbilical cord. Ironically, McEwan's narrator ponders suicide because he cannot bear the sexual encounters of Trudy and Claude. Every time they have sex, the baby is apparently running a risk of being injured because of the advanced state of pregnancy and, consequently, intercourse should be avoided at this stage: 'I'll say it fast: I'm going to kill myself. An infant death, a homicide in effect, due to my uncle's reckless assault'.[40] As the foetus does not profess religious faith, nothing prevents him from attempting to kill himself: 'To take the life I'll need the cord, three turns around my neck of the mortal coil', although he eventually fails.[41] Because of his condition as a hedonist, this unborn baby is certainly eager to enjoy the pleasures of the world he is about to join: 'I want my *go*. I want to *become*'.[42] Undoubtedly, it is 'life after birth' that he pursues, and surrender cannot be contemplated.[43] His hedonism is at odds with the commandments of God, since he enjoys small pleasures like the intake of alcohol. The atheist condition of the author is also present in the treatment of sex, including fornication and female pleasure, since Trudy, as a *monstrous mother*, cannot restrain her sexual instincts, resulting in incestuous behaviour.

In McEwan's fiction, one hardly ever finds representations of the nuclear family. The function of the family is destructive, rather than constructive, as the death of one or both parents, as well as voluntary abandonments, conditions the later development of the children, rendering them devoid of the affection needed.[44] Not only does isolation exert influence over his characters, but so do childhood traumas caused by physical and sexual abuse, domestic violence and inadequate relationships among relatives. Consequently, these figures undergo insufficient growth, which ends up spoiling their relations when they become adults. One of the most impressive examples is found in 'Dead as They Come', belonging to the collection *First Love, Last Rites*. It is the story of a wealthy man who, after three failed marriages, falls in love with a mannequin in a shop window. He behaves as if they were a real couple, making love to her and getting angry at her silence. This insane behaviour is obviously the consequence of childhood traumas and an inadequate sexual education: 'my father's death rattle, my mother's terror of sexuality, my own sexual initiation with an elder cousin'.[45]

In *Nutshell*, the unborn baby witnesses the progressive separation of his parents as his mother's adulterous affair acquires importance, jeopardising his possibilities of joining a united family: 'His [Claude's] existence denies my rightful claims to a happy life in the care of both parents'.[46] The source of the problems of this disrupted family seems to be the childlike jealousy felt by Claude: 'You hated your brother because you could never be the man he was'.[47] Therefore, this relationship between the estranged brothers in their infancy brings about inadequate parental and sexual behaviour in adulthood. Certainly, apart from an uncontrollable sexual desire, Claude shows no further evidence of affection towards his lover: 'Nothing tender, no fond dozing in a lovers' tangled clasp'.[48] This insensitivity is also the culprit of the loathing felt for the baby to the extent of endangering his life through inappropriate sexual practices posing a risk to the foetus: 'By this last stage they should be refraining on my behalf. Courtesy, if not clinical judgement demands it'.[49]

In *The Comfort of Strangers*, McEwan introduces two prototypical couples of his fiction epitomising different affective and social roles. Mary and Colin, the protagonists, make the acquaintance of a sadomasochist local couple, Robert and Caroline, who posit that women should yield to their husbands on the grounds that they all 'enjoy being beaten up'.[50] This extreme sexual violence derives from the physical abuse Robert suffered every time his father punished him. Although these strangers distort the visitors' image of a usual relationship, this unexpected factor makes their lovemaking thrilling, recovering sexual desire. Indeed, in *Nutshell*, Trudy only feels aroused by maintaining the secret relationship with Claude. Throughout McEwan's fiction, incestuous relationships are explored in a number of ways, from the immoral affair between a wife and her brother-in-law, as exemplified in *Nutshell*, to the discovery of sexuality among inexperienced siblings. In the short story 'Homemade', McEwan introduces a teenager who is willing to touch a woman's genitals and, in order to get practice, induces his ten-year-old sister to have sex with him. Unlike this initiatory sexual ritual, the incestuous relationship found in *The Cement Garden* is a way to meet the affectional needs inherent in being orphaned.[51] In this novel, Jack and Julie maintain a secret relationship, even when the latter is in a relationship with a boy named Derek, who catches them in bed: 'it is sick, ... he's your *brother*'.[52]

Biographical details about McEwan's family also help us to fully comprehend the configuration of Trudy's character. His mother, Rose Moore, married Ernest Wort, who died during the Normandy landings in 1944. While he was away, she maintained an extramarital relationship with David McEwan, an army officer. An undesired child was the fruit of this secret affair, who was handed over to strangers in a railway station. After her former husband's death, Rose married her lover David McEwan and gave birth to Ian in 1948. Unfortunately, Ian did not encounter his brother, David Sharp, until recently, when the latter decided to trace his origins.[53] Probably because of his background, McEwan's women are not submissive; they 'regularly mutilate the men physically, emotionally, materially – denying their existence as meaningful human beings, depriving them of their children ... Men are unable to cope with adult women'.[54] In Shakespeare's *Hamlet*, Gertrude is portrayed as an old woman and, as such, she can no longer experience sexual desire. On the contrary, McEwan's Trudy regains full possession of her female body and of her sexuality, reversing the gender ideology of female chastity and male promiscuity. Despite McEwan's supposed feminism, 'the women he presents are often far from admirable themselves', and 'many of McEwan's female figures echo very traditional feminine stereotypes'.[55] Trudy represents the archetype of the *monstrous mother*, encoded as 'an emblem of lust', reinforcing the Christian negative reading of fertility which regards the fecund female body as the site of sin.[56] These mothers are unable to repress their sexual desires and, consequently, they refuse to accept the passive female role. But their acts are 'presented as physically disgusting or psychologically damaging and often both'.[57]

As a consequence of their sexual behaviour, they tend to reproduce often, which is not the case with Trudy as she is already pregnant with her first child at the start of the action. However, the fact that this pregnancy is undesired evidences the frequency of her lovemaking as a source of mere pleasure. Although *monstrous mothers* are usually depicted with 'physical characteristics of animals, dragons, dogs and asses',[58] Trudy is a symbol of beauty. She is constantly eroticised and conceived as a modern Lolita, 'corrupted and corrupting', whose daily garments are shorts and bikini tops and 'pink-framed, heart-shaped sunglasses'.[59] Moreover, her genitals are negatively described as 'the Wall of Death' until she eventually gives birth: 'What was in his day a vagina, is now proudly a birth canal'.[60]

Not only does Trudy cause psychological harm to the foetus by being unfaithful to John Cairncross, but she also causes physical harm by drinking wine despite her advanced state of pregnancy. Certainly, the intake of alcohol can bring about disabilities in the foetus, such as foetal alcohol spectrum disorders (FASDs), an issue that the narrator is aware of: 'I know that alcohol will lower my intelligence. It lowers everybody's intelligence'.[61] Not only does Trudy seem to forget about her baby, but she also considers the possibility of getting rid of him once he has been born: '*And... We've placed the baby somewhere. ... Placed* is the lying cognate of *dumped*. As *the baby* is of me. *Somewhere* is a liar too. Ruthless mother!'.[62] The baby suffers by his mother's subversion of his plan to join a united family: 'My mother has preferred my father's brother, cheated her husband, ruined her son. My uncle has stolen his brother's wife, deceived his nephew's father, grossly insulted his sister-in-law's son'.[63] This soliloquy recalls the passage in the original play when Hamlet confronts Gertrude so as to decry her wrong choice in substituting King Hamlet: since Trudy is not at all offended by the foetus' offences because of the obvious lack of communication between them, she does not react or defend herself, echoing the Shakespearean Gertrude who is silenced.

McEwan had previously employed this monstrous female figure in his early works, such as the short story 'Disguises', belonging to his collection *First Love, Last Rites*. A ten-year-old orphan, Henry, is delivered to his aunt Mina – an old actress whose last role on stage was Goneril – who intends to replace her mother in order to fill the void caused by being unmarried and childless. Although she considers the boy to be in need of a 'real mother', she is a 'surreal mother'. Mina forces her nephew to transgress the boundaries of masculinity by dressing up like a woman, which apparently arouses her to the extent of groping his body: 'She was excited by his presence and appearance, for twice in the meal she got up from her place to come to kiss and hug him where he sat and run his fingers through the fabric'.[64]

An extreme case of inadaptation caused by a progenitor's death and a *monstrous mother* is expressed in 'Conversation with a Cupboard Man'. The trait of fertility related to this sort of mother is made explicit at the very beginning of the story: 'All she wanted was to have children'.[65] Indeed, all the protagonist's social problems as he grows up stem from the atrocities committed by the *monstrous mother*, altering the proper development of her offspring: 'I never saw my father because he died before I was born. I think my problems started right there – it was my mother who brought me up and no one else'.[66] This mother prevents her son from learning to speak until he turns eighteen, and certainly prevents him from growing up, but he cannot run away because her reality is the only world he is acquainted with: 'I don't want to be free. That's why I envy these babies I see in the street being bundled and carried about by their mothers'.[67] All she seemingly wants is to have him back in her womb: 'She was too busy trying to push me back up her womb'.[68] Apart from the obvious relation of the uterus, the author draws parallels between this story and *Nutshell* because the unborn baby cannot prevent himself from loving his evil mother: 'the mystery of how love for my mother swells in proportion to my hatred'; because he is also physically and psychologically dependent on her: 'She made herself my only parent. I won't survive without her'.[69]

The mistreatment John Cairncross has to endure in *Nutshell* can only be understood in relation to McEwan's previous works because of his recurrent configuration of mothers and wives as authoritative and destructive, especially for the natural growth of their offspring. John Cairncross plays the role of the betrayed father, prevented from taking care of the baby the *monstrous mother* is gestating. This updated version of King Hamlet struggles to maintain his position in the family every time he sees his chances of a happy marriage dwindling: 'My father longs for ... his wife and, surely, his son'.[70] At the start of the action, the unborn narrator takes his parental love for granted: 'No need for an umbilical cord. My father and I are joined in hopeless love', and assumes his fatherhood.[71] Nevertheless, the baby surmises that he shares part of his genome with Claude, which, unfortunately, joins them together: 'My uncle – a quarter of my genome ... What depictable part of myself is Claude and how will I know?'[72] His conjecture goes a step further, to the extent of defying heredity, as he is frightened of his uncle's sperm 'seed[ing] his thoughts': 'Then, brain-damaged, I'll think and speak like him. I'll be the son of Claude'.[73] Although in the beginning the narrator takes his father's love for granted and would prefer to be poisoned with him instead of being placed somewhere else, he ends up realising that not even John awaits his birth: 'What was I in my father's peroration? Dead. ... Not even a mention, not in an aside, not even dismissed as an irrelevance'.[74] Therefore, it is implied that once the baby is born, he will lack parental affection, as is the case for the majority of McEwan's characters.

The reason McEwan chose *Hamlet* as the basis for his reinterpretation seems to be the themes it develops, as they are similar to the central issues of his narratives. Thus, despite the fact that he is rewriting a Shakespearean work, the author remains faithful to his style and favourite topics. *Nutshell* does not tamper with the original play, but offers a renewed version that amplifies the source text and 'brings together McEwan's enduring strengths – lurid imagination, black humour and the ability to put these at the service of a compelling narrative'.[75] In *Nutshell*, McEwan masterfully blends together themes and characters from *Hamlet* with aspects of his previous works, so as to create a unique literary work entirely his own.

Acknowledgements

The research for this work has been funded by the project 'La recepción de las obras de Shakespeare en la cultura española y europea III' [Ref.: PID2022-139809NB-I00]. We are grateful to the Spanish Ministry of Science, Innovation and Universities for its support.

Elena Bandín is Associate Professor at the University of León where she teaches undergraduate and postgraduate courses focused on English Literature and Gender Studies. She has done extensive research on the reception of Shakespeare's works in Spain with a particular interest in translation, performance, censorship and media adaptation. She has published articles in national and international journals such as *SEDERI Yearbook and Cognitive Linguistics*. More recently, she has co-edited, with Francesca Rayner and Laura Campillo, *Othello in European Culture* (John Benjamins, 2022) and has contributed chapters to volumes including *Shakespeare and Cultural Appropriation* (Routledge, 2023) and *Shakespeare and Comics: Negotiating Cultural Value* (The Arden Shakespeare, Bloomsbury, 2024).

Elisa González is a graduate from the University of León. She later completed her MA in Translation and Intercultural Mediation at the University of Salamanca in 2019. She has lectured in Specialised Translation at the European University of the Atlantic. She is currently a PhD candidate at the University of Salamanca.

Notes

1. Dominic Dromgoole, 'Shakespeare: The Playwright Who Brings the Word Closer', *The Guardian*, 23 April 2016, https://www.theguardian.com/stage/2016/apr/23/shakespeare-globe-dominic-dromgoole-complete-walk-william-hamlet.
2. Viv Groskop, 'Vinegar Girl by Ann Tyler Review – Skilled but Pointless Shakespeare Retread', *The Guardian*, 12 June 2016, https://www.theguardian.com/books/2016/jun/12/anne-tyler-vinegar-girl-review-taming-shrew-update.
3. On *Vinegar Girl*: 'Maybe there's fun to be had in working out how Tyler can stay true to the original while still creating something in her own voice. But instead of a tribute, it just feels like tying the hands of an author who's perfectly capable of creating her own world and really doesn't need to borrow someone else's. No, not even Shakespeare's. Verdict? Fun, accomplished, readable, enjoyable. But Anne Tyler originals do all this and so much more'. Groskop, 'Vinegar Girl by Ann Tyler Review'. On *Hag-Seed*: 'Set all that aside, though, as this is written with such gusto and mischief that it feels so much like something Atwood would have written anyway. The joy and hilarity of it just sing off the page. It's a magical eulogy to Shakespeare, leading the reader through a fantastical reworking of the original but infusing it with ironic nods to contemporary culture, thrilling to anyone who knows *The Tempest* intimately, but equally compelling to anyone not overly familiar with the work'. Viv Groskop, 'Hag-Seed Review – Margaret Atwood Turns The Tempest into a Perfect Storm', *The Guardian*, 16 October 2016,

https://www.theguardian.com/books/2016/oct/16/hag-seed-review-margaret-atwood-tempest-hogarth-shakespeare. On *New Boy*: 'But, deprived of the complex opacity of Shakespeare's theatrical vision, and lacking the wild teenage darkness of, for instance, *Lord of the Flies*, her novel becomes linear, reductive and almost banal – a playground scrap, in which a prized strawberry pencil case must stand in for Desdemona's fatal handkerchief'. Robert McCrum, 'New Boy by Tracy Chevalier Review – A Vexed Retelling of Othello', *The Guardian*, 14 May 2017, https://www.theguardian.com/books/2017/may/14/new-boy-tracy-chevalier-review-othello.
4. Ángeles de la Concha, 'Shakespeare en la imaginación contemporánea: reescrituras en su cuarto centenario' (lecture, University of León, León, Spain, 24 November 2016). Retrieved from https://videos.unileon.es/video/1461.
5. The names of the characters are not completely preserved. McEwan shortens the name of Gertrude and modifies the spelling of Claudius: Trudy and Claude. In addition, the third member of the love triangle, King Hamlet, is renamed as John Cairncross, who was an essayist about the self in Shakespeare's time. Ironically, although the unborn narrator evokes the figure of Hamlet, the author renders the main character unnamed throughout the novel.
6. Rosemary Neill, 'Ian McEwan on New Novel *Nutshell*, Hamlet, His Brother and the Bard', *The Australian*, 27 August 2016.
7. Ian McEwan, *Nutshell* (London: Jonathan Cape, 2016), 62.
8. Ibid., 3.
9. Ibid., 12.
10. Ibid., 3.
11. As in Carlos Fuentes' *Christopher Unborn* (1987), a catastrophic story set in Mexico whose narrator ponders whether being born in such a destroyed setting is worthy or not. Even in exotic literature traditions, such as the Indian, some parallels can be found: in a version of the epic *Mahābhārata*, Abhimanyu, in his mother's womb, eavesdrops on his father planning a battle strategy with his wife.
12. Julie Sanders, *Adaptation and Appropriation* (Oxon: Routledge, 2006), 54.
13. Linda Hutcheon, *A Theory of Adaptation* (New York: Routledge, 2006).
14. John Updike, *Gertrude and Claudius* (London: Penguin Books, 2000).
15. Margaret Atwood, 'Gertrude Talks Back', in *Good Bones and Simple Murders* (New York: Nan A. Talese, 1994).
16. Cindy Chopoidalo, 'The Possible Worlds of *Hamlet*: Shakespeare as Adaptor, Adaptations of Shakespeare' (PhD diss., University of Alberta, 2009), 133.
17. Atwood, 'Gertrude Talks Back', 19.
18. Ian McEwan, 'Ian McEwan on His Novel Nutshell – Books Podcast', *The Guardian*, 2 September 2016, https://www.theguardian.com/books/audio/2016/sep/02/ian-mcewan-on-his-novel-nutshell-books-podcast.
19. McEwan, *Nutshell*, 1.
20. Jon Cook, Sebastian Groes and Victor Sage, 'Journeys without Maps: An Interview with Ian McEwan', in *Ian McEwan: Contemporary Critical Perspectives*, ed. Sebastian Groes (London: Continuum, 2009), 133.
21. Claire Colebrook, '*The Innocent* as Anti-Oedipal Critique of Cultural Pornography', in Groes, *Ian McEwan: Contemporary Critical Perspectives*, 43.
22. Ibid., 45.
23. Cook et al., 'Journeys without Maps', 124.

24. Colebrook, 'The Innocent as Anti-Oedipal Critique', 47.
25. Ibid., 45.
26. Ian McEwan, The Child in Time (London: Vintage, 1992 [1987]), 81.
27. Ibid., 117.
28. McEwan, Nutshell, 2.
29. Ibid., 1.
30. Ibid., 100.
31. Kate Clanchy, 'Nutshell by Ian McEwan Review – An Elegiac Masterpiece', The Guardian, 27 August 2016, https://www.theguardian.com/books/2016/aug/27/nutshell-by-ian-mcewan-review.
32. McEwan, Nutshell, 4.
33. Colebrook, 'The Innocent as Anti-Oedipal Critique', 53.
34. McEwan, The Child in Time, 57.
35. Ibid., 190.
36. McEwan, Nutshell, 2.
37. Biwu Shang, 'Ethical Literary Criticism and Ian McEwan's Nutshell', Critique: Studies in Contemporary Fiction 59, no. 2 (2018), 142–53, here 153.
38. FRONTLINE, 'Faith and Doubt at Ground Zero', Ian McEwan interviewed by Helen Whitney, April 2002, http://www.pbs.org/wgbh/pages/frontline/shows/faith/interviews/mcewan.html.
39. Omar Abdulaziz Alsaif, 'The Significance of Religion in Hamlet', International Journal of English and Literature 3, no. 6 (2012), 132–35, here 132.
40. McEwan, Nutshell, 127.
41. Ibid., 127.
42. Ibid., 129.
43. Ibid., 160.
44. Fernando Galván, Formas nuevas de la ficción británica contemporánea: David Lodge, Ian McEwan y Salman Rushdie (Universidad de La Laguna: Secretariado de Publicaciones, 1998), 55.
45. Ian McEwan, First Love, Last Rites (London: Vintage, 1997 [1975]), 69.
46. McEwan, Nutshell, 20.
47. Ibid., 120.
48. Ibid., 23.
49. Ibid., 21.
50. Ian McEwan, The Comfort of Strangers (London: Vintage, 2001 [1981]), 71.
51. Galván, Formas nuevas de la ficción británica contemporánea, 61.
52. Ian McEwan, The Cement Garden (London: Vintage, 1997 [1978]), 136.
53. Alan Cowell, 'Ian McEwan's Life Takes Twist with Discovery of a Brother', The New York Times, 17 January 2007, https://www.nytimes.com/2007/01/17/arts/17iht-brother.4240717.html. McEwan's personal background has exerted a powerful influence over his narrative: he reflects his own mother, Rose Moore, in some way on many of his female main characters, such as Trudy. The possibility of the narrator being abandoned once he is born recalls the handing over of the author's brother at a railway station in order to conceal the infidelity of his mother. Indeed, the author acknowledged the unborn baby of Nutshell to be the fruit of the extramarital affair, unambiguously pointing at himself because his father is not his mother's first husband, but the lover with whom she contracted marriage afterwards.

54. Jack Jr. Slay, *Ian McEwan* (New York: Twayne Publishers, 1996), 81.
55. David Malcolm, *Understanding Ian McEwan* (Columbia: University of South Carolina Press, 2002), 14.
56. Marilyn Francus, 'The Monstrous Mother: Reproductive Anxiety in Swift and Pope', *Elh* 61, no. 4 (1994), 829–51, here 829.
57. Ibid., 830.
58. Ibid., 830.
59. Clanchy, '*Nutshell* by Ian McEwan Review'.
60. McEwan, *Nutshell*, 196.
61. Ibid., 7.
62. Ibid., 43.
63. Ibid., 33.
64. McEwan, *First Love, Last Rites*, 133.
65. Ibid., 89.
66. Ibid., 89.
67. Ibid., 105.
68. Ibid., 91.
69. McEwan, *Nutshell*, 109.
70. Ibid., 34.
71. Ibid., 16.
72. Ibid., 33.
73. Ibid., 21. Later on, McEwan himself acknowledged during a talk that the unusual narrator is not even John's biological child, but the fruit of the incestuous relationship. According to the author, what arouses suspicion about the actual fatherhood is the fact that John is given £5,000 in order to keep him away from the house. However, there is no explicit allusion to this surprising declaration throughout the novel, apart from the fact that the baby is constantly referred to as undesired.
74. McEwan, *Nutshell*, 71.
75. Orlando Bird, 'Nutshell by John McEwan, Review – Lectures from the Womb', *The Telegraph*, 23 September 2016, http://www.telegraph.co.uk/books/what-to-read/nutshell-by-ian-mcewan-review--lectures-from-the-womb/.

Chapter 3
Modernising Misogyny in Shakespeare's *Shrew*

Natalie K. Eschenbaum

An NPR review of *Vinegar Girl* states that Anne Tyler's modernisation of Shakespeare's *The Taming of the Shrew* is a 'fizzy cocktail of a romantic comedy, far more sweet than acidic, about finding a mate who appreciates you for your idiosyncratic, principled self'.[1] The reviewer suggests that Tyler's novel is successful, 'despite [*Shrew's*] ever-controversial sexism'.[2] In this article, I consider how Tyler's novel fits into the critical debate concerning the play's misogyny. Katherine Sirluck summarises the range of readings and performances of Shakespeare's play:

> It has been seen as a rollicking comic flyting match between a resourceful suitor and a dangerous man-hater. Some productions have encouraged the idea that Katharina secretly longs for a man too strong for her, one who can awaken her true feminine nature.... [Some feminists] ... are ready to accord Shakespeare a trans-patriarchal perspective. Others present the play as a brutally frank celebration of patriarchal power, or as a despairing recognition of the same.[3]

In my reading, *Vinegar Girl* ends up 'far more acidic than sweet', because it reveals how *any* tale about taming a woman has an underlying message of male dominance. In Tyler's novel, misogynistic values are sometimes romanticised, sometimes criticised, and frequently both simultaneously. In this contradictory way, it is very much like Shakespeare's original play.

I originally decided to assign *Vinegar Girl* to address a teaching 'problem' I encountered in 2017.[4] A healthy number of undergraduate English majors in my upper-division Shakespeare class boldly stated that studying *Shrew* and its informing histories reinforces the patriarchy and normalises misogyny. They came to this conclusion after a full discussion of multiple readings regarding the shrew-taming plot. One of these included Sirluck's richly argued conclusion that 'Shakespeare did not intend merely to represent the institutionalized power relations in his society, let alone to celebrate them; but that instead he set out to represent them satirically'.[5] The students focused on the fact that Petruchio abuses his new wife via sleep deprivation and starvation, and insisted that this abuse overshadows any critical reading. They were not convinced – as I had been – by Sirluck's argument that the extreme nature of Petruchio's actions indicates its artificiality: 'In allowing Petruchio to demonstrate the extremes of behaviour that are ultimately ratified by social codes, towards both women and servants, the veil of paternal care-taking and rational order is torn, and the brute reality of vindictive proprietorship is made manifest'.[6] There was nothing amiss with Sirluck's argument, *per se*; rather, the students stated that any argument pushed against their critical, political and social understanding of domestic abuse; any readings that explained Petruchio's behaviour were also, in some way, excusing it. Today, it is not enough to say something like, the play has 'problematic gender politics'.[7] Students respond disgustedly: 'These are not "problematic gender politics"; this is flat out domestic abuse!'

My post post-feminist students were smartly reconstructing parts of Emily Detmer's argument from 'Civilizing Subordination: Domestic Violence and *The Taming of the Shrew*', now over two decades old, but newly relevant in this #MeToo movement. Detmer explains that, in the late sixteenth and early seventeenth centuries, cultural laws were discouraging husbands from using physical violence as a means of controlling wayward wives, and thus *Shrew* may be, in part, an exploration of how men can gain control over their wives using forms of non-physical violence. Detmer argues 'that the play signals a shift toward a "modern" way of managing the subordination of wives by legitimizing domination as long as it is not physical'.[8] She predicts my students in her claim: 'If readers and teachers fail to take seriously the experience of Petruchio's abuses, and thus identify more strongly with him than with Kate, they risk complicity with an ideology that authorizes oppression as long as it is achieved without physical violence'.[9] Detmer includes an important footnote – 'naming and defining violence, physical or otherwise, is a political act' – which reminds us that when students define Petruchio's treatment of Kate as 'domestic abuse', they are not just doing literary criticism, but they are doing political work and contributing to social justice activism.[10] Peter Erickson also encouraged us to do this work in *Rewriting Shakespeare, Rewriting Ourselves* when he stated: 'political analysis and intellectual complexity are not mutually exclusive. One does not cease to be scholarly when one starts to be political'.[11]

Essentially, my students made me reconsider how, and more importantly why, I teach this controversial play. The stated purpose of the MLA's *Approaches to Teaching Shakespeare's The Taming of the Shrew* is to 'help students more fully appreciate the witty complexities of *The Taming of the Shrew*', although the editors admit that the sexism of the play makes it difficult to teach.[12] Readings of *Shrew* continue to be published that work to minimise apparent misogyny, because, as Rachel McLennan notes, 'Shakespeare's cultural authority is privileged'.[13] What if instructors' primary concern were instead to fully appreciate the play's misogyny? What if we leaned into the play's controversies rather than skirted around them? Erickson argues that our readings and rewritings of Shakespeare's works should never defend him, but should aim to make his works 'part of the change'.[14]

Erickson also argues that 'no study of the past is totally separated from, or uninformed by, the present, [and] the historical distinction between past and present is relative rather than absolute'.[15] Reading *Vinegar Girl* alongside Shakespeare's controversial play helps students discover that we do not exist outside of history, and that understanding the complexity of the past does not excuse it. *Vinegar Girl* tells the story of Kate Battista, a preschool teacher who has been kicked out of college and is living at home, caring for her father and flirtatious sister, Bunny. Kate's father, a Johns Hopkins scientist, proposes a marriage between Kate and his lab assistant,

Pyotr Scherbakov, to extend Pyotr's visa. When critics claim that Tyler 'tamed the Bard's shrewish battle of the sexes into a far more politically correct screwball comedy of manners', this may be true by some measures, but to say that *Vinegar Girl* is more – even far more – progressive than *Shrew* when it comes to sexism is not saying much.[16] Detmer argues that when 'we "historicize" [*Shrew*] – for ourselves or for our students – we should not only account for sixteenth- and seventeenth-century notions of domestic violence; we need to consider twentieth-century notions of violence as well'.[17] The story of *Shrew* is a story of violence against women that extends through to today and reverberates with *any* narrative about the dominance of men over women. *Vinegar Girl* is also a narrative about the ways in which men abuse women. Katherine Scheil says that, 'Through the ways that Shakespeare has been reworked for later generations, we can trace changing aesthetic taste, shifts in literary forms, and developing ideas about Shakespeare himself'.[18] More, we can trace the shift in what readers and audiences think is most important to address *today*. In *Shakespeare and Millennial Fiction*, Andrew James Harley asserts that contemporary novels of the plays

> challenge Shakespeare's contribution as a cultural touchstone for Western literary production. They wrestle with what Shakespeare is, what his work finally means for our present moment, and the extent to which the plays might be usefully invoked as mirrors of contemporary reality and possibility .... [T]hese novels meditate ... on the problems his works pose for current ideologies, and on the imaginative and linguistic spaces he opens up for both authors and readers.[19]

Shrew poses 'problems ... for current ideologies', especially feminist ones, but if *Vinegar Girl* 'mirrors ... contemporary reality', then complications exist today too. Tyler's exclusion of the scenes of domestic abuse fixes some of the obvious problems, but doing so allows students to notice there are more subtle 'problematic gender politics' that persist. Marjorie Garber's powerful, chiasmatic statement, 'Shakespeare makes modern culture and modern culture makes Shakespeare', is apt here.[20]

Critical analyses of *Vinegar Girl* published to date actually praise Tyler's revisions. Two recent Master's theses (Colleen Etman, College of Charleston, 2017, and Renee Drost, Radboud University, 2018) examine the same three Hogarth series novels (Margaret Atwood's *Hag-Seed*, Jeanette Winterson's *The Gap of Time*, and *Vinegar Girl*) to separately conclude that *Vinegar Girl* is the only adaptation that successfully addresses problematic gender politics. And, in 'The Hogarth Shakespeare Series: Redeeming Shakespeare's Literariness', Douglas M. Lanier suggests that Tyler is able to find a 'solution' to the problem of *Shrew* through 'three revisions to Shakespeare's narrative'.[21] First, Tyler focuses on the Battista family and their commitment to scientific thinking; second, she makes 'Pyotr comically inept rather than misogynistically motivated'; and third, 'Kate tames herself'.[22] Certainly, there is much to praise about Tyler's revisions, but I disagree that she is able to fully distance Pyotr 'from the unsavory elements of Petruccio's misogyny' by making him 'comically inept' and treating his 'chauvinism as a matter of unexamined cultural heritage'.[23] Pyotr's foreignness helps to explain some of his misogynistic gaffes, but it does not excuse his repeated mistreatment of Kate, as I will argue. I also disagree that taming oneself solves the taming plot. It is true that Kate decides 'voluntarily to engage in a sham marriage to Pyotr to get out from under her oppressive home situation', and she may well end up in a better situation than she was in with her father, but the plot still reveals numerous examples of dominance and abuse.[24]

Tyler's purposeful use of the powerful term 'girl' throughout her novel helps to reveal how the taming plot is modernised, but remains misogynistic. In *Shakespeare and the Performance of Girlhood*, Deanne Williams tells us that 'the girl has become a hot topic in contemporary sociology, psychology, and cultural studies'.[25] Undergraduates may just be discovering that girlhood studies is an area of academic interest, but they will have known since elementary school how the word is used to reveal pride ('girl power') or to throw an insult ('cry like a girl'). *Vinegar Girl* opens with Kate Battista gardening and then hearing her father speaking into the family's answering machine. He asks her to bring his lunch to his lab. Kate protests – as one would expect considering her character model – but when her father says, 'Ah, Kate, don't be like that. Just hop in the car and zip over; there's a good girl', Kate responds 'Sheesh', slams down the phone, grabs the lunch bag and essentially does as she is told.[26] Williams explains how 'the term "girl" often appears in Shakespeare as a label for a young woman's independence, willfulness, and resistance: examples include ... the recalcitrant Kate in *The Taming of the Shrew*'.[27] But when Louis Battista asks a twenty-first-century Kate to be a 'good girl', her resistance falters. Dr Battista may simply be using 'girl' as a term of endearment for his daughter. But, as Williams outlines, the term has a 'history of ambiguous gender, sexuality, and domestic service', and, in this case, Kate may feel obligated because she also functions as the household help.[28] She is responsible for all of the shopping, cooking and laundry for the family.

At twenty-nine, Tyler's Kate is likely older than Shakespeare's Katherine. By most definitions, she is not a 'girl', but she tolerates being called one by her father and her Uncle Barclay. When Pyotr calls her 'girl', though, Kate is quick to correct him. Dr Battista's request for the lunch delivery ends up being a ploy for him to introduce Kate to Pyotr, who needs a fast marriage to secure an extension on his work visa. In their first exchange – and well before Kate knows the marriage plans – Pyotr reacts to Kate's cheeky response to her father's request that she join them for lunch. Pyotr laughs loudly:

> 'Just like the girls in my country', he said, beaming. 'So rude-spoken'.
> 'Just like the *women*', Kate said reprovingly.
> 'Yes, they also. The grandmothers and the aunties'.[29]

Kate may tolerate her elders calling her 'girl', but not an equal or lesser who should know better. Pyotr's response clarifies that he knows the difference between girls and women, but he believes all girls, women, grandmothers and aunties are rude-spoken like Kate. Pyotr continues to refer to Kate as 'girl', even after this correction. When the marriage plot is revealed, Kate is livid. Pyotr visits her in her garden; they sit together, share her sandwich and end up having a relatively pleasant conversation that includes the following exchange:

> 'Was a foolish notion anyhow', he said, speaking to the lawn in general. 'It is evident you could choose any husband you want. You are very independent girl'.
> 'Woman'.
> 'You are very independent woman and you have the hair that avoids beauty parlors and you resemble dancer'.[30]

Pyotr marks Kate's independence and then compliments her hair and body as the things that would allow her the choice of any husband. Later, at their engagement party, discussing whether or not she will change her surname, Pyotr once again calls Kate 'girl':

> Aunt Thelma asked Kate if she were planning to be Kate Cherbakov (pronouncing it as her brother-in-law did). 'Definitely not', Kate said. Even if this marriage had not been temporary, she was opposed to the notion of brides changing their names. And Pyotr, to her

relief, chimed in with '*No*, no, no'. But then he added, 'Will be Shcherbakov-*ah*. Female ending, because she is girl'.

'Woman', Kate said.

'Because she is woman'.

'I'm sticking with Battista', Kate told her aunt.[31]

In both of these scenes, Pyotr does not fight against Kate re-identifying herself as a woman. Kate is training him in the culturally appropriate language, and he quickly corrects himself. But the second scene reveals subtler gender politics that end up having a great effect on how we read the novel's outcome. Pyotr does not listen to Kate. He completely misses her statement that she will 'definitely not' change her name. And Kate seems more interested in fixing Pyotr's use of 'girl' than the substance of the conversation. Throughout the novel we are reminded of Kate's independence, and Pyotr's unwillingness to listen to something as important as a discussion of her name – her identity – signals the subtle way in which dominance and oppression remain the themes of this story, even in its attempts to modernise the 'taming' tale.[32]

When Pyotr is late to their wedding, Kate hopes that something has gone wrong at the lab, revealing her vulnerabilities:

> She honestly wanted to know, because whatever it was would be preferable to Pyotr's simply deciding he found it too off-putting to marry her no matter how advantageous it was. 'Would not be worth it', she could hear him saying. 'Such a *difficult* girl! So unmannerly'.[33]

The fact that Kate imagines Pyotr using the term 'girl' demonstrates that she knows him, which creates an intimacy, albeit a perverse one. She imagines that he still has not learned how she likes to be categorised. But Kate – not Pyotr – is the one who pictures herself as a 'girl' here, and as a difficult one too. The fact that Kate quickly questions her worthiness suggests that she has internalised Pyotr's, her father's and the culture's expectations of her, and Kate's use of the word 'girl' to describe herself suggests that she is on her way to being 'tamed'. Detmer explains that the 'heterosexual romance plot of [*Shrew*] encourages readers to see this bonding as "love" and to disregard the violence as taming'.[34] The same is true in *Vinegar Girl* in that the romantic context of the novel encourages us to read this moment as an expression of Kate's true love for Pyotr, instead of (or at least at the same time) as a revelation of the loss of her independence and an admission that she now wants to be Pyotr's 'girl', no matter the cost.

The other person who categorises Kate as a 'girl' consistently is Tyler herself. The very title of the book, *Vinegar Girl*, suggests that even the omniscient narrator denies this twenty-nine-year-old womanhood. Kate is described as immature and childish at her workplace, where she is an assistant preschool teacher. For instance, when a four-year-old complains that somebody called her a 'weirdo', Kate's response is, 'What do you care? ... Tell her she's weird herself'.[35] In addition, 'If a child refused to lie down at Quiet Rest Time, Kate just said, "Fine, be that way", and stomped off in a huff'.[36] And when Kate eats with the preschoolers, she tells them the pasta 'smells like wet dog'.[37] Tyler summarises Kate's relationship with her wards: 'they seemed to view her as just an extra-tall, more obstreperous four-year-old'.[38] Her supervisor explains that she sees her 'in charge of a classroom' one day, once she 'mature[s]'.[39] Sirluck argues that wife-training is shown to be like child-rearing in Shakespeare's play, when Petruchio 'proffers these humiliations as a natural and necessary corollary of her shrewishness. Like a parent training a child, he seems to suggest that the child itself chooses the parent's behaviour, enforces its own punishment'.[40] One of the many complexities of *Shrew* is that it examines the ways in which society trains girls to behave in certain ways. In *Vinegar Girl*, Kate can run a household, but this neither entitles her to womanhood, nor grants her maturity. As Williams argues, in *Shrew*, '"girl" signals, not peevish independence, but pliant, even tearful, obedience'.[41] Kate is not supposed to mature into womanhood; she is supposed to learn how to properly perform girlhood.

Throughout the novel, Kate is very aware that girlhood is a performance. She has a crush on Adam, her co-worker, and we are told that 'she always tried to look like a nicer person than she really was when Adam was around'.[42] And, 'Walking home at the end of the day, she reviewed her conversation with Adam. "Ooh!" she had said, not once but twice, in that artificial, girlie way she detested, and her voice had come out higher-pitched than usual and her sentences slanted upward at the end. Stupid, stupid, stupid'.[43] When Kate becomes aware of this specific performance of girlhood, she is frustrated because it is similar to the performance of girlhood she observes in her fifteen-year-old sister, Bunny: 'Kate could tell it was a boy [Bunny] was talking to because of the breathy, shallow voice she put on'.[44]

In *Shrew*, performance is a key component to Katherine's 'taming'.[45] Consider, for instance, the scene when Petruchio and

Katherine are on their way to Baptista's house and he makes her call the sun the moon:

> Katherine: And be it moon, or sun, or what you please.
> And if you please to call it a rush candle,
> Henceforth I vow it shall be so for me.
> Petruchio: I say it is the moon.
> Katherine: I know it is the moon.
> Petruchio: Nay, then you lie. It is the blessed sun.
> Katherine: Then God be blest, it is the blessed sun.
> But sun it is not, when you say it is not,
> And the moon changes even as your mind.
> What will have it named, even that it is,
> And so it shall be so for Katherine. (4.5.15–25)

Petruchio threatens Katherine, saying that unless she agrees with him, he will turn the carriage around, but her responses demonstrate that she is not simply obeying. She obeys, yes, but she explains that obedience is a performance. When Petruchio says that the sun is now the sun again, she repeats him verbatim, but not without saying that she will also immediately agree it is the moon if he changes his mind again. As if to reinforce the fact that obedience itself is a performative aspect attached to gender, Petruchio next has Katherine address Vincentio, an old man, as a girl:

> Young budding virgin, fair and fresh and sweet
> Whither away, or where is thy abode?
> Happy the parents of so fair a child!
> Happier the man whom favorable stars
> Allots thee for his lovely bedfellow. (4.5.40–45)

Katherine embraces the performance, giving five full lines of absurd compliment that focus on an old man's femininity, immaturity and sexuality; there is a 'playful kind of empowerment [that] underpin[s] her performance of obedience'.[46] Williams wonders if 'the outcome of Petruchio's brutality', including scenes of forced obedience such as this one, is 'to liberate Kate from the strictures of traditional girlhood which are founded on gender difference'.[47] By discovering the performative aspects of femininity, Kate gains some control over them.

The adapted sun/moon scene in Tyler's novel also incorporates the tailor scene from Shakespeare's play and occurs when Pyotr rushes home, late, the evening of the wedding, after the fiasco involving stolen lab mice. When Kate realises they need to get to the reception, but neither of them is dressed appropriately, she says:

'But I'm not changed. *You're* not changed'.
'We go as we are; it is family'.
Kate spread her arms to reveal the wrinkles across the front of her dress from her nap, and the mayonnaise stain near her hem. 'Just give me half a second, okay?' she said. 'This dress is a disaster'.
'Is a beautiful dress', he said.
She looked down at it and then dropped her arms.
'Fine, it's a beautiful dress', she said. 'Have it your way'.
But he was already out on the landing now, heading toward the stairs, and she had to run to catch up with him.[48]

Tyler's adaptation is open to at least a couple of readings, and one could be perceived as romantic: Pyotr shows Kate that he does not care about our culture's trappings of femininity; a dress may be wrinkled and stained, but it is 'beautiful' because it is on Kate. Kate's acceptance of Pyotr's definition may not be obedience, but rather the realisation that she does not need to *act* like anything with him. But this reading was unacceptable to most of my students, who were troubled that Pyotr does not even wait around to hear her response. Kate is literally left chasing after him. She asks for 'half a second' and he gives her none. This scene echoes the 'conversation' Pyotr had about Kate's choice of surname, when Pyotr failed to hear Kate's desires about her identity. Kate has no choice but to bend to Pyotr's will because he does not even stay to hear her responses.

Pyotr tames Kate through neglect, and Kate recognises that this behaviour is abusive. Immediately after their wedding, when Pyotr is trying to figure out who has stolen the lab mice, Kate asks Pyotr a series of questions (Where are you going? Why don't you have lunch first? What are you doing?) and asks if she can come with him on his detective mission, but he does not respond and 'all she heard was the slapping sound of his flip-flops descending the stairs'.[49] She muses: 'She should *make* him take her with him. She should run after him and fling herself into the car. It was hurt feelings, probably, that stopped her. Ever since the wedding he had been downright abusive, as if now that they were married he thought he could treat her however he liked'.[50] Detmer explains that 'domestic violence is any act of coercion that aims to nullify a person's will or desire in order for the abuser to gain dominance'.[51] Pyotr's dominance over Kate is subtle in comparison to Petruchio's over Katherine's, but ignoring Kate again and again has a profound effect on Kate's person. Her feelings are hurt, as she says, but she is also changing how she acts. She has learned that he will not listen to her so it is not worth chasing after the car, asking him to wait while she changes her dress, or to do anything else she might perceive is important. In other words, she is silenced and frozen; she is 'tamed'.

Kate has also started making excuses for Pyotr's rude behaviours. When Pyotr forgets his keys and snaps at the landlady, Mrs Liu, Kate says:

> 'Sorry... We didn't mean to disturb you. Monday I'm getting an extra key made, so this shouldn't happen again'.
> '*He* is the one is very rude', Mrs. Liu said.
> 'He's had a really hard day'.
> 'He has many hard days', Mrs. Liu said.[52]

Kate is concerned that Mrs Liu feels sorry for her that she married Pyotr, and perhaps she should be.[53] Because the assumption of the novel is that Pyotr will not change – he will continue to be rude and to have 'many hard days' – but Kate will need to change if she is to remain married. Is Pyotr's rudeness abuse or violence? Perhaps not. But it sits on a sliding scale with abuse and violence, because his behaviour affects others in profound and negative ways. Rudeness and neglect can be – indeed, frequently are – forms of oppression.

Kate's concluding speech explains, in part, why she excuses some of Pyotr's selfish and dominating behaviours. Tyler's version of one of the most controversial moments in *Shrew* parallels Shakespeare's in that it comes as a bit of a surprise and focuses on the woes of men. The contemporary update is that Kate speaks of the emotional traumas men face on account of the pressures of masculinity. She says, 'It's *hard* being a man', because men are 'a whole lot less free than women are, when you think about it. Women have been studying people's feelings since they were toddlers; they've been perfecting their radar – their intuition or their empathy or their interpersonal whatchamacallit. ... It's like men and women are in two different countries! I'm not "backing down", as you call it; I'm letting him into my country. I'm giving him space in a place where we can both be ourselves'.[54] Lanier argues that Tyler's novel is a 'tale of developing empathy and intimacy', and this speech would support such an argument.[55] But the speech, like Katherine's in *Shrew*, is ambiguous because it is difficult to tell how much of it she honestly believes. She spends much of the time critiquing the 'country' occupied by gossipy girls and women, and her concerns about men's emotions come from a conversation with her father, not Pyotr.

Williams argues that Petruchio's 'abusive actions may ... be read as a campaign against a system of marriage negotiations, illustrated by Baptista's treatment of his daughters, and an entire social structure in which the girl is treated as little more than a "bauble, a silken pie"'.[56] In *Vinegar Girl*, Kate and Bunny are horrified that Kate is being offered up for marriage to save their father's lab, but this is not the system or social structure that receives the greatest critique. The greatest critique falls on the system that requires people to *perform* in some way in order to marry. Thus, the performative aspects of gender provide Katherine some freedom in *Shrew*, but the opposite is true in *Vinegar Girl*. The fact that Kate is required to become someone she not – the fact that 'taming' is still part of the narrative at all – is the problem that cannot be unwritten in this story.

When I taught Tyler's novel for the first time in 2018, my students were interested in the gender politics in *Vinegar Girl*, in part because they are more familiar, and in part because they are, frankly, less devastatingly abusive than they are in Shakespeare's *Shrew*. But the subtle abuse of Pyotr's inability (or refusal) to listen to Kate, and his selfish rudeness, could not simply be explained away with a speech about the vulnerabilities of masculinity; nor could students ignore the gentle romance between two people who discover they *think* they don't need to act 'like a girl' or 'like a man' to be loved. They worked to reconcile such contradictory readings of Tyler's novel, which helped the students to discover the necessity of reading the similarly complex gender politics in *Shrew* less reactively and more critically.

Natalie K. Eschenbaum is professor of English and Dean of the School of Interdisciplinary Arts and Sciences at the University of Washington Tacoma. She teaches Shakespeare, early modern literature and culture and writing. Her research focuses on disgust and the bodily senses, as well as on Shakespeare and adaptation. Publications include the co-edited *Disgust in Early Modern English Literature* (Routledge, 2016) with Barbara Correll and 'Sense, Reason, and the Animal–Human Boundary in *A Midsummer Night's Dream*', in Simon Smith, ed., *Shakespeare/Sense* (Bloomsbury Arden, 2020). She is currently working on a new co-edited collection on humanities-informed higher education leadership with Ariane Balizet and Marcela Kostihova titled 'Applied Shakespeare'

Notes

1. Heller McAlpin, 'Fizzy "Vinegar Girl" Tames Shrewishness to Sparkle', www.npr.org, 21 June 2016.
2. Ibid.
3. Katherine Sirluck, 'Patriarchy, Pedagogy, and the Divided Self in *The Taming of the Shrew*', *University of Toronto Quarterly* 60, no. 4 (1991), 417–34, here 417, https://doi.org/10.3138/utq.60.4.417.
4. I use 'problem' to associate this work with Scholarship of Teaching and Learning (SoTL) work, but the 'problem' I encountered, like most teaching 'problems', was an opportunity to rethink how I was teaching this material.
5. Sirluck, 'Patriarchy, Pedagogy, and the Divided Self', 431.
6. Ibid., 428.
7. Rachel McLennan, 'To Count as a Girl: Misdirection in *10 Things I Hate About You*', *Borrowers and Lenders* 9, no. 1 (2014), 1–18, here 2, http://www.borrowers.uga.edu/1215/show#top.
8. Emily Detmer, 'Civilizing Subordination: Domestic Violence and *The Taming of the Shrew*', *Shakespeare Quarterly* 48, no. 3 (1997), 273–94, here 274, https://doi.org/10.2307/2871017.
9. Ibid., 275.
10. Ibid.
11. Peter Erickson. *Rewriting Shakespeare, Rewriting Ourselves* (Berkeley: University of California Press, 1991), 3.
12. Margaret Depuis and Grace Tiffany, eds, *Approaches to Teaching Shakespeare's The Taming of the Shrew* (New York: MLA, 2013), xii.
13. McLennan, 'To Count as a Girl', 4.
14. Erickson, *Rewriting Shakespeare*, 5.
15. Ibid., 3.
16. McAlpin, 'Fizzy "Vinegar Girl"'.
17. Detmer, 'Civilizing Subordination', 283.
18. Katherine Scheil, 'Adapting Shakespeare's Comedies', in *The Oxford Handbook of Shakespearean Comedy*, ed. Heather Hirschfeld (Oxford: Oxford University Press, 2018), 439–54, here 454.
19. Andrew James Harley, 'Introduction: "Reason Not the Need!"', in *Shakespeare and Millennial Fiction*, ed. Andrew James Harley (Cambridge: Cambridge University Press, 2018), 1–12, here 7–8.
20. Marjorie Garber, 'Introduction', in *Shakespeare and Modern Culture* (New York: Pantheon, 2008), xiii–xxxv, here xiii. Garber's thesis that Shakespeare helps to create our contemporary realities makes the charge for reading Shakespeare through a social justice–oriented lens all the more pressing. If Shakespeare's woman-taming narrative helped – in any way – to establish systems of male dominance or abuse of women, then our current readings must work to undo this.
21. Douglas M. Lanier, 'The Hogarth Shakespeare Series: Redeeming Shakespeare's Literariness', in Harley, *Shakespeare and Millennial Fiction*, 230–50, here 241.
22. Ibid., 241.
23. Ibid., 242, 241.
24. Ibid., 241.

25. Deanne Williams, *Shakespeare and the Performance of Girlhood* (New York: Palgrave, 2014), 3.
26. Anne Tyler, *Vinegar Girl* (New York: Hogarth, 2016), 18.
27. Williams, *Shakespeare and the Performance of Girlhood*, 6.
28. Ibid., 5.
29. Tyler, *Vinegar Girl*, 22.
30. Ibid., 102.
31. Ibid., 161–162.
32. We never find out if Kate takes Pyotr's last name or remains Battista, but in the Epilogue we do discover that Pyotr and Kate have a son named Louie Scherbakov. The names of both Kate's father (Louie) and Pyotr (Scherbakov) represent the fully patrilineal society that dominates Kate, who might have chosen Battista-Scherbakov or, simply, Battista for her son's last name, but did not.
33. Tyler, *Vinegar Girl*, 190.
34. Detmer, 'Civilizing Subordination', 289.
35. Tyler, *Vinegar Girl*, 30.
36. Ibid., 32.
37. Ibid., 34.
38. Ibid., 32.
39. Ibid., 41.
40. Sirluck, 'Patriarchy, Pedagogy, and the Divided Self', 429.
41. Williams, *Shakespeare and the Performance of Girlhood*, 37.
42. Tyler, *Vinegar Girl*, 43.
43. Ibid., 86.
44. Ibid., 69.
45. William Shakespeare, *The Taming of the Shrew*, ed. Barbara A. Mowat and Paul Werstine (New York: Washington Square Press, 1992).
46. Williams, *Shakespeare and the Performance of Girlhood*, 39.
47. Ibid., 42.
48. Tyler, *Vinegar Girl*, 223.
49. Ibid., 211.
50. Ibid.
51. Detmer, 'Civilizing Subordination', 283.
52. Tyler, *Vinegar Girl*, 206.
53. Ibid., 206.
54. Ibid., 240.
55. Lanier, 'The Hogarth Shakespeare Series', 242.
56. Williams, *Shakespeare and the Performance of Girlhood*, 41.

Chapter 4
Almost Shakespeare – But Not Quite

Keith Jones

Kenneth S. Rothwell provides a taxonomy for the study of Shakespeare and film in his *History of Shakespeare on Screen*.[1] It includes four degrees of Shakespearean adaptation (delineated throughout the book) and seven kinds of Shakespearean derivatives.[2] For Rothwell, an adaptation is a film that largely retains Shakespeare's language, and a derivative is one that abandons the language of Shakespeare but retains one of a number of connections to the work from which it's derived. These 'Shakespeare derivatives of seven kinds'[3] are extremely useful for thinking about film versions of Shakespeare:

> There are seven kinds of Shakespeare derivatives, which take protean shapes in plot, theme, language, design, purpose, and camera work. Those of the first kind (recontextualizations) will keep the plot but move Shakespeare's play into a holy new era and jettison the Elizabethan language (*Joe Macbeth*); the second kind (mirror movies) will meta-cinematically make the movie's backstage plot about the troubled lives of actors run parallel to the part of the Shakespearean play that the actors are appearing in (*A Double Life*); the third kind

Notes for this section begin on page 66.

(music/dance) will turn the plays into musicals (*West Side Story*), or ballets and operas such as Zeffirelli's *Otello* (1986) ... the fourth kind (revues) will use the excuse of a biography (*Prince of Players*) or of a documentary (*Looking for Richard*), or even a horror show (*Theater of Blood*) to showcase scenes from Shakespeare's plays; the fifth (parasitical) will exploit Shakespeare for embellishment, and/or graft brief visual or verbal quotations onto an otherwise unrelated scenario (Katherine Hepburn in *Morning Glory*); the sixth kind (animations) – at this point the scheme does begin sounding like Polonius' – will put Shakespeare into cartoon images (*The Lion King*); and finally the seventh kind (documentaries and educational films) will make a variety of pedagogical films that in turn may overlap with any of the permutations and combinations in the previous categories.[4]

Quoted in full, it is clear how that schema can account for a wide range of Shakespeare films.

When we turn to the category 'Shakespearean Fiction', we find ourselves almost exclusively in the 'derivative of Shakespeare' category. After all, if a work retains most of Shakespeare's language, it would be an edition of a play rather than a fictional version of a play.[5] And we also find ourselves in a field that could use a thoroughgoing taxonomy of its own – both so that we can tell each other what we're dealing with and so that we can draw some significant conclusions based on the genres of the works in question.

By way of example, let me run through a few works that relate, in one way or another, to *Macbeth*. A. J. Hartley and David Hewson's *Macbeth: A Novel*[6] recasts the plot of *Macbeth* in the genre of the novel. It might be classified as a retelling (or, more precisely, a straightforward retelling – or, more flippantly, a novelisation) of the play. It makes no significant alterations to the plot; it does not focus on any particular aspect of the play; it doesn't provide commentary on the play or its characters. Stewart Kenneth Moore's graphic novel of *Macbeth*[7] may be the closest to Rothwell's 'adaptation' that we get in the category of Shakespearean fiction. It retains much of Shakespeare's language; the illustrations and layout involve interpretation of the play itself. In Moore's case, the retelling is based on a specific performance of *Macbeth* by the Prague Shakespeare Company, making it something of an adaptation of an adaptation. Rebecca Reisert's *The Third Witch*[8] retells the plot of *Macbeth* from the first-person point of view of one of the Weïrd Sisters. It's a parallel narrative from the perspective of a secondary (or tertiary) character. Similarly, Caroline B. Cooney's *Enter Three Witches*[9] offers the plot from alternate third-person perspectives, but these are largely from characters who are not in *Macbeth* itself. Further, it's a young adult novel, a genre which has multiple sub-categories of its own. Lisa Klein's *Lady Macbeth's Daughter*[10] imagines a daughter for Macbeth and Lady Macbeth – one Macbeth, suspecting Lady Macbeth of infidelity, orders killed. Another book in the general young adult genre is Neil Arksey's *MacB*,[11] a brief and loose retelling that abandons the setting of *Macbeth* as well as its language (and – forgive the spoiler here – its tragic conclusion). Set on the modern football pitch (that's 'soccer field' to US readers), the novel is concerned with rivalry over who will be team captain that year. *MacB* could be called a recontextualisation, as could Alan Gratz's book: he also finds a new setting for *Macbeth* in his *Something Wicked: A Horatio Wilkes Mystery*.[12] A murder at a Scottish heritage competition needs to be solved: is Mac responsible? Or could his girlfriend, Beth, have something to do with it? *Macbeth* does seem to lend itself to the murder mystery genre; more frequently, it does so in 'mirror novel' guise. Both Cindy Brown's *Macdeath*[13] and Ngaio Marsh's *Light Thickens*[14] are narratives about murders that are committed during productions of *Macbeth*. In a 'tangential' category, Susan Fraser King has written *Lady Macbeth*,[15] a historical novel that owes very little – if anything – to Shakespeare's play. Finally, works that draw their titles from *Macbeth* without engaging with its plots or its characters might be considered parasitical. Eleanor Brown's *Weird Sisters*,[16] even though it has Shakespeare in it, doesn't retell the plot of any of the plays. Perhaps Ray Bradbury's *Something Wicked This Way Comes*[17] and William Faulkner's *The Sound and the Fury*[18] would fit this category. I've chosen those titles deliberately to indicate that 'parasitical' need not be disparaging. Still, I'm not altogether satisfied with the term since works like these are seriously engaging with Shakespeare, not just appropriating a Shakespeare quote for a good-sounding title (as Agatha Christie's *By the Pricking of My Thumbs*[19] or Paul Bowles' *Let It Come Down*[20] might be considered to do).

The scope that 'Shakespearean Fiction' covers is immense, and some formal system of classification seems indeed to be warranted. In the meantime, what interests me in this article are those works that defy such classification: works that are clearly indebted to Shakespeare in one way or another but which do not retell or even reflect on one particular plot.

In *Shakespeare and the Problem of Adaptation*, Margaret Jane Kidnie suggests that we should not measure adaptations or derivatives of Shakespearean plays against the text of the plays.[21] In Kidnie's view, to do so is to ascribe too much authority to that text. Instead, she argues that any production – adaptation – derivative – should be looked at as 'a dynamic process that evolves over time in response to the needs and sensibilities of its users'.[22] I agree with this to a point, but I also find that the best works of Shakespearean fiction invite us and encourage us to return to Shakespeare's text – not to evaluate the work of fiction by what we find there but to see how reading a work of Shakespearean fiction affects or interacts with our re-reading of a play.

That's one reason why I'd like to examine some works that grapple deeply with Shakespeare but that do not retell or recontextualise the plot of any one play. Doing so will help us get away from evaluating the work based on how closely it sticks to or how far it deviates from Shakespeare's narrative.

Gary Schmidt's *Wednesday Wars*[23] is just such a book. Schmidt sets his young adult novel in Long Island during the 1967–1968 school year, and the book doesn't pull any punches about the time period. Yet the seriousness of the time period provides a tremendous counterpoint to the hilarity of our narrator's seventh-grade school year. Holling Hoodhood, our hero, is the only Presbyterian in his class. On Wednesday afternoons, all the Catholic students head to Catechism lessons at the Catholic church; at the same time, all the Jewish students head to Temple for Hebrew School. That leaves Holling and his teacher, Mrs Baker. He's convinced that she hates him, though she probably just hates having what might otherwise have been a free afternoon filled with one student. At first, she has him clean chalkboards and clean the rats' cage.

Then she considers that their time might be better employed studying Shakespeare. And that's where, for the Shakespeare buff, the novel really gets rolling. Mrs Baker has Holling read several plays – in an attempt, he believes, to bore him to death and get her Wednesday afternoons back. If that's her intent, it backfires. He's intrigued by *The Merchant of Venice*, though he says that it's not as good as *Treasure Island*, and he admires *The Tempest* as a place to pick up Shakespearean curses. Later, he uses his knowledge of the play to earn cream puffs: the baker, it turns out, is a Shakespeare fan who needs someone to play the part of Ariel.

The novel covers a good number and a wide range of Shakespeare plays: *The Merchant of Venice, The Tempest, Macbeth, Romeo and Juliet, Julius Caesar, Hamlet* and *Much Ado About Nothing* are all incorporated between its covers. In doing so, the novel covers a range of genres, and that invites us to consider the novel's own genre. The novel ends on a happy note, which is not quite the same as saying it ends happily. It certainly doesn't end unhappily, but there are complexities to the ending. In short, its genre might be either tragicomedy or problem play.

I don't want to give away too much of the plot, but here's one place where the novel considers the complexities of endings. Two of the main characters have family members fighting in Vietnam, and Mai Thi, one of Holling's classmates, is a recent émigré from Vietnam who has to face prejudice and hatred from some of the staff and students at the school. After the words 'Go Home Viet Cong' are written on Mai Thi's dwelling, our narrator reflects on the event:

> At the happy ending of *The Tempest*, Prospero brings the king back together with his son, and finds Miranda's true love, and punishes the bad duke, and frees Ariel, and becomes a duke himself again. Everyone – except for Caliban – is happy, and everyone is forgiven, and everyone is fine, and they all sail away on calm seas. Happy endings.
> That's how it is in Shakespeare.
> But Shakespeare was wrong.
> Sometimes there isn't a Prospero to make everything fine again.
> And sometimes the quality of mercy *is* strained.[24]

This passage is characteristic of the novel's complexity. There may be happy endings, but they certainly aren't simple.

The historical setting also adds to the generic complexity of the work. The assassination of Dr Martin Luther King and the assassination of Bobby Kennedy both find their tragic way into the novel. The war in Vietnam (and protests about the war in Vietnam) figure prominently, as does the Cold War–era fear of nuclear annihilation. This historical accuracy provides tremendous depth to the plot and the characterisation.

And that characterisation also takes on a complex life of its own. Holling isn't, at the end of the novel, certain about what he'll do with his life, and his difficult relationship with his father remains unresolved. Further, his parents' marriage has grown increasingly rocky through the pages of the novel, and his own grade-school romance, though happy enough, may prove ephemeral. But it's through this complexity that we see the genuine depth of the human being and the human condition. As in the problem plays of Shakespeare – whichever ones fit that category – sorrow and joy are complicatedly intermingled in *The Wednesday Wars*, creating intensely three-dimensional characters in whom we can find ourselves.

Station Eleven[25] both fits and transcends its genre. Emily St. John Mandel has written a profound work that uses the idea of a post-apocalyptic world to transcend the genre of post-apocalyptic novel completely.

The novel opens with an actor putting on *King Lear* – and dying from a heart attack in the middle of Act IV, Scene VI. That night, a devastating pandemic (the Georgia flu) arrives in America. It sweeps across America and around the world, killing nearly everyone who is exposed to it.

The novel then explores what takes place twenty years later – but without leaving the time just before and just after the Georgia flu unexplored. Indeed, that's what I found so masterful and so genre-breaking about this novel: what happens twenty years after and what happens two weeks before the breakout are explored nearly equally in order to make sense out of the flu breakout, civilisation (and its downfall) and the human condition. In this, *Station Eleven* is both a post- and a pre-apocalyptic novel.

In the section set twenty years after the Georgia flu, we mostly follow the experiences of The Traveling Symphony, a group of actors and musicians who have come together in the wake of the collapse of civilisation:

> The Symphony performed music – classical, jazz, orchestral arrangements of pre-collapse pop songs – and Shakespeare. They'd performed more modern plays sometimes in the first few years, but what was startling, what no one would have anticipated, was that audiences seemed to prefer Shakespeare to their other theatrical offerings.
> 'People want what was best about the world,' Dieter said.[26]

The Traveling Symphony has, as a sort of motto, *Survival is insufficient*, which, one of the characters says, 'would be way more profound if we hadn't lifted it from *Star Trek*'.[27] The motto implies that there's more to life than mere survival, and the novel explores that theme in all its intricacies and mysteries. In that (and in its use of Shakespeare), it's a bit like Jean-Luc Godard's film *King Lear*,[28] suggesting that Shakespeare could help rebuild a civilisation that has fallen.

But it also questions the premise repeatedly. Late in the novel, for example, we learn this: 'The truth was, the clarinet hated Shakespeare'.[29] The notion that music can help a civilisation rebuild appealed to her, but she 'found the Symphony's insistence on performing Shakespeare insufferable. She tried to keep this opinion to herself and occasionally succeeded'.[30] Her argument is that the Symphony is limiting itself by performing plays by Shakespeare exclusively:

> Survival might be insufficient, she'd told Dieter in late-night arguments, but on the other hand, so was Shakespeare. He'd trotted out his usual arguments, about how Shakespeare had lived in a plague-ridden society with no electricity and so did the Traveling Symphony. But look, she'd told him, the difference was that they'd seen electricity, they'd seen everything, they'd watched a civilization collapse, and Shakespeare hadn't. In Shakespeare's time the wonders of technology were still ahead, not behind them, and far less had been lost.[31]

Station Eleven does not retell the plot of any Shakespeare play. Nor does it serve as much of a 'mirror novel', even though several sections describe the production of *King Lear* that begins the narrative. But it does reflect philosophically on the purposes of Shakespeare – and of things like Shakespeare. It may not ask us to re-examine a specific play, but it does ask its readers to consider what they value, and why, and how.

Briefly, Linda Lê's *The Three Fates*[32] provides a challenging but fascinating post-post-modern approach to a single play, but in utterly unexpected ways. Even though one of the main characters goes by the soubriquet 'King Lear', the plot is not the same as Shakespeare's play. The plot plays with Shakespeare's play by telling the story of three granddaughters (two sisters and their cousin) who were brought to France from Vietnam by their grandmother and who are planning to get the two sisters' father (who stayed in Vietnam) to visit them in France.

The passage below describes Long Legs, who is pregnant, and her journey to her pregnancy. It captures some of the manic madness of King Lear and others in the play and invites unlikely comparisons to Shakespeare.

> For while waiting for the demigod who would devote his little barb to her alone, the brazen hussy had flailed like a regular banshee, jumped one joker after another, scraped every string with her bow, learned the guitar in ten easy lessons, danced the jig, bought a drum that went chica-boom, ordered paint sets, set up an easel, bought a box

that went click-clack, designed dresses, bought a machine that went zigzag, nursed dwarf trees, bought a miniature fountain that went splish-splash, crammed basic Japanese easy-peasy, mimicked the art of tea, bought a rare tea service financed in a hugger-mugger, but try as she might to go clickclackchicaboomzigzag, the days went by willy-nilly, the detritus of failed vocations piled up pell-mell, and it was always the same bric-a-brac of boredom that found itself waiting for the fortuitous smish-smash of a savior who burst in lickety-split to cure these fits and untangle this mish-mash of whim-whams. Said whim-whams had spun my cousin's head round and round, emptied her pockets, left her still yearning to stock her little boutique with an extra measure of heart. The savior who fell from heaven reached under the detritus of failed vocations and pulled out a lost soul eager to be branded, to sell off her cartload of whim-whams, swap the extra measure of heart for a gleaming kitchen, trade in the boxes that went clickclackchicaboom for a mewling blob of jelly that went waah waah at any hour of the day or night. For in all her zigzagging, the lost soul had forgotten the tick-tock of age. While she was frolicking, time had pursued its game of tic-tac-toe. And once the clickclackchicaboom was over and done, the clock began tick-tocking something fierce in the whim-wham graveyard. The savior dropped in just in time to pluck the ripe fruit. The green was turning mauve. The pink was getting dusky. The bell was tolling for her youth, drowning out the caterwaul of strings fiddled a-go-go. Her whim-whams now stowed in the attic, the lost soul devoted her life to the savior who had dropped into her bed, calm block here fallen from a celestial joy. A flawless brick, all smooth, square, and dry, the heart of the wall, which had reared up without warning, blocking out the sun. But behind the wall, the lost soul had her spanking new enclosure, bricks of good sense on which to lay her head and, soon, a demi-god who would go waah waah then clickclack-chicaboomsplishsplash, carving out his own little slice of heart before getting his own spanking new enclosure and, inside it, a mewling demigod who'd go waah waah before sounding all the bells and whistles. All super-duper and hunky-dory, everything ship-shape.[33]

Unlike *The Three Fates*, neither *The Wednesday Wars* nor *Station Eleven* points us back to a specific Shakespeare play. But all three novels are continually involved in saying, 'Here's Shakespeare. What do you intend to do with it?' – both with their plots (here are characters grappling with Shakespeare) and in their very existence (here are authors doing something with Shakespeare). Careful classification of such works is significant, particularly when it aids comparative study. And the issues such works bring up are far more than questions of evaluation. They are questions of how adaptations invite us to consider both themselves and the works they are adapting.

Keith Jones is a Professor at the University of Northwestern–St. Paul and the author of *Bardfilm: The Shakespeare and Film Microblog*. His current interests are in Global Shakespeares, particularly in Asia and Africa. He teaches Shakespeare, Shakespeare and Film, and other courses in the Department of English and Literature at the University of Northwestern, and he is also a freelance editor.

Notes

1. Kenneth S. Rothwell, *A History of Shakespeare on Screen: A Century of Film and Television*, 2nd ed. (Cambridge: Cambridge University Press, 2004).
2. Ibid., 209–210.
3. Ibid., 208.
4. Ibid., 209.
5. For convenience, I shall continue to use *play* as the term for the source of a work of Shakespearean fiction. Though plays are the primary works that inspire Shakespearean fiction, the sonnets, the longer poems, and the biography of or the myths surrounding Shakespeare are other conceivable source material.
6. A. J. Hartley and David Hewson, *Macbeth: A Novel* (Las Vegas: Thomas & Mercer, 2012).
7. Stewart Kenneth Moore, illus., *The Tragedie of Macbeth by William Shakespeare: A Graphic Novel by Stewart Kenneth Moore based on an abridged version of 'The Scottish Play' produced and performed by the Prague Shakespeare Company* (CreateSpace Independent Publishing Platform, 2016).
8. Rebecca Reisert, *The Third Witch* (New York: Washington Square Press, 2002).
9. Caroline B. Cooney, *Enter Three Witches* (New York: Scholastic Press, 2007).
10. Lisa Klein, *Lady Macbeth's Daughter* (New York: Bloomsbury, 2009).
11. Neil Arksey, *MacB* (New York: Pearson Longman, 2004).
12. Alan Gratz, *Something Wicked: A Horatio Wilkes Mystery* (New York: Dial Books, 2007).
13. Cindy Brown, *Macdeath* (Dallas: Henery Press, 2015).
14. Ngaio Marsh, *Light Thickens* (New York: HarperCollins, 1994).
15. Susan Fraser King, *Lady Macbeth* (New York: Crown Publishers, 2008).
16. Eleanor Brown, *The Weird Sisters* (New York: Amy Einhorn Books, 2011).
17. Ray Bradbury, *Something Wicked This Way Comes* (New York: Avon Books, 1997).
18. William Faulkner, *The Sound and the Fury* (New York: Modern Library, 2012).
19. Agatha Christie, *By the Pricking of My Thumbs* (New York: Dodd, Mead, 1968).
20. Paul Bowles, *Let It Come Down* (Santa Rosa: Black Sparrow Press, 1997).
21. Margaret Jane Kidnie, *Shakespeare and the Problem of Adaptation* (London: Routledge, 2009).
22. Ibid., 2.
23. Gary D. Schmidt, *The Wednesday Wars* (Boston, MA: Houghton Mifflin, 2007).
24. Ibid., 72.

25. Emily St. John Mandel, *Station Eleven* (New York: Vintage, 2015).
26. Ibid., 37–38.
27. Ibid., 119.
28. *King Lear*, dir. Jean-Luc Godard (1987, DVD, Lear Media).
29. Mandel, *Station Eleven*, 288.
30. Ibid., 288.
31. Ibid., 288.
32. Linda Lê, *The Three Fates*, trans. Mark Polizzotti (New York: New Directions, 2010).
33. Ibid., 49–50.

Chapter 5

Canon Fodder and Conscripted Genres
The Hogarth Project and the Modern Shakespeare Novel

Laurie E. Osborne

> While there is certainly value in attending to the dynamics at work in [specific] examples, it is equally important to acknowledge that individual works also always participate in collective acts of Shakespearean adaptation, acts that considered as an aggregate are reshaping our conceptions of Shakespeare in response to energies, paths of flow, tensions, pressures, and blockages within the larger social and cultural matrix, itself constantly in flux. ... In short, by thinking of Shakespeare as a collectively created, adaptational rhizome rather than a body of texts appropriated by single adaptors, we may be able better to chart the ever-nomadic paths of Shakespearean cultural capital.[1]

Drawing on Pierre Bourdieu and Gilles Deleuze, Douglas Lanier has argued that the reciprocal relationship between popular culture and Shakespeare is rhizomatic: the ways that they grow towards each other reveal how Shakespeare's cultural capital is shifting.[2]

Notes for this section begin on page 82.

The recent commemorative novelisations of Shakespeare by the Hogarth Press both embody Shakespeare as the 'collectively created, adaptational rhizome' and contribute to our understanding of the twenty-first-century migration of Shakespeare from film to fiction as a site for adaptation. Beyond the overt moves 'redeeming Shakespeare's literariness' that Lanier details, Hogarth's ostensibly 'new' version of serial Shakespearean publication intersects in provocative ways with both historical adaptive strategies and current but less high-profile Shakespearean novels.[3] The first Hogarth novel, *The Gap of Time*, also participates in the recent adapters' choices of lesser-known Shakespearean sources, a noteworthy trend in modern Shakespeare novels.[4] As 'collective acts of Shakespearean adaptation', the Hogarth novels even underscore the recent proliferation and blurring of genres that are now broadly evident in Shakespearean fiction making. The concurrent publication of Hogarth's 'literary' Shakespeare novels and 'popular genre' adaptations that draw on the same plays signals generic intersections and duplications that register Shakespeare's cultural impact in early twenty-first-century fiction. As these contexts suggest, the Hogarth series sharpens our focus on several emergent dimensions in the encounter between modern fiction writing and Shakespeare.

This confluence of features suggests that, in addition to reaching the post-textual Shakespeare that Lanier so ably analyses, we have also entered a period of *re-textual* Shakespeare. Represented in a concentrated way by the Hogarth project, recent Shakespeare-based novels are interconnected despite varied age targets and genres; as a result, they appeal to increasingly fragmented yet coalescing reading audiences and participate in genre proliferation in important ways. Because the Hogarth series is more culmination than innovation, it makes visible the movement in Shakespearean cultural capital, but the emerging contours of the cultural matrix are often equally evident in less 'literary' Shakespeare novels.

When the Hogarth press launched their series of Shakespeare novel adaptations, the editors pointed to the distinctiveness of their project and promoted its 'literariness' by commissioning several well-established novelists to write their adaptations, each with a different style and set of literary credentials.[5] Despite the apparent novelty of producing a series of Shakespeare novels, Hogarth Press was hardly the first to do so. Almost two hundred years earlier, between 1850 and 1852, Mary Cowden Clarke, arguably the first novelist of

Shakespearean fictional adaptations for adults, published her series of fifteen novellas, *The Girlhood of Shakespeare's Heroines*.[6] She garnered her authority for these adaptations from her reputation as the Shakespearean critic who researched and published the first Shakespeare concordance, a scholarly achievement often mentioned beneath her name on the title page of the novellas.

In contrast, the Hogarth editors anchor their Shakespeare novels in the literary status and varied styles of their writers' other published work. With the possible exception of Howard Jacobson who wrote his first book, *Shakespeare's Magnanimity*, with Wilbur Sanders, the Hogarth authors' distinctive literary skills as novelists, not their critical knowledge of Shakespeare's works, qualify them for the task and in turn drive the interest and publicity for the series.[7] Paul Joseph Zajac's analysis in 'Distant Bedfellows: Shakespearean Struggles of Intimacy in Winterson's *The Gap of Time*' underscores this point. Focusing on aspects of *The Gap of Time* that intersect with Jeanette Winterson's earlier novels, Zajac explores how she adapts Shakespeare's *Winter's Tale* in response to features in the play that resonate with her artistic sensibility.[8] As Zajac's approach suggests, Hogarth's choice of creative rather than critical expertise emphasises a cultural shift in Shakespearean narrative adaptation, away from celebrating 'quintessential' Shakespearean artistic insight in the mid-nineteenth century and towards valuing recognised novelistic artistry in the early twenty-first century. This redirection of artistic energies marks Shakespeare's works more as raw materials than inspiration, as canon fodder rather than canon father.

As much as the different strategy evident in Cowden Clarke's Shakespearean series, the temporal distance between *The Girlhood of Shakespeare's Heroines* and the Hogarth Shakespeare novels might seem to ensure the uniqueness of the latter. However, their highly publicised series follows after and ultimately participates in a surprisingly large array of current 'Shakespeare series', including less high-profile series published by single authors or persistent partnerships. Perhaps we can discount the trilogies by Lesley Livingston, Lisa Mantchev and L. Jagi Lamplighter, whose serial narratives emerge from the multi-volume conventions of recent YA and science fiction.[9] Nonetheless, trilogies like Livingston's, which highlights three different plays, do represent reiterative narrative adaptations of Shakespeare's plays. The would-be serial novelisations of Shakespeare by authors like Alan Gratz, David Bergantino and

Tessa Gratton might also seem like tenuous examples, since each wrote only two books, hardly enough to constitute a series. Even so, Gratz's Horatio Wilkes detective novels, Bergantino's *Bard's Blood* horror adaptations and Gratton's historical *Queens of Innis Lear* duology signal strong, if abbreviated, intentions to serialise Shakespeare while at the same time exploiting his works as a source for different genres.[10] In the process they combine the swift emergence of genres and genre-blending with the narrative (and marketing) prevalence of the series.

Even these potential series demonstrate that treating Shakespeare's works as a linked array of source materials for serial novel-writing not only predates but also extends well beyond the Hogarth project. Kim Askew and Amy Helmes's *Twisted Lit* adaptations, Jackie French's growing array of younger YA Shakespeare fiction, and Sophie Masson's more eclectic *Shakespeare Collection* actively embraced the principle of the Shakespeare series before and during the Hogarth project. US authors Askew and Helmes launched their *Twisted Lit* series, entirely grounded on Shakespearean novelisation, in 2012. They even followed up the conventional publication of their reimagining of *Macbeth* in *Exposure* (2012), *The Tempest* in *Tempestuous* (2012), and *Romeo and Juliet* in *Anyone But You* (2014), with *Puck*, a self-published adaptation of *A Midsummer Night's Dream*, in 2016.[11] Askew and Helms adapt each play individually but frame the array collectively as Shakespearean. At the same time that their YA approach appeals to the still-dominant educational market identified by Lanier,[12] this array of independent novels deploys Shakespeare as both a serial source and a unifying structure for varied fictions.

In addition to preceding the Hogarth Shakespeare with their own collected novelisations, Australian authors Jackie French and Sophie Masson illustrate the global scope of Shakespearean series. French actually identifies her Shakespeare adaptations as a 'Shakespeare series' on her webpage, which lists *Ophelia, Queen of Denmark* (2014), *I Am Juliet* (2014), *Third Witch* (2017) and *The Diary of William Shakespeare, Gentleman* (2016).[13] In a 2019 author's newsletter, she describes the series' scope in the context of its final book, *My Name is NOT Peaseblossom* (2019):

> I began the Shakespeare Series writing about Romeo and Juliet from the point of view of Juliet, adding scenes that might have happened, while staying true to the play. *Ophelia, Queen of Denmark* is *Hamlet* but with a happy ending and a lot of cheese – but true to the play too.

> *Third Witch* is *Macbeth*, but with no witchcraft, only pretense and
> mistakes – and a happy ending (for some, at least). *My Name is NOT
> Peaseblossom* is the last in the series ... [L]ike *A Midsummer Night's
> Dream*, *My Name is NOT Peaseblossom* has deeper questions at its
> heart. ... Which would you rather have, real life or faked happiness?[14]

French simultaneously identifies her novels as 'true to the play' and details notable variations that she has incorporated. That move resembles Cowden Clarke's assertions about her novellas, which she backs up with footnotes to the plays as the sources of her extrapolative fictions. French makes similar claims for *The Diary of William Shakespeare, Gentleman* (2016): 'The world knows the name of William Shakespeare. This book reveals the man – lover, son and poet. Based on new documentary evidence, as well as textual examination of his plays, this fascinating book gives a tantalising glimpse at what might have been: the other hands that helped craft those plays, the secrets that must ever be hidden but – just possibly – may now be told'.[15] This book represents yet another genre, the fictional biography. Like French, Australian YA novelist Sophie Masson, who has written five Shakespeare novels, started to embrace varied styles and approaches well before Hogarth Press envisioned their eclectic array of novels. Masson lists her books as 'The Shakespeare Collection' and includes novels that range from historical fiction to fantasy to mystery.[16] Like the Hogarth novelists, French and Masson embrace varying approaches to his work, adding biographical fiction, mystery and fantasy into the mix.

At the same time, like Cowden Clarke, these authors envision their Shakespearean adaptations as a series or a collection. The difference between these two designations is significant: while collections include works loosely allied by authorship – both the novelists' and Shakespeare's – a series implies coherent, intentional planning, perhaps grounded in multi-book contracts, like that of Askew and Helms. The envisioned multi-narrative coherence associated with series also often derives as much from genre as from authorship – the YA fantasy/science fiction trilogy or the detective and horror genre reiterative structures adopted by Gratz and Bergantino. French's self-defined series falls somewhere between the two. Her adaptations of different plays take Young Adult literature as their genre. By omitting her fictionalised biography in the description of her novels as a series, French identifies Shakespeare's works as a governing connection for novels written over the space of several years.

The unannounced Shakespearean collections of established US novelists like Lisa Klein and Grace Tiffany, both with academic credentials reminiscent of Cowden Clarke's, also register genre changeability. Both authors vary their approach and have published several adaptations of Shakespeare's plays and sometimes of his life story. While Klein adapts particular plays in *Ophelia* (2006) and *Lady Macbeth's Daughter* (2009), her most recent novel, *Love Disguised* (2013), is 'a comic romp featuring young Will Shakespeare' and his invented cross-dressing friend Meg/Mack.[17] Tiffany, a multi-talented Early Modern scholar, has written five novels with varying connections to Shakespeare: two novelistic adaptations of specific plays – a YA novel *Ariel* (2005) and a historical novel *The Turquoise Ring* (2006) intended for adult readers; two historical novels centring around women associated with Shakespeare, *My Father Had a Daughter* (2004) and *Paint* (2013); and one fictional biography of Shakespeare himself, *Will* (2005).[18] Though these authors lay no claims to be creating series or collections, their novels nonetheless demonstrate the authors' sustained interest in Shakespeare and his works as source material for fiction.

Some writers create or sustain *ad hoc* series by resorting to self-publishing, in the same way that Askew and Helms extended their series. After conventionally publishing *Falling for Hamlet* (2011), praised by Erika Hateley for its adaptive approach, Michelle Ray created a *de facto* Shakespearean series with two self-published novels, *Mac/Beth* (2015) and *Much Ado about Something* (2016).[19] Some self-published authors, like Alison May (*Choc Lit: 21st Century Bard*), C. E. Wilson (*Shakespeare for Everyone Else*) and Marian Cheatham (*Stratford High*), announce in their subtitles their intentions to serialise Shakespeare in novel form.[20] In the 'high-interest/low pages series' of *Unbarred* novels, *Duty or Desire*, *Fight or Flee*, *Friend or Foe* and *Heart or Mind* (2016), Patrick Jones reimagines four different Shakespearean tragedies in the context of adolescent encounters with incarceration, gang violence and racial conflict.[21] As his focus suggests, thematic considerations as much as Shakespearean sources and educational intentions can drive such series.

Even Hogarth's decision to commission several authors rather than one for their Shakespearean adaptations has earlier, though less high-brow precursors in the 2005 Silhouette Romance 'Shakespeare in Love' series, in which three different romance authors write Shakespearean novels, all set in Avon, Texas: Myrna MacKenzie's

Much Ado About Matchmaking, Elizabeth Harbison's *The Taming of the Two* and Karen Rose Smith's *Twelfth Night Proposal*.[22] A & C Black's *Shakespeare Today* series hired six authors to 'retell' ten of Shakespeare's plays 'in consultation with The Centre for Literacy in Primary Education' with the advice that the novels 'can be used in the White Wolves guided reading programme with experienced readers in Year 6'.[23] Given these acknowledged and expanded Shakespearean novel series, the Hogarth Shakespeare project is clearly a follower rather than a leader in publishing Shakespeare fiction collectively.

At least as interesting a phenomenon as the novels themselves, in fact more intriguing than some of the books mentioned above, this current trend in reiterative Shakespearean novel-writing coincides with developments in serialisation currently dominating cinematic and televisual art. Reciprocal influence is certainly possible, given several recent Shakespeare-inflected television series: ABC Family's *10 Things I Hate about You: The Series* (2009–2010, one season), CW's *Star-Crossed* (2014, one season), TNT's *Will* (2017, one season), the BBC's *Upstart Crow* (2016+), TNT's *The Royals* (2014, four seasons) and ABC's *Still Star-Crossed* (2017, one season).[24] The last two are themselves adaptations of Shakespearean YA fiction. *The Royals* started its broadcast life as a loose adaptation of Michelle Ray's *Falling for Hamlet*, while *Still Star-Crossed* is based on Melinda Taub's YA novel of the same title.[25] Such connections suggest that collective adaptation, specifically in the case of serialisation, does indeed provide important access to Shakespeare's cultural impact.

Drawing on serial narrative as renewable cultural capital does not, however, assure success, either for Shakespeare-based television or novel series. After examining the shortened broadcast life of *Star-Crossed*, Kinga Földáry concludes that the strong dramatic arcs in the plays and in particular the high stakes in *Romeo and Juliet* as a source undermine the rhythms and impetus for continuity that are necessary in series television.[26] Even so, at least one series based on the tragedy, the Japanese anime *Romio X Jurieto* has been very successful.[27] However, its longevity may derive from its capacious adaptive reach as it incorporates elements from multiple plays. Certainly, the very popular and critically acclaimed Canadian TV series *Slings and Arrows* thrived by simultaneously staging and adapting three different individual plays in its three successive seasons.[28] These televised Shakespeare series, both successful and unsuccessful, support what the Hogarth project foregrounds: serial artwork as a mode of adaptation has increasingly contributed to Shakespeare's cultural presence.

At the same time, the Hogarth project participates in the unexpected retrieval of less canonically obvious Shakespearean sources. Much as Shakespearean filmmakers have begun to take up unusual play choices like Ralph Fiennes' *Coriolanus* and Michael Almereyda's *Cymbeline*, authors have begun to adapt plays other than the ubiquitous *Hamlet, Romeo and Juliet* and *Macbeth*.[29] Some Hogarth plays, like *The Taming of the Shrew* and *Othello*, which already have some novelistic history, have experienced a resurgence in the last five years. However, *The Winter's Tale*, chosen by Jeanette Winterson for the first novel of the Hogarth series, has not been adapted in fiction, as far as I can discover, since Mary Cowden Clarke's *The Girlhood of Shakespeare's Heroines*.

Hogarth's blend of currently popular and less obvious plays actually resembles Cowden Clarke's incorporation of a range of heroines. Her character choices reflect their popularity in her Victorian context: *Portia; The Heiress of Belmont* (*Merchant*), *The Thane's Daughter* (*Macbeth*), *Imogene; The Peerless* (*Cymbeline*) and *Meg and Alice; The Merry Maids of Windsor* (*Merry Wives*) were contemporaneously greeted with enthusiasm on stage and in literary criticism.[30] Many of her subjects, particularly Portia and Lady Macbeth as the first two heroines, seem designed to initiate and maintain interest in the series. Even so, interspersed among her novellas, she included more surprising female heroines, like *Hermione, The Russian Princess* (*The Winter's Tale*) and the bed-trick participants, *Helena, The Physician's Orphan* (*All's Well that Ends Well*) and *Isabella, the Votress* (*Measure for Measure*).[31]

Winterson's adaptation of *The Winter's Tale* was clearly not selected in order to open the Hogarth series with a currently popular play. In line with the precedence of authors over sources, Hogarth contacted Winterson and then asked which play she wished to adapt. According to the reviews, Winterson surprised the publishers by choosing *Winter's Tale* because of her personal interest in it. Like Perdita, Winterson was a foundling and therefore had always been drawn to the play.[32] Though not a currently popular or obviously adaptable play, the novelist's idiosyncratic choice garnered its own level of promotional interest, particularly since *The Gap in Time* was the opening salvo of the series. One result of her unusual choice was that the Hogarth series seemed to be directing new attention to plays often ignored by novelists since Cowden Clarke.

However, perhaps unexpectedly, this interest in relatively underexplored plays is hardly unique to the Hogarth adaptations. Almost simultaneously, *The Winter's Tale* also inspired E. K. Johnston's YA novel, *Exit, Pursued by a Bear* (2016).[33] Johnston eschewed the common YA strategy of incorporating high school performance or academic study at the heart of recent YA adaptations of *Othello*, Shakespeare's other newly popular jealousy play. Instead, she deploys the tactics of adaptive translation and intermittent linguistic similarities and citations that have come to characterise the Hogarth Shakespeare novels. Lanier identifies this strategy with the Hogarth series' literary aspirations,[34] but Johnston's novel fits solidly in the less literary category of YA fiction, with high school and cheerleading camp as its principal social contexts. Other less frequently novelised Shakespearean plays have also recently inspired fiction writers. While *The Tempest* has been fruitful adaptive material for many years, two recent novels, Ali Smith's *Spring: A Novel* (2019) and Mark Haddon's *The Porpoise* (2019), turn to another, more obscure late Shakespearean play, *Pericles*.[35] The press releases for Haddon's novel suggest one significant advantage to adapting less well-known Shakespearean materials:

> This contemporary story mirrors the ancient legend of Antiochus, whose love for the daughter of his dead wife was discovered by the adventurer Appolinus [*sic*] of Tyre. The tale appeared in many forms through the ages; Apollinus becoming the swashbuckling Pericles in Shakespeare's eponymous play. In *The Porpoise*, as Angelique comes to terms with a life imprisoned on her father's estate, Darius morphs into Pericles, voyaging through a mythic world. In a bravura feat of storytelling, Haddon recounts his many exploits in thrilling fashion, mining the meaning of the old legends while creating parallels with the monstrous modern world Angelica inhabits.[36]

As this description suggests, Shakespeare's play has not as completely superseded the mythic source material as his most popular plays, like *Romeo and Juliet*, have displaced their source materials from cultural currency.

This move to less well known plays also appears in YA novels like Patrick Jones' retelling of *Antony and Cleopatra* in *Duty or Desire* (2016), C. E. Wilson's *All's Well that Ends Well* (2014) and Tessa Gratton's *Lady Hotspur* (2020).[37] While it is far too early to suggest a shift away from the narrative dominance of the usual Shakespearean plays, adapting less widely known materials tends to increase the circulation of the Shakespearean 'brand' rather than shifting less familiar plays into positions of greater cultural influence, as one might argue that a linguistically and narratively faithful film like Fiennes' *Coriolanus* does.

Of the several comedies that have recently enjoyed their first appearance in narrative form since Cowden Clarke's *Girlhood* novellas, *Twelfth Night*'s extensive renewal in novelistic adaptation foregrounds the pervasiveness of genre variation. Sophie Masson's YA theatrical fiction *Malvolio's Revenge* (2005) led the way, but Elizabeth Hand's magical realist novel *Illyria* (2007) soon followed.[38] A few years later, a small flurry of more directly plot-driven *Twelfth Night* adaptations hit the market in twenty-four months: Celia Rees's historical novel, *The Fool's Girl* (2010), Michelle Mankin's self-published rock romance, *Love Evolution* (2012) and Lev A. C. Rosen's *All Men of Genius* (2011), a YA cross-dressing steampunk mash-up of *Twelfth Night* and *The Importance of Being Earnest*.[39] Adapting the same play into so many different novelistic sub-genres and with such different intended audiences not only suggests the current relevance of the gender ambiguities and homoeroticism in its love plots but also shows that Shakespearean adaptations participate in genre evolution.

Joss Whedon's recent *Much Ado about Nothing* and *Shakespeare ReTold*'s newsroom adaptation register the same popular interest in that comedy that inspired eleven *Much Ado* novels published in only thirteen years: Jody Gehrmann's *Triple Shot Betty* (2008), Kjersten Beck's *Much Ado about Magic* (2012)*, Michelle Mankin's *Love Revolution* (2012)*, Alison May's *Much Ado about Sweet Something* (2013)*, C. E. Wilson's *Much Ado about Nothing: Shakespeare for Everyone Else* (2013)*, Marion Cheatham's *Ruined* (2014)*, Marina Fiorato's *Beatrice and Benedick* (2014), Michelle Ray's *Much Ado about Something* (2016)*, Lily Anderson's *The Only Thing Worse than Me is You* (2016), McKelle George's *Speak Easy, Speak Love* (2017) and Molly Booth's *Nothing Happened* (2018) (*self-published novels).[40] Despite their various forms from YA to historical fiction, these works, like the *Twelfth Night* novels, implicitly affirm Shakespeare's potential social and cultural relevance as a strong factor in adaptation. For example, Gehrmann, Cheatham, Wilson, Mankin, Ray and Anderson all adapt the comedy in ways that appropriate new concerns about the use of technology in public sexual shaming. Almost concurrently these authors explore the dangerous consequences of slander within a new context where, as in Shakespeare's play, the manipulation of appearances can ruin reputations and naïve young lives.

Such narrative adaptations enact what Ariane Balizet identifies in teen film as re-cognition, or re-making and thus re-understanding Shakespeare's play in a wholly new cultural context. According to Balizet, the point of re-cognition is not to incite audiences – or readers – to uncover the Shakespearean core or celebrate the familiarity of recognising Shakespearean elements.[41] Instead these novels, like the films that Balizet examines, show Shakespeare's plays remade in ways that encourage audiences to reimagine the Shakespearean original as a means of understanding more fully contemporary cultural and social pressures. Following Balizet's logic, we might suspect that this noticeable shift in desirable Shakespearean sources reflects the influence of current Western social and cultural issues more than an investment in Shakespeare's works.

In *William Shakespeare's Much Ado about Mean Girls* (2019), by Ian Doescher, the current cultural matrix completely outweighs the apparent Shakespearean source.[42] Rather than adapting Shakespeare's comedy, Doescher translates Tina Fey's *Mean Girls* screenplay into pseudo-Shakespearean iambic pentameter. Current culture obviously dominates when the only residual aspect of Shakespeare's play is the first three words of the title. Despite this radical departure from any Shakespearean source, Doescher's ongoing strategy of importing Shakespearean linguistic features and imposing Shakespearean authorship upon current cultural works aligns with the other patterns explored here. The screenplay's subtitle, '*Pop Shakespeare, Book 1*', offers yet another promise of serial adaptation, supported by the simultaneous release of *William Shakespeare's Get Thee . . . Back to the Future!* (2019).[43] Because Doescher's adaptive approach inverts the normal trajectory – he revises the language of popular and cult filmscripts to position those works as retroactively Shakespearean – he is demonstrably incorporating, even creating, 'new' Shakespearean materials. While claiming Shakespeare as a unifying principle in popular culture and possibly marking an outer boundary for adaptation, his *William Shakespeare's Much Ado*, *Get Thee* and *Star Wars* books also embrace yet another genre: the screenplay.

The proliferation of genres evident in the *Twelfth Night* and *Much Ado* adaptations pervades the Hogarth series structurally because of its choice of authors. The Hogarth novelists range from those with stellar literary credentials, including Pulitzers, Booker prizes or nominations to both, to writers whose cultural authority is more likely to derive from Oscar nominations or smaller, more specialised prizes for comic novels or site-specific crime fiction. While the incorporation of varied genre fiction in the series may be most obvious in the Hogarth *Macbeth*, written by Nordic crime novelist Jo Nesbø, other Hogarth authors include futuristic writer Margaret Atwood and thriller-writer Gillian Flynn, whose adaptation of *Hamlet* seems to be on hold.[44] By commissioning these writers and offering them the choices of which plays to adapt, Hogarth not only reinforces the generic flexibility evident within Shakespearean novelisations but locates that flexibility within the Shakespearean canon, which provides both the common ground and the potential for generic variation.

In fact, concurrently published adaptations beyond the Hogarth novels make the trend of multiplying adaptation genres especially clear. Consider the near simultaneous publication of Hogarth 'literary' Shakespeare novels and adaptations of the same plays in other genres. Winterson's and Johnston's adaptations of *The Winter's Tale* merely initiate this trend. Ann Tyler's adaptation of *Taming*, *Vinegar Girl* (June 2016), was published slightly after Stephanie Kate Strohm's YA novel *The Taming of the Drew* (April 2016), and Tracey Chevalier's reimagining of *Othello* in *New Boy* (May 2017) came out one month after Sonia Belasco's adaptation of the same play in *Speak of Me As I Am* (April 2017).[45] Essentially, the literary adaptations of specific plays commissioned by Hogarth reach the market almost simultaneously with independent YA novels based on those same plays.

Winterson's and Johnston's novels comfortably inhabit their own distinct genres – literary 'magical realism' and YA fiction respectively – but these adaptations explore current sexual preoccupations and problems in ways that ally them. Winterson grounds the loss of Perdita in a fully realised, if repressed, homoerotic relationship between Leo and Zeno as young men, while Johnston characterises her Paulina as explicitly gay. Whereas Winterson is most concerned with the effects of her parents' troubles on Perdita, the baby Perdita is literally lost to abortion in *Exit, Pursued by a Bear*. Johnston concentrates on Hermione's experience of social ostracism, soiled reputation and persistent anxiety about her violator; she represents her cheerleader captain Hermione as simultaneously virginally pure, as far as she knows, and as sexually compromised by date rape, though she has no memory of her violation because she was drugged. With these adaptive choices, more than the common source and publication date align these two novels. Released within six months of each other, Jeannette Winterson's *The Gap of Time* and E. K. Johnston's *Exit, Pursued by a Bear* both modernise the core dysfunctions in Shakespeare's play.

This multi-genre novelistic synchronicity coincides with a blending of novel forms even evident in *The Gap of Time*. The memoir-inflected interest that drives Winterson's novel surfaces overtly in its final pages with an authorial intrusion into the narrative such that her novel resonates with the current enthusiasm for creative nonfiction. Two Hogarth novels, Ann Tyler's *Vinegar Girl* and Tracey Chevalier's *New Boy*, participate in genre blurring that becomes merely more obvious in their concurrent publication with explicitly YA novels. Tyler's *Vinegar Girl* restages Shakespeare's Kate as twenty-something Katherine Battista, whose father is a professor and researcher; in translating *Shrew* into this situation, Tyler's novel closely fits with the recently established genre of 'New Adult fiction', a category designed to capture adolescent readers as they age out of YA fiction by offering protagonists and issues centring on their experiences. Using one characteristic situation of that readership – working through separation from paternal authority – Tyler reshapes Katherine's story around the demands of her scientist father. With his insistence that she marry his Russian research assistant to keep him in the country, the novel reframes the arranged marriage and Pyotr's sexist assumptions within a plausible contemporary context. Using the increasingly familiar YA setting of a youth summer theatre, Strohm transfers the taming strategies from Shakespeare's play into the techniques that her heroine uses to control and torment the arrogant young man cast as Petruchio to her Kate. Both novels concentrate their negotiations with *Taming* around younger protagonists dealing with exasperating but inescapable male expectations. Perhaps such alignment between announced literary fiction and New Adult and YA novels in Shakespearean adaptations of *Taming* is unsurprising. However, Tracy Chevalier's transposition of *Othello* into playground competition and the quick-paced instant love and break-ups of eleven-year-olds frames that adaptation in the context of children's literature as much as does the school theatre context of Sonia Belasco's *Speak of Me As I Am*. These concurrent publications of Hogarth novels and YA novels adapting the same source underscore the genre variations within the Hogarth series itself. As a result, despite the pursuit of 'literariness' that Lanier diagnoses, the individual Hogarth novels end up revealing that Shakespearean adaptations currently challenge distinctions between literary fiction and genre fiction.

The Hogarth Shakespeare series, as a culminating reflection of collective and individual narrative Shakespeare adaptations, gives focused evidence of several significant interactions between Shakespeare as a cultural force and Shakespeare as a cultural raw material. While Lanier has grounds for claiming that Hogarth's 'coherent program to update Shakespeare in "literary retellings" ... seems rather different from the idiosyncratic one-off adaptations that have tended to characterize novelizations up to this point. It is an escalation rather than just another manifestation of it',[46] this escalation exposes more than the constraints of literariness and narratives of redemption that Lanier identifies in the opening novels. The Hogarth series both contributes to and emphasises Shakespeare's participation in the three zones of cultural capital explored here: our individual and collective artistic investment in series, the culturally provoked shifts in adaptive choice, and evolving genres that increasingly test former lines between literary and genre fiction.

In the context of the striking number of adaptations that are or become series, the Hogarth novels foreground Shakespeare as a principle of collectivity, a gesture towards coherence in works whose larger alliances reside in genre or authorship. Hogarth's Shakespearean frame draws attention to new adaptive choices, like *Winter's Tale* and *Pericles*, which expand but perhaps dilute Shakespeare as a useful collective canon. In its concurrent publication with those supposedly 'idiosyncratic one-off adaptations', the Hogarth project underscores how emerging and shifting narrative genres deploy the same plays to target varied reading audiences while registering similar social and cultural concerns. What the Hogarth series shows is that Shakespeare's works are both fictional fodder at the service of contemporary narrative artistry and conscripted ground troops in the competition over narrative genres, social relevance and cultural influence.

Laurie E. Osborne is the Zacamy Professor of English, Emerita at Colby College. Her research has ranged from nineteenth-century performance editions to Shakespeare on film, on television and in contemporary popular culture. Her recent publications include 'Reviving Cowden Clarke: Rewriting Shakespeare's Heroines in YA Fiction', in *Shakespearean Echoes* (Palgrave, 2015), 'The Paranormal Bard: Shakespeare Is/As Undead', in *Shakespeare and Millennial Fiction* (Cambridge, 2018) and 'Teaching Global Shakespeare: Visual Culture Projects in Action', in *Global Shakespeares* (Routledge, 2019). She is also co-editor and contributor to *Shakespeare and the 'Live' Theatre Broadcast Experience* (Routledge, 2018).

Notes

1. Douglas Lanier, 'Recent Shakespeare Adaptations and the Mutations of Cultural Capital', *Shakespeare Studies* 38 (2010), 104–113, here 113.
2. Ibid., 101–102.
3. Douglas Lanier, 'The Hogarth Shakespeare Series: Redeeming Shakespeare's Literariness', in *Shakespeare and Millennial Fiction*, ed. Andrew James Hartley (Cambridge: Cambridge University Press, 2017), 230–50, here 230.
4. Jeanette Winterson, *The Gap of Time: A Novel* (London: Hogarth Shakespeare, 2015).
5. Lanier, 'The Hogarth Shakespeare Series', 231–32.
6. Mary Cowden Clarke, *The Girlhood of Shakespeare's Heroines* (London, 1850–1852).
7. Wilbur Sanders and Howard Jacobson, *Shakespeare's Magnanimity: Four Tragic Heroes, Their Friends, and Families* (New York: Oxford University Press, 1978.
8. Paul Joseph Zajac, 'Distant Bedfellows: Shakespearean Struggles of Intimacy in Winterson's *The Gap of Time*', *Critique: Studies in Contemporary Fiction* 59, no. 3 (2018), 332–45.
9. L. Jagi Lamplighter, *Prospero in Hell* (New York: Tor Books, 2010), *Prospero Lost* (New York: Tor Books, 2010), and *Prospero Regained* (New York: Tor Books, 2011); Lesley Livingston, *Darklight* (New York: HarperCollins, 2009), *Tempestuous* (New York: HarperCollins, 2010), and *Wondrous Strange* (New York: HarperCollins, 2009); and Lisa Mantchev, *Eyes Like Stars: Theatre Illuminata* (New York: Feiwel & Friends, McMillan, 2009), *Perchance to Dream: Theatre Illuminata #2* (New York: Feiwel & Friends, McMillan, 2010), and *So Silver Bright: Theatre Illuminata #3* (New York: Feiwel & Friends, McMillan, 2011).
10. Alan Gratz, *Something Rotten: A Horatio Wilkes Mystery* (New York: Dial, 2007) and *Something Wicked* (New York: Dial, 2008); David Bergantino, *Hamlet II: Ophelia's Revenge – Bard's Blood #1* (New York: Pocket Books, 2003) and *A Midsummer Night's Scream: Bard's Blood #2* (New York: Pocket Books, 2003); and

Tessa Gratton, *The Queens of Innis Lear* (New York: Tor Books, 2018) and *Lady Hotspur* (New York: Tor Books, 2020).
11. Kim Askew and Amy Helmes, *Exposure: A Twisted Lit Novel* (Blue Ash, OH: Merit Press, 2012), *Tempestuous: A Twisted Lit Novel* (Blue Ash, OH: Merit Press, 2012), *Anyone But You* (Blue Ash, OH: Merit Press, 2014), and *Puck* (Doublet Press, 2016).
12. Lanier, 'Recent Shakespeare Adaptations', 105.
13. Jackie French, *Ophelia, Queen of Denmark* (Sydney: HarperCollins Australia, 2014), *I Am Juliet* (Sydney: HarperCollins Australia 2014), *The Third Witch* (Sydney: HarperCollins Australia, 2017), *Diary of William Shakespeare, Gentleman* (Sydney: HarperCollins Australia, 2016), and *My Name is NOT Peaseblossom* (Sydney: HarperCollins Australia, 2019).
14. Jackie French, 'The wonder of the oldest profession of them all', Author's Newsletter, promotions@harpercollins.com (7 May 2019).
15. Jackie French, Shakespeare Series (http://www.jackiefrench.com/shakespeare-series).
16. Sophie Masson, *The Shakespeare Collection* (http://www.sophiemasson.org/books.html).
17. Lisa Klein, *Ophelia* (New York: Bloomsbury USA Children's Books, 2006) and *Lady Macbeth's Daughter* (New York: Bloomsbury USA Children's Books, 2009); Lisa Klein, *Love Disguised* (New York: Bloomsbury USA Children's Books, 2013), as subtitled on Klein's author's website (http://www.authorlisaklein.com/love-disguised.html).
18. Grace Tiffany, *Ariel* (New York: HarperTeen, 2005), *The Turquoise Ring* (New York: Berkley Trade, 2006), *My Father Had a Daughter: Judith Shakespeare's Tale* (New York: Berkley Trade, 2004), *Paint* (New York: Bagwyn Books, 2013), and *Will* (New York: Berkley Trade, 2005).
19. Michelle Ray, *Falling for Hamlet* (New York: Poppy, 2011); Erica Hateley, 'Sink or Swim? Revising Ophelia in Contemporary Young Adult Fiction', *Children's Literature Quarterly Association* 38, no. 1 (2013), 435–48, here 444–46; Michelle Ray, *Mac/Beth: The Price of Fame Should Not Be Murder* (Amazon Digital Services, 2015), and *Much Ado About Something* (Amazon Digital Services, 2016).
20. Marion Cheatham, *Ruined: Stratford High* (Amazon Digital Services, 2014) and *4Ever Girl: Stratford High* (Amazon Digital Services, 2016); Alison May, *Midsummer Night Dreams* (UK: Choc Lit, 2014) and *Much Ado about Sweet Nothing* (UK: Choc Lit, 2015); and C. E. Wilson, *All's Well that Ends Well: Shakespeare for Everyone Else* (Amazon Digital Services, 2014), *Much Ado about Nothing: Shakespeare for Everyone Else* (Amazon Digital Services, 2013), and *Othello: Shakespeare for Everyone Else* (Amazon Digital Services, 2013).
21. Patrick Jones, *Duty or Desire, Fight or Flee, Friend or Foe,* and *Heart or Mind*, *Unbarred Series* (Minneapolis: Darby Creek, 2016).
22. Elizabeth Harbison, *The Taming of the Two: Shakespeare in Love* (New York: Silhouette Romance, 2005); Myrna MacKenzie, *Much Ado about Matchmaking: Shakespeare in Love* (New York: Silhouette Romance, 2005); and Karen Rose Smith, *Twelfth Night Proposal: Shakespeare in Love* (New York: Silhouette Romance, 2005).
23. Franzeska G. Ewert, *William Shakespeare's The Tempest, Retold* (London: A & C Black, 2007), cover, 2.

24. *10 Things I Hate about You: The Series*, creator Carter Covington (ABC Family, 2009–2010); *The Royals*, creator Mark Schwahn (TNT, 2014–2017); *Star-Crossed*, dir. Meredith Averill et al. (USA CW, 2014); *Still Star-Crossed* (ABC, 2017); *Will*, creator Craig Pierce (TNT, 2017); and *Upstart Crow*, creator Ben Elton (BBC 2016–2018). See also *Shakespeare ReTold*, dir. Brian Percival (BBC, 2005).
25. Ray, *Falling for Hamlet* and *The Royals* (TNT, 2014–2017); Melinda Taub, *Still Star-Crossed* (New York: Random House, 2013) and *Still Star-Crossed* (ABC, 2017).
26. Kinga Földáry, 'Serial Shakespeare: The Case of *Star-Crossed* (2014)', in *Forme, strategies e mutations serial*, ed. A. Bernardelli et al., *Between* 6, no. 11 (2016), http://www.betweenjournal.it.
27. *Romio X Jurieto*, dir. Fumitoshi Oizaki (Chubu-nippon Broadcasting Company: Japan – CBC, 2007–).
28. *Slings and Arrows*, seasons I–III, creators Susan Coyne, Bob Martin and Mark McKinney (Toronto: Rhombus Media, 2003, 2005, 2006).
29. *Coriolanus*, dir. Ralph Fiennes (Icon Entertainment, 2012) and *Cymbeline*, dir. Michael Almereyda (Lionsgate, 2014).
30. Cowden Clarke, *The Girlhood of Shakespeare's Heroines*, Tales I, II, V and XV.
31. Ibid., Tales III, VI and XIII.
32. Alexandra Alter, 'Reimagining Shakespeare's Plays', *International New York Times*, 8 October 2015, 11.
33. E. K. Johnston, *Exit, Pursued by a Bear* (New York: Dutton Books for Young Readers, 2016).
34. Lanier, 'The Hogarth Shakespeare Series', 238.
35. Mark Haddon, *The Porpoise* (New York: Doubleday, 2019); Ali Smith, *Spring: A Novel* (London: Pantheon Books, 2019).
36. https://booksandbookskw.com/the-porpoise-mark-haddon/.
37. Jones, *Duty or Desire*; Gratton, *Lady Hotspur*; Wilson, *All's Well that Ends Well*.
38. Sophie Masson, *Malvolio's Revenge* (London: Hodder Children's Books, 2005); Elizabeth Hand, *Illyria* (New York: Viking, 2007).
39. Celia Rees, *The Fool's Girl* (New York: Bloomsbury USA Children's Books, 2010); Mankin, *Love Evolution*; Lev A. C. Rosen, *All Men of Genius* (New York: Tor Books, 2011).
40. *Much Ado About Nothing*, dir. Joss Whedon (Bellwether Pictures, 2012), and *Much Ado about Nothing: Shakespeare ReTold* (BBC, 7 November 2005); Jody Gehrman, *Confessions of a Triple Shot Betty* (New York: Dial Books for Young Readers, 2008); Kjersten Beck, *Much Ado about Magic* (Amazon Services, 2012); Mankin, *Love Revolution*; May, *Much Ado about Sweet Nothing*; Wilson, *Much Ado about Nothing: Shakespeare for Everyone Else*; Cheatham, *Ruined*; Marina Fiorato, *Beatrice and Benedick* (London: Hodder & Stoughton, 2014); Ray, *Much Ado about Something*; Lily Anderson, *The Only Thing Worse than Me is You* (New York: St. Martin's Griffin, 2016); McKelle George, *Speak Easy Speak Love* (New York: HarperCollins: Greenwillow Books, 2017); Molly Booth, *Nothing Happened* (New York: Little Brown Books for Young Readers, 2018).
41. Ariane Balizet, 'Teen Scenes: Recognizing Shakespeare in Teen Film', in *Almost Shakespeare: Reinventing His Worlds for Cinema and Television*, ed. James R. Keller and Leslie Stratyner (Jefferson, NC: McFarland, 2004), 122–136, here 123. See also Ariane Balizet, *Shakespeare and Girls' Studies: Routledge Studies in Shakespeare* (New York: Routledge, 2019).

42. Ian Doescher, *William Shakespeare's Much Ado about Mean Girls: Pop Shakespeare, Book 1* (New York: Quirk Books, 2019).
43. Ian Doescher, *William Shakespeare's Get Thee ... Back to the Future!* (New York: Quirk Books, 2019).
44. Jo Nesbø, *Macbeth* (London: Hogarth Shakespeare, 2018); Margaret Atwood, *Hag-Seed* (London: Hogarth Shakespeare, 2016).
45. Ann Tyler, *Vinegar Girl* (London: Hogarth Shakespeare, 2016); Stephanie Kate Strohm, *The Taming of the Drew* (New York: Sky Pony Press, 2016); Tracy Chevalier, *New Boy* (London: Hogarth Shakespeare, 2017); Sonia Belasco, *Speak of Me As I Am* (New York: Philomel Books [Penguin Random House], 2017).
46. Lanier, 'The Hogarth Shakespeare Series', 231.

Chapter 6

Loving Shakespeare
Anne Tyler's *Vinegar Girl* and the Hogarth Shakespeare Project

Elizabeth Rivlin

Near the end of a promotional video that Vintage Books produced to launch the Hogarth Shakespeare Project, novelistic retellings of seven of Shakespeare's plays, several of the participating authors take turns reciting the famous closing couplet of Sonnet 18: 'So long as men can breathe, or eyes can see / So long lives this, and this gives life to thee'.[1] The authors' collective recitation suggests that the purpose of the project (the second 'this') is to participate in an ongoing, continuous revivification of Shakespeare ('thee'). In turn, the publisher's website connects Shakespeare's continued survival to his lovableness: 'For four hundred years, Shakespeare's works have been performed, read, and loved throughout the world. They have been reinterpreted for each new generation, whether as teen films, musicals, science-fiction flicks, Japanese warrior tales, or literary transformations'.[2] The project justifies itself through its participation

Notes for this section begin on page 99.

in a history of widespread adaptation, dissemination and reception, in which Shakespeare must be made perpetually new and fresh 'for each new generation' so that readers and audiences will continue to have an emotional bond with him. The key to keeping Shakespeare alive is making readers and audiences love him, and in this way the Hogarth Shakespeare is concerned above all with promoting a positive affective response in its readers.[3]

If the Hogarth Shakespeare positions itself as a labour of love, Anne Tyler had a problem: *The Taming of the Shrew*, which she elected to retell for the Hogarth Shakespeare as *Vinegar Girl* (2016), strikes many people today as distinctly unlovable.[4] The play's open misogyny, which displays how a husband subordinates his wife and brings her to accept her submission in public, threatens to make the work unpalatable and even unacceptable to contemporary fiction readers, especially considering that the most likely American buyer of trade fiction like the Hogarth Shakespeare is an upper-middle-class, college-educated woman.[5] Affective descriptors such as exasperation, loathing and rage might even apply to a reader's expected reactions to the play's gender politics. Moreover, Tyler is on record as having negative feelings about the play, and more generally about Shakespeare. A feature piece by Ron Charles in the *Washington Post* begins: 'Anne Tyler hates Shakespeare's plays. All of them. But she hates "The Taming of the Shrew" the most. So she rewrote it'.[6] Given her antipathy, why did she agree to join the project and why did she choose this play in particular? Tyler reveals in this feature that the publishers gave her first pick of the plays, so it seems particularly perverse that she chose the play that she hates above all others. Rather than inspiring readers to love Shakespeare through her own love of the Bard, Tyler begins from an estranged, oppositional position that seems antithetical to the project's mandate to help Shakespeare live and be loved.

In this article, I argue, however, that for Tyler, the point of retelling *Taming* is precisely to make Shakespeare lovable to readers today by converting their and her own hate to love, though the quality of that love may be surprising. Tyler recognises that it is *Taming*'s gender politics that prove objectionable to a contemporary readership, and so it is this 'problem' that she sets out to solve. However, her solution lies not in countering or opposing Shakespeare directly, but rather in moderating and mediating the play's troublesome elements: she turns Petruchio's coercions and abuse into eccentric affection and recasts Katharina's shrewishness as a sometimes too rigid, but also admirable, indifference to social convention. Her narrative favours the production of empathy and understanding between its characters and pushes against ideological certainties. Some of the novel's critics objected to its temperate approach: *Kirkus* complained that the novel was 'neither a faithful retelling nor a trenchant countertale, though agreeable enough as an afternoon's entertainment', and *Publishers Weekly* concluded: 'It is not the shrew who is tamed, but the tale itself'.[7] Surprisingly for a novel whose impetus was the uncluttered emotion of hatred, *Vinegar Girl* seems to model its relation to Shakespeare on more modest, positive feelings. In Tyler's retelling, 'love' is not, as readers might expect, strong, powerful or overwhelming. It is, rather, tempered, understated, even tepid. The hate that gives rise to that love is likewise evacuated of its charge. I suggest that trafficking in middling, mild emotions constitutes a deliberate aesthetic strategy on Tyler's part to provoke similar feelings in her readers, and that under the auspices of bringing her readers to love Shakespeare, she in fact strengthens the bonds between herself and them.

The generating of readerly communities based in affect is a main priority of the middlebrow fiction with which Tyler has been associated and is relevant more broadly to the Random House/Crown/Chatto & Windus Hogarth Shakespeare series, which I claim also emerges as a certain kind of middlebrow enterprise. For the Hogarth 'project', as the website refers to it, the publishers recruited authors who occupy varied cultural and literary positions within the contemporary publishing field, 'acclaimed and bestselling novelists of today'.[8] Out of the seven participating novelists, Jeanette Winterson perhaps most thoroughly represents literary fiction, with Margaret Atwood, Edward St. Aubyn and Howard Jacobson close to that status, while Tracey Chevalier and Jo Nesbø hail more from the location of popular bestsellers and genre fiction. Within this continuum, Tyler's *Vinegar Girl* may have a fair claim to be considered as the most middlebrow of the offerings – the middle of the middle, and thus, as I will return to in the conclusion, an intriguing representation of what the Hogarth Shakespeare is trying to do and why and how it is doing it.

'Humour and gentleness'

I begin by unpacking the emotional disposition – 'hate' – that prompted Tyler to retell *Taming*. Her public comments about *Vinegar Girl* have been few, but they nevertheless give some indication about how she decided which affects were appropriate to bring to her reading of the play. In the *Washington Post* piece, Tyler elaborates on her understanding of Shakespeare's characters: 'People behave so inexplicably that you just know there's another side to it. Someone's exaggerating; somebody's putting his own spin on things. Let's just figure out what really happened'.[9] 'Someone' and 'somebody' stand in euphemistically for Shakespeare; they also gesture to the idea that the play is biased towards the perspectives of Petruchio, Baptista and other male characters. Notably, Tyler does not say that she will provide a different subjective perspective. Instead, she promises an objective view: 'what really happened'. In Hogarth's promotional video, she uses somewhat different phrasing when she reflects in voiceover: 'You know how sometimes a friend will tell you something that happened to her, and you think, "Wait, there must be more to it than that. I'm sure there's another side to this." Well, that's how I've always felt about *The Taming of the Shrew*'.[10] Here, she falls back on the convention that there are two sides to every story. Interestingly, too, Shakespeare is characterised as the female friend rather than as a male author, transformed from dead icon to living peer as a way of downplaying the magnitude of adapting Shakespeare. When coupled with her comments in the *Washington Post* piece, the effect is to give a more privileged, quasi-objective status to *her* side of the story, the one that she is suggesting has remained untold until *Vinegar Girl*. Tyler's rhetoric bespeaks curiosity, bemusement and scepticism, but not much hate.

In fact, there is something exceedingly temperate and moderate, and at the same time authoritative, in how Tyler goes about redressing her hatred for *Taming*, even as she sometimes recalls bolder feminist histories of adaptation. The language of 'telling the other side of the story' can be traced back to Adrienne Rich and Lee R. Edwards, and further back still to Virginia Woolf, all of whom called for revising Shakespeare's and other canonical writers' patriarchal stories in ways that would allow suppressed women's voices to speak.[11] And yet, so unlike, for example, Jane Smiley's viscerally raw, angry rewriting of *King Lear* in *A Thousand Acres* (and despite the fact that Smiley blurbs Tyler's novel on the front cover of the paperback edition), *Vinegar Girl* does not tell a story charged with passion or other strong emotions – in Tyler's characters or in her narrative voice.[12] Although Kate is clearly the protagonist, the third-person narrative is detached and observational, almost studiedly neutral in relation to Kate as well as the other characters, and thus congruent with Tyler's possible claim to objectivity, to telling the 'real' story.[13] Her narrative stance is not devoid of emotion, but it does not readily lend itself to strong, unqualified emotions like hate or love.

What Tyler produces is an oxymoron: a hate infused with humour and gentleness, one that helps readers love Shakespeare in the mildest of ways by evading the bluntness of gender and class conflicts in *Taming*. I borrow these words – 'humour' and 'gentleness' – from Charles' use of them in his *Washington Post* piece on the novel. He describes Tyler's 'ingenious resetting of the plot' as allowing the characters 'to behave with considerably more humor and gentleness than in the Bard's version'.[14] Is this 'more'ness in *Vinegar Girl* a rebuke to *The Taming of the Shrew* or a rescue of it? The answer seems to be 'yes' and 'yes'. Charles seems to mean that the author softens the difficult temperaments of Shakespeare's characters, making them better humoured and giving the story a more truly comedic tone. There is an unacknowledged irony in Charles' choice of words, however, since he has hit upon two of the more astringent words in Shakespeare's play. 'I'll curb her mad and headstrong humor' (4.1.189), Petruchio threatens of Katharina, while Petruchio's servant, Grumio, advises Petruchio's friend Hortensio to 'Let him go while the humour lasts' (1.2.104), that is, to let Petruchio have his way while he is in an intractable mood.[15] To have a humour in Shakespeare is to be subject to a bodily imbalance and an extremity of emotion, an excess of affect. As for 'gentleness', Shakespeare continually plays between two adjectival forms of the word. 'Gentle' is the disposition that Petruchio is trying to create in Katharina – 'Of an animal: tame, quiet, easily managed' (*OED* 'gentle, adj.', A.4.b) and 'Of persons: Mild in disposition or behaviour; kind, tender' (*OED* 'gentle, adj.', A.8). At the same time, 'gentle' signifies elevated social standing. Upon meeting her, Petruchio insists to Katharina that 'I finde you passing gentle' (2.1.235), a line that mocks her resistance to his courtship yet simultaneously gestures to the social capital he hopes to gain in marrying her. Her gentleness enriches him but disempowers her.[16] In *Taming*, then, 'humour' and 'gentleness' index competing pressures, individual and structural, that inform the characters' motivations and behaviour. Charles' use of these words to compare Tyler's novel to Shakespeare's play strips away the complexity. This usage reflects the way in which Tyler avoids talking back to Shakespeare's abrasive gender and class politics and instead substitutes more benign, moderate terms that mitigate readers' perceptions of Shakespeare, taming hate to provide an opening for positive affects that can go by the name of love. In effect, Tyler works in the mode that Hortensio urges upon Katharina: 'No mates for you, / Unless you were of gentler, milder mold' (1.1.59–60).

Tyler as middlebrow

It is helpful to contextualise Anne Tyler's authorial strategies in *Vinegar Girl* within definitions of middlebrow fiction, since her adaptation of Shakespeare participates in the cultural and literary categories that organise the field of contemporary fiction. In some respects, Tyler seems an unlikely candidate for middlebrow authorship. Clearly, she does in part belong to the highbrow world of literary fiction: she has received critical praise and awards, and when she comes out with a new book, it is all but guaranteed a review in the country's leading publications. Her output has been major: since 1964, she has published twenty-two novels, in addition to numerous short stories and two children's books. A number of her novels have been bestsellers.[17] Yet her work nowadays meets with a mixed critical reception, and her reputation is quieter and considerably more neglected than peers such as Philip Roth, Toni Morrison or Joyce Carol Oates.[18] The combination of commercial success and lukewarm critical credentials makes her authorial identity susceptible to the middlebrow label.[19]

What qualifies as 'middlebrow' requires further definition, especially in its implications for the relationship between author, text and readers. There are important material constituents to the word, with its connotations of a hierarchical sorting of 'high', 'middle' and 'low' culture. The word as an adjective characterises 'a person' as 'only moderately intellectual; of average or limited cultural interests (sometimes with the implication of pretensions to more than this)' and applies to 'an artistic work, etc.: of limited intellectual or cultural value; demanding or involving only a moderate degree of intellectual application, typically as a result of not deviating from convention'

(*OED* 'middlebrow, adj.'). Middlebrow works are for middlebrow people, those who have limits that they wish they did not have or aspire to transcend. Thus, any discussion of middlebrow aesthetics and their limitations falls back on perceptions of the audience for whom the work is produced, or in this case for whom the author writes. Material judgements often masquerade as aesthetic judgements, with gender, in addition to class, historically demarcating the middlebrow. By this logic, because Tyler's novels revolve around the interiority of solidly middle-class people, they project a middle-class, middlebrow readership.[20] And because feelings are understood in American culture to be largely the provenance of women, as Lauren Berlant observes, a novel like *Vinegar Girl* that narrates its heroine's evolving feelings towards the man she ultimately marries, seems, whether fairly or not, to be directed towards women.[21] Furthermore, reviews of *Vinegar Girl* use genre terms that separate it from Shakespeare and signal a feminised readership, calling the novel 'a politically correct screwball comedy of manners that actually channels Jane Austen more than Shakespeare' and 'more like a New Age romantic comedy than a Shakespearean production'.[22] These freighted notions of audience are pivotal to the cultural classification of Tyler's fiction as middlebrow.[23]

At stake are not only the feelings that the novel represents in its characters, but also those that it cultivates in its readers. One put-down of Tyler has it that 'she allows the middle-brow middle class to love itself for all its poignant insufficiency'.[24] Tyler is damned here for encouraging in her middle-class, apparently mediocre readers an unearned, positive affect towards themselves. Even one of her more consistent champions, John Updike, echoed this criticism, writing that her work had 'one possible weakness: a tendency to leave the reader just where she found him. Acceptance, in her fiction, is the sum of the marvellous … the impending moral encloses the excitements of her story in a circle of safety that gives them the coziness of entertainment'.[25] In its 'safety' and 'coziness', Tyler's work urges 'acceptance' of the status quo rather than embrace of the new, the experimental or the destabilising. Without coming out and saying so, Updike manages to suggest that Tyler's fiction does not demand too much exertion on the part of readers to affirm the feelings that they like to have.

Although she might contest the pejorative tone of these discussions, Tyler would likely agree that she puts her readers first.

She noted in one interview that she tries to view her final drafts from a reader's perspective.[26] Elsewhere, she contrasted her style to Faulkner's: 'I want everyone to understand what I'm getting at'.[27] Surveying decades' worth of Tyler's published reviews of other authors' works, Elizabeth Evans observes that 'her views are based less on technical matters than on responses created in the reader,' and concludes of her novelistic impact that 'she wants her fiction to be *readable* – that is, to be understood'.[28] The emphasis on accessibility chimes with Beth Driscoll's claim that 'middlebrow institutions not only invoke critics, but also disavow them: middlebrow values are above all intensely reader-oriented, dedicated to the pleasure and the usefulness of reading'.[29] In *Vinegar Girl*, Tyler gives readers new access to Shakespeare's *The Taming of the Shrew* by fostering a sense of positive affect in them. Tyler thus takes on the role of mediator between Shakespeare and her readers.

'It's not that bad': Tyler's taming

To create positive affects, Tyler resists confronting *Taming of the Shrew*'s misogyny. While a direct approach might elicit readers' hate, her substitution of 'gentle' and 'humorous' dynamics facilitates a milder response. As Doug Lanier says, Tyler's Kate 'tames herself'.[30] Even when Kate's sharp edges are preserved, as in the case of the novel's title, they are reinterpreted in a different light. Pyotr, Tyler's Petruchio, points out the flaw in the proverb that 'you can catch more flies with honey than with vinegar', asking, 'But why you would want to catch flies, huh? Answer me that, vinegar girl' (135).[31] Although the appellation 'vinegar girl' could create an impression of sourness, Pyotr suggests that she is not shrewish so much as intelligent and discriminating. Notably, the title has excised all references to 'taming' as well as to 'the shrew'. Staying close to Shakespeare's plot, Tyler does have Kate marry Pyotr by her father's instigation, to procure him a Green Card that will allow him to stay in the US to assist her father, Dr Louis Battista, with his important but obscure immunological research. From this stilted situation, Kate gradually develops genuine feelings for Pyotr, and we learn at the end of the novel that the marriage is a happy, fulfilled, and notably non-patriarchal one.

In addition to its ending, which I will return to later, the novel does contain some moments of feminist counter-narrative: Kate's father selfishly expects that his daughter should not only continue to tend his household and act as a substitute mother for her teenaged sister, Bunny, which she has been doing since she dropped out of college ten years before, but also now should enter into a sham marriage (he still expects her to live at home and keep house for him, it emerges) to advance his research. Kate agitates over his treatment of her, but it is the fifteen-year-old Bunny who voices many of the novel's anti-patriarchal statements, expressing horror at the plan for Kate to marry Pyotr: 'What are you? ... Chattel?' (131). In *Taming*, it is Petruchio who declares of Katharina that 'She is my goods, my chattels' (3.2.221). Reassigning the word to Bunny allows Tyler to appropriate and thus invert Petruchio's derogation of Katharina to the status of 'household stuff', his 'anything' (3.2.222; 223). In the novel, Bunny and sometimes other women call out misogynistic and sexist formations; they don't allow male characters to get away with that kind of behaviour or thinking, where arguably Shakespeare rewards it. At such moments, the novel seems to take Shakespeare to task.

But while *Vinegar Girl* affirms the basic principle that women do have independent value as human beings and are not simply objects of transfer between men, it endorses only a mild critique of patriarchy. When on the same page as the 'chattel' comment, Bunny continues to lambast their father – 'He's making a human sacrifice of you, don't you get it?' – Kate responds: '"Oh, now, it's not that bad ... This [the marriage] will only be on paper, remember." But Bunny was so upset that her Taylor Swift ringtone played nearly all the way through before she could think to answer her phone' (131). Kate's 'Oh now, it's not that bad' is the epitome of a moderate – and moderating – comment. While readers know that Kate has entertained doubts about how her father perceives her, she tempers her response in the face of her sister's open defiance. At this point, she has already told her father that she will marry Pyotr, after her father's reassurance that the marriage will indeed be 'only on paper' (119). But Kate's response also seems to stand in for her author's approach, as if Tyler is glancing sidelong at Katharina and Petruchio's union and wryly concluding that 'it's not that bad', or perhaps, 'I can turn this marriage into a pretty good one' that readers can ultimately embrace. If 'it's not that bad' hardly sounds like a clarion call, I think that its tepidness is actually part of Tyler's *modus operandi*: to situate her characters in grey areas that admit of no certainty and issue in few definite commitments. In the context of adapting Shakespeare, her method results in an agnostic stance that does not lend itself to strong ideological gestures; it tries, rather, to locate and occupy a middle space where a community of readers might recognise feelings in common.[32] The pointed jab at Bunny, who is all about feminist principles in this scene, but whose concept of feminism is apparently limited to the Taylor Swift self-empowerment variety, invites readers to laugh at Bunny's youthful 'excesses'. Bunny's strength of conviction is comically – or 'gently' – undermined throughout the novel.[33]

In place of Bunny's certainty, Tyler privileges empathy, a sharing of affect. Empathy registers in the benefit of the doubt that Kate begins to extend to Pyotr. Although on the whole, Pyotr is portrayed as caring, authentic and absent-minded, there are episodes in which he tracks more closely with Petruchio: he arrives unacceptably late for the wedding, dressed in his oldest, mismatched clothes; he whisks Kate away unceremoniously as soon as the vows are read; his household is in disarray with no accommodation made for her; he rushes her back to the reception without giving her the time to put on a clean dress. Yet good explanations are given for Pyotr's inconsiderate, arguably sexist actions. These reasons occur on the plot level – Pyotr learns just before the wedding that an animal rights advocate (not coincidentally, Bunny's boyfriend) has illegally freed the mice that are the experimental subjects in his and Dr Battista's research – and also on the level of character, since as Lanier has suggested, Tyler psychologises her characters.[34] In fact, readers gain access to Pyotr's psychology through Kate's developing capacity for empathy: 'It occurred to her suddenly that he *was* thinking – that only his exterior self was flubbing his *th* sounds and not taking long enough between consonants, while inwardly he was formulating thoughts every bit as complicated and layered as her own' (106). Later, as she dresses for her wedding, Kate finds that she understands her father's awkward attempts to express his love for her, in contrast to her long dead mother's inability to decipher his intentions: 'She knew what he was trying to say. It crossed her mind that if her mother had known too – if she had been able to read the signals – the lives of all four of them might have been much happier. For the first time, it occurred to her that she herself was getting much better at reading signals' (182). Kate's new emotional and social intelligence is thus forecast to be responsible for the success of her marriage. The moral emphasis that Tyler gives to Kate's empathy suggests that it is a way of negotiating the friction between men and women and a generous alternative to what the novel presents as the inauthentic rigidity of Bunny's feminism.

In suggesting that women have a responsibility to be empathetic with the struggles of men, Tyler displays what might be seen as a retrograde sensibility, but one that is calculated to forge connections with readers from across the ideological and political spectrum. Tyler's version of Katharina's showstopper final speech makes explicit that women are emotionally superior to men and thus have the responsibility to understand them: 'It's *hard* being a man. ... Anything that's bothering them, men think they have to hide it ... They're a whole lot less free than women are, when you think about it. Women have been studying people's feelings since they were toddlers; they've been perfecting their radar – their intuition or their empathy or their interpersonal watchamacallit' (239). This sort of affirmation of women's emotional labour is central to a good deal of 'middlebrow' contemporary fiction, in ways that Berlant has suggested are tied to women's tactics of adaptation and reconciliation to patriarchal structures: 'middlebrow popular genres are about the management of ambivalence, and not the destruction of pleasures or power'.[35] As one dimension of such management, fictions that promote women's empathy 'enact a fantasy that my life is not just mine, but an experience understood by other women, even when it is not shared by many or any'.[36] In this sense, empathy is not just that held by one character for another but also that which serves as connective tissue between author, characters and readers. Kate's speech can model not only how women see their own relationships but also how Tyler situates herself and her readers in relation to Shakespeare: with Tyler's aid, they can read Shakespeare with tolerance in order to glean, perhaps, the insecurity that undergirds *Taming*'s bravura performances of masculinity. In her speech, Kate does not say that women should be subordinate to men, but neither does she confront patriarchal structures governing marriage. What she does do is gesture to a mutual sphere: 'I'm not "backing down" ... I'm letting him into my country. I'm giving him space in a place where we can both be ourselves' (240). The idea of making space for others is what Tyler seems to be enacting in her gentle, humorous approach to Shakespeare: crafting an accommodating space, based on shared affect, for reading him *without* the perceived need to debate or combat issues like gender politics.

The epilogue, which flashes forward eleven years and is told from the perspective of Kate and Pyotr's six-year-old son, Louie, reassures readers that the marriage has been a success, hitting one more time the novel's positive, yet understated, affective notes. The final paragraph describes Louie looking at his parents: 'they were both in the one door side by side and very close together, neither one in front or behind, and they were holding hands and smiling' (245). This ending has no analogue in *Taming*; it is supplementary, and implicitly opposed, in its vision of mutuality and equality. Tyler might be borrowing from the final lines of *A Comedy of Errors*: 'We came into the world like brother and brother, / And now let's go hand in hand, not one before the other' (5.1.426–427) as if discovering there a more palatable alternative to *Taming*'s closing emphasis on the miraculously successful taming of the shrew (''Tis a wonder, by your leave, she will be tamed so' [5.2.193]).[37] Going to a source from outside the play, as well as, interestingly, outside the bounds of heteronormative marriage, allows Tyler to provide a more satisfying mode of closure on Kate and Pyotr's marriage. No direct rebuke to Shakespeare's play is necessary – and in fact would be counter-productive – to secure readers' good feelings. There is contentment portrayed here at the end, but in keeping with *Vinegar Girl*'s overall ethos, there are no highly charged emotions, just two happy people in close proximity to each other.

Conclusion

I have been arguing that in *Vinegar Girl*, Tyler mediates Shakespeare for readers: she changes those elements of *Taming* that are unacceptable to many readers in a contemporary context to mitigate their discomfiting effects and to introduce positive feelings in their place. As Birte Christ has argued of John Irving's *The World According to Garp* (1978), Tyler's novel 'represents narrator, characters, author, and readers as part of one affective community – a hallmark of middlebrow literary practices'.[38] Christ extrapolates from *Garp* to a larger group of later twentieth-century novels, inheritors of mid-century realism, that strive 'to represent and imagine reality in such a way that it can model a better reality for the reader'.[39] The Hogarth Shakespeare is similarly sincere and aspirational in its mission to make Shakespeare work as a living model for readers, and similar, too, in forging communal bonds through the cultivation of affects like affection and empathy. That the publishers refer to the series as a 'project' is itself revealing, with the word's denotation of a 'planned undertaking' or 'collaborative enterprise' (*OED* 'project, n', 2.a., 2.c). It reminds us that the Hogarth Shakespeare is a collected work, industrial in its production, requiring the participation of multiple agents, and seeking a large, actively engaged audience. Reading the 'project' within the framework of the middlebrow shows how affective communities can shape the appropriation of Shakespeare in contemporary fiction.

Ultimately, the concept of the middlebrow gives us material context for studying Shakespearean appropriations, a kind of scholarship that Roger Chartier argues requires 'a social history of the uses and understandings of texts by communities of readers who, successively, take possession of them'.[40] Chartier's social history, alongside the growing scholarship of middlebrow literature and culture, helps to elucidate enterprises such as the Hogarth Shakespeare, which need to be interpreted in terms of the communities that their various institutional and authorial agents try to reach and the versions of Shakespeare that are constituted from such projected communities' imperatives and demands. Too often we have stipulated a readership or audience for Shakespearean productions without examining exactly how the work imagines the communities it will reach and its uses in the world, and how, in turn, those real or imagined communities and uses shape the work. Shakespearean adaptation and appropriation are a part of social history, to an extent which has not yet been fully appreciated in the field of Shakespeare studies. In this article, I have tried to briefly sketch how a social history of a Shakespeare novel might inform an interpretation of the text.

In the case of the Hogarth Shakespeare, while the survival of Shakespeare is certainly a cultural desire, it is even more fundamentally a commercial and economic priority which can only be accomplished through articulating and appealing to substantial communities of readers. By banking on well-known and highly credentialed authors (rather than, say, newcomers like Preti Taneja, whose *We That Are Young* (2017), an adaptation of *King Lear*, has created considerable buzz), Random House/Crown/Chatto & Windus have invested in the fan bases that each of these authors brings to the project.[41] The opening freeze-frame on the promotional video greets visitors to the Hogarth website with 'The world's favourite playwright / Today's best-loved novelists / Timeless stories retold', a tag line that links Shakespeare's universal popularity to the love that readers have for the novelists.[42] A blurb from *The New York Times*, just above the video, similarly calls attention to the series' 'all-star roster'.[43] Fandom often entails the possession of shared affects, and the Hogarth Shakespeare parlays that existing emotional investment into the reading of Shakespeare fiction, where an author's reading community meets and merges with groups of readers who have found their way to the Hogarth Shakespeare through other routes.[44] Hogarth seeks to construct new, expansive communities of readers, but that doesn't change the fact that it is built on a bedrock of pre-existing communities. The appeal of each novelist differs, and I have focused on how Anne Tyler in particular orients a community of readers around positive affects that encourage a modest, moderate love. For her audience to have these feelings about Shakespeare, the novel must first make the audience feel comfortable with itself, and one question that this analysis invites is whether it is Shakespeare whom she brings readers to love or whether it is primarily love for Tyler, and for the images of themselves that they see in her fiction, that ends up being reinforced. Returning once more to Sonnet 18, 'So long as men can breathe or eyes can see, / So long lives this, and this gives life to thee', we can notice that 'this' and 'thee' compete for primacy, and that both depend for their continued survival on those who 'breathe' and 'see'.

Elizabeth Rivlin is an associate professor of English at Clemson University. She is the author of *The Aesthetics of Service in Early Modern England* (Northwestern University Press, 2012) and co-editor, with Alexa Alice Joubin, of *Shakespeare and the Ethics of Appropriation* (Palgrave Macmillan, 2014). She is completing a book titled *Middlebrow Shakespeare: American Reading Publics*.

Notes

1. Vintage Books, 'The Hogarth Shakespeare', YouTube video, uploaded 5 October 2015, https://www.youtube.com/watch?time_continue=1&v=n6qGtAlufFw (accessed 25 March 2021).
2. Hogarth Shakespeare, 'About', http://hogarthshakespeare.com/about/ (now obsolete).

3. Deidre Shauna Lynch traces the historical institutionalisation of readers' intimate affective relation to literature in *Loving Literature: A Cultural History* (Chicago: University of Chicago Press, 2015), 7. She pays attention to how Shakespeare became a privileged example of the possessive, personalised love that so many readers in the nineteenth century began to declare for certain authors and that generated their canonicity (9; 65; 118–19). It is this legacy of love for Shakespeare that the Hogarth Shakespeare takes as its premise but also that which it conveys as endangered.
4. Previous adaptations of *Taming*, in particular Samuel and Bella Spewack's and Cole Porter's *Kiss Me Kate* (1948) and Gil Junger's *10 Things I Hate About You* (1999), have laid the groundwork for *Vinegar Girl* in 'updating' the play's gender politics. As several critics have pointed out, the process of abating the problems of Shakespeare's text almost invariably raises new gender issues. In 'Taming "10 Things I Hate About You": Shakespeare and the Teenage Film Audience', L. Monique Pittman argues that the teen film 'works hard to soften the obvious gender inequities of the original, but in many ways silences honest and serious debate over gender in the process', *Literature/Film Quarterly* 32, no. 2 (2004), 144–52, here 146. And in 'Katherina Bound; or, Play(K)ating the Strictures of Everyday Life', Barbara Hodgdon observes that 'it is one thing to reconstruct past acts of comprehension with imaginary bodies and theorized spectators; it is quite another when *Shrew* is played out by and on the bodies of real women and observed by historically situated spectators of either gender', *PMLA* 107, no. 3 (May 1992), 538–53, here 538, https://doi.org.10.2307/462760.
5. The National Endowment for the Arts last conducted an Annual Arts Basic Survey in 2020. At that time, 46 per cent of US women and 33 per cent of US men reported having read at least one work of literature in the past 12 months. 55 per cent of college graduates had done so, though this percentage was not broken down by gender. 'Demographic Table 2020 Arts Basic Survey,' National Endowment for the Arts, December 2022, https://www.arts.gov/impact/research/arts-data-profile-series/adp-32 (accessed 21 March 2024).
6. Ron Charles, 'Anne Tyler Loathes Shakespeare. So She Decided to Rewrite One of His Plays', *Washington Post*, 21 June 2016, https://www.washingtonpost.com/entertainment/books/in-a-rare-interview-anne-tyler-talks-about-her-unusual-new-novel/2016/06/21/640b99c0-3311-11e6-8ff7-7b6c1998b7a0_story.html?utm_term=.32bd7f493bc7 (accessed 25 March 2021).
7. 'Vinegar Girl', *Kirkus*, 15 March 2016, https://www.kirkusreviews.com/book-reviews/anne-tyler/vinegar-girl/; 'Vinegar Girl', *Publishers Weekly*, 29 February 2016, https://www.publishersweekly.com/978-0-8041-4126-0 (accessed 25 March 2021).
8. Hogarth Shakespeare, 'Books', http://hogarthshakespeare.com/books/ (now obsolete).
9. Charles, 'Anne Tyler Loathes Shakespeare'.
10. 'The Hogarth Shakespeare', YouTube video.
11. Adrienne Rich, 'When We Dead Awaken: Writing as Re-Vision', *College English* 34, no. 1 (1972), 18–30, here 18, https://doi.org.10.2307/375215; Lee R. Edwards, 'Women, Energy, and Middlemarch', *Massachusetts Review* 13, no. 1/2 (1972),

223–238, here 228; Virginia Woolf, *A Room of One's Own* (Orlando, FL: Harcourt, 2005 [1929]). Virginia and Leonard Woolf's Hogarth Press, originally founded in 1917, 're-launched in 2012 as a partnership between Chatto & Windus in the UK and Crown in the U.S.' The Crown Publishing Group, 'Hogarth', http://www.randomhousebooks.com/imprints/ (accessed 25 March 2021). One of the press's principal calling cards has been the Hogarth Shakespeare series. There is thus a material link, as well as thematic ones, between *A Room of One's Own* and *Vinegar Girl*.

12. Jane Smiley, *A Thousand Acres* (New York: Random House / Ballantine, 1991).
13. Patricia Rowe Willrich describes Tyler's detached narrative voice in 'Watching Through Windows: A Perspective on Anne Tyler', *VQR: A National Journal of Literature and Discussion* 68, no. 3 (1992), https://www.vqronline.org/essay/watching-through-windows-perspective-anne-tyler (accessed 25 March 2021).
14. Charles, 'Anne Tyler Loathes Shakespeare'.
15. William Shakespeare, *The Taming of the Shrew*, ed. Dympna Callaghan (New York: Norton, 2009).
16. On the competing claims of gender and class on 'gentle', see Lynda E. Boose, '*The Taming of the Shrew*, Good Husbandry, and Enclosure', in *Shakespeare Re-read: The Texts in New Contexts*, ed. Russ McDonald (Ithaca, NY: Cornell, 1994), 193–225, here 218–219.
17. A number of her twenty-four published novels have been *New York Times* bestsellers, spanning the period from 1982 to 2022 (*Vinegar Girl* is not one of them). 'Books', Anne Tyler, http://annetyler.com/books (accessed 21 March 2024).
18. In part, Tyler seems to have fallen out of fashion. There have been scholarly books and essays published about her, but very few in the past twenty years. See *Critical Essays on Anne Tyler*, ed. Alice Hall Petry (New York: G. K. Hall & Co., 1992); Elizabeth Evans, *Anne Tyler* (New York: Twayne, 1993); and Paul Bail, *Anne Tyler: A Critical Companion* (Westport, CT: Greenwood Press, 1998).
19. Reviews of *A Spool of Blue Thread* (2015), the novel Tyler published right before *Vinegar Girl*, allude to the consensus that her oeuvre is considered middlebrow. See Michiko Kakutani, 'Ordinary People, Wayward Son', *The New York Times*, 5 February 2015, https://www.nytimes.com/2015/02/06/books/anne-tylers-20th-novel-a-spool-of-blue-thread.html (accessed 25 March 2021); and Kevin Nance, 'Review: "A Spool of Blue Thread" by Anne Tyler', *Chicago Tribune*, 12 February 2015, http://www.chicagotribune.com/lifestyles/books/ct-prj-spool-of-blue-thread-anne-tyler-20150212-story.html (accessed 25 March 2021).
20. Timothy Aubry, *Reading as Therapy: What Contemporary Fiction Does for Middle-Class Americans* (Iowa City: University of Iowa Press, 2011), 25.
21. Lauren Berlant, *The Female Complaint: The Unfinished Business of Sentimentality in American Culture* (Durham, NC: Duke University Press, 2008), 1–2.
22. Heller McAlpin, 'Fizzy "Vinegar Girl" Tames Shrewishness to Sparkle', *NPR Book Reviews*, 21 June 2016, https://www.npr.org/2016/06/21/482023595/fizzy-vinegar-girl-tames-shrewishness-to-sparkle (accessed 25 March 2021); Carol Memmott, 'Anne Tyler's "Vinegar Girl" Reinvents 'The Taming of the Shrew' for Modern Audiences', *The Chicago Tribune*, 28 June 2016, https://www.chicagotribune.com/entertainment/books/ct-prj-vinegar-girl-anne-tyler-20160628-story.html (accessed 25 March 2021).

23. Nicola Humble argues that 'a predominantly female readership very often automatically consigned a text to the category of the middlebrow' in 'The Reader of Popular Fiction', in *The Cambridge Companion to Popular Fiction*, ed. David Glover and Scott McCracken (Cambridge: Cambridge University Press, 2012), 86–102, here 93. Taking this line of argument to the present day, Beth Driscoll argues that 'the feminization of certain kinds of reading is one of the clearest indicators that middlebrow logics still operate in twenty-first century literary culture', in *The New Literary Middlebrow: Tastemakers and Reading in the Twenty-First Century* (New York: Palgrave Macmillan, 2014), 30; while Birte Christ connects thematics with perception of a gendered audience: 'The middlebrow is typically both "female" (in subject matter and reader address) and "feminized" (in terms of extrinsic judgment)', in 'The Aesthetics of Accessibility: John Irving and the Middlebrow Novel after 1975', *Post45*, 'The Middlebrow: A Special Cluster', ed. Cecilia Konchar Farr and Tom Perrin (July 2016), http://post45.research.yale.edu/2016/07/the-aesthetics-of-accessibility-john-irving-and-the-middlebrow-novel-after-1975/#identifier_1_7037 (accessed 25 March 2021).
24. Vivian Gornick, 'Anne Tyler's Arrested Development', *Village Voice*, 30 March 1982, 40–41.
25. John Updike, 'Loosened Roots', in Petry, *Critical Essays*, 88–91, here 88.
26. Wendy Lamb, 'An Interview with Anne Tyler', in Petry, *Critical Essays*, 53–58, here 58.
27. Quoted in Katharine Whittemore, 'Ordinary People', *The Atlantic*, May 2001, https://www.theatlantic.com/magazine/archive/2001/05/ordinary-people/302225/ (accessed 25 March 2021).
28. Evans, *Anne Tyler*, 17, 20.
29. Driscoll, *New Literary Middlebrow*, 28.
30. Douglas Lanier, 'The Hogarth Shakespeare Series: Redeeming Shakespeare's Literariness', in *Shakespeare and Millennial Fiction*, ed. Andrew James Hartley (Cambridge: Cambridge University Press, 2018), 230–250, here 241.
31. Anne Tyler, *Vinegar Girl: William Shakespeare's* The Taming of the Shrew *Retold* (New York: Hogarth/Crown/Penguin Random House, 2016).
32. Cornel Sandvoss, *Fans: The Mirror of Consumption* (Malden, MA: Polity Press, 2005), 53–61.
33. Tyler's representation of Bianca recalls the tradition of interpreting her as a site of feminist resistance to patriarchy. See Patricia Parker, 'Mastering Bianca in *The Taming of the Shrew*', in *The Impact of Feminism in English Renaissance Studies*, ed. Dympna Callaghan (New York: Palgrave Macmillan, 2007), 193–209, here 206; Lynn Enterline, 'The Cruelties of Character in *The Taming of the Shrew*', in *Shakespeare's Schoolroom: Rhetoric, Discipline, Emotion* (Philadelphia: University of Pennsylvania Press, 2011), 95–119, here 100; and Christopher Bertucci, 'Rethinking Binaries by Recovering Bianca in *10 Things I Hate About You* and Zeffirelli's *The Taming of the Shrew*', *Literature/Film Quarterly* 42, no. 2 (2014), 414–426, here 419.
34. Lanier, 'The Hogarth Shakespeare Series', 238.
35. Berlant, *The Female Complaint*, 4–5.
36. Ibid., x.
37. William Shakespeare, *The Comedy of Errors*, in *The Norton Shakespeare*, 3rd ed., ed. Stephen Greenblatt et al. (New York: Norton, 2016), 745–797.

38. Christ, 'The Aesthetics of Accessibility'.
39. Ibid.
40. Roger Chartier, *Forms and Meanings: Texts, Performances, and Audiences from Codex to Computer* (Philadelphia: University of Pennsylvania Press, 1995), 92.
41. Preti Taneja, *We That Are Young* (New York: Knopf, 2018).
42. 'The Hogarth Shakespeare', YouTube video.
43. Hogarth Shakespeare, 'About'.
44. On shared affect in fandom, see 'Excerpts from "Matt Hills Interviews Henry Jenkins"', in Henry Jenkins, *Fans, Bloggers, and Gamers: Exploring Participatory Culture* (New York: New York University Press, 2006), 9–36, here 14.

Chapter 7
Millennial Dark Ladies

Katherine Scheil

In August of 2017, Globe Theatre director Michelle Terry commissioned a new play by Morgan Lloyd Malcolm. Entitled *Emilia*, this play about Aemilia Lanyer was performed with an all-female cast, and purported to reveal 'the life of Emilia: poet, mother and feminist'. The Globe website proclaimed: 'This time, the focus will be on this exceptional woman who managed to outlive all the men the history books tethered her to'.[1] The play opened a year later in August of 2018 for an initial sold-out run of eleven performances and had an extended run in London's West End. Critic Michael Billington remarked that Lloyd Malcolm's play turns Lanyer 'into a symbol of women down the ages who have struggled to make their voices heard'. Even though there is no evidence that Lanyer met Shakespeare, Billington notes that 'the play's most contentious assertion ... is that she was Shakespeare's lover, the inspiration for the dark lady of the sonnets and, as a fellow poet, someone whose words the bard freely borrowed'. In this play, Shakespeare and Lanyer are lovers, but he steals her words for his character Emilia's monologue in *Othello*,

Notes for this section begin on page 117.

prompting her to storm onstage and reclaim her poetry. According to Billington, this imagined relationship 'allows Lloyd Malcolm to turn Emilia into a living symbol of exploited women'.[2] While Morgan Lloyd Malcolm's 2017 play *Emilia* has been described as 'an outright feminist triumph and a brilliant call-to-arms',[3] not all imaginary Dark Ladies embody this same progressive stance.

Morgan Lloyd Malcolm is not the first to build a history of the imaginary 'Dark Lady', the fictional figure originating in Shakespeare's Sonnets, who has taken on a life of her own over the last century or so.[4] Writers from George Bernard Shaw to Anthony Burgess have explored the idea of a female muse who inspires Shakespeare's poetry and invigorates him romantically, to illustrate what Paul Franssen has termed 'Shakespeare as a sexual being'.[5] Likewise, many biographers of Shakespeare posit some sort of sexual relationship between Shakespeare and an invented woman derived from the Sonnets. Jonathan Bate, for example, in *Soul of the Age* (2009), argues that the relationship between the speaker of the Sonnets and the Dark Lady is 'intensely sexual', though 'there is no way of knowing whether the dark lady was created out of an imagined relationship or inspired by a real affair'.[6] Stephen Greenblatt, in his blockbuster biography *Will in the World* (2004), contends that Shakespeare's obsession with a Dark Lady 'has everything to do with the compulsions of "lust in action" (129.2), the rhythm of tumescence and detumescence that defines for him what it means to be with her ... This sexual rhythm, yoking vitality and death, pleasure and disgust, longing and loathing, is not a mere recreation or an escape. As the sonnets insist again and again, the poet's witty, anxious, self-conscious embrace of his own desires defines what it means to be Will'. In spite of the dearth of evidence about a Dark Lady 'in real life', Greenblatt uses this fantasy woman to contrast to the actual historical women in Shakespeare's life – his wife and daughters: 'there is no room in the way in which Shakespeare represented himself in the sonnets, for his wife or his children', so 'the figures of the young man and the dark lady seem to displace and absorb emotions that we might have conventionally expected Shakespeare to feel in and for his family. About Anne Shakespeare he is silent ...'.[7] For Greenblatt, the Dark Lady is a substitute wife and sexual outlet, a conduit for his Shakespeare's emotional expressions.

Given that his novel *Nothing Like the Sun* (1964) depends on a fleshed out Dark Lady, it is no surprise that Anthony Burgess's biography of Shakespeare spends substantial time expanding this imaginary lover. During his time in London, this Shakespeare was 'heavily in love', his wife Anne 'in Stratford was forgotten, or if remembered, remembered guiltily', and his dark beloved was 'either a lady of some social position' or 'a high-class courtesan equipped with geisha skills'. Burgess speculates that 'Shakespeare's mistress' may indicate that he was 'falling for a dark skin', and that 'the transports Shakespeare knew with his Dark Lady were very violent and wholly carnal'. In the end, Burgess argues that 'it is best to keep the Dark Lady anonymous, even composite', since it is unlikely that Shakespeare 'limited himself to one affair'. Instead, he knew 'the tugging of the black and white spirits, and the irresistible lure of the primal darkness that resides in all women, whether white or black'.[8] Like Greenblatt's Dark Lady, Burgess's version is intensely sexual but also dangerously exotic.

These male biographers are not the only ones who have imagined a libidinous (and often disturbing) story to fill in the gaps in Shakespeare's London life, and to provide a passionate muse. What happens when contemporary women authors do this for women readers? What might an imaginary Dark Lady look like, if she is created *by* women *for* women?[9]

Recently, the mysterious Dark Lady has become a fruitful subject in a series of modern novels by women writers, designed primarily for a female reading audience: Meredith Whitford's *Shakespeare's Will* (2010), Alexa Schnee's *Shakespeare's Lady* (2012), Victoria Lamb's *His Dark Lady* (2013), Grace Tiffany's *Paint: A Novel of Shakespeare's Dark Lady* (2013), Sally O'Reilly's *Dark Aemilia* (2014), Andrea Chapin's *The Tutor* (2015) and Mary Sharratt's *The Dark Lady's Mask* (2016). These seven novels, ranging from 2010 to 2016, saw print not long after the founding of the #MeToo movement (2006), and are part of a group of women-centred biographical works that update Shakespeare's life story for women readers.[10] Four of the seven novels imagine a relationship between Shakespeare and Lanyer. Alexa Schnee, who wrote *Shakespeare's Lady* when she was eighteen, tells the story of Lanyer, who falls in love with Shakespeare when he comes to London. Shakespeare encourages her to write, but ends up stealing *A Midsummer Night's Dream* from her. In Grace Tiffany's *Paint: A Novel of Shakespeare's Dark Lady*, Lanyer paints her skin and dyes her hair to look more Italian, and attracts a number of men, including Shakespeare. Lanyer is also the central character in Sally O'Reilly's *Dark Aemilia*.[11] Here she carries on an affair with Shakespeare, who later helps to save her son Henry from the plague. In Mary Sharratt's *The Dark Lady's Mask: A Novel of Shakespeare's Muse*, Shakespeare and Lanyer fall in love and leave London for Italy, where they write comedies together, but their subsequent return to London entails an acrimonious relationship.

Victoria Lamb's *His Dark Lady* focuses on Lucy Morgan, a member of Elizabeth's court, often linked to 'Lucy Negra' or 'Black Luce', who ran a brothel in Clerkenwell.[12] Morgan is a dark-skinned lady-in-waiting to Queen Elizabeth, who also inspires Shakespeare's writing when they fall in love with each other. The last two novels of the group reject these historical figures, in favour of creating fictional women to serve as Dark Ladies. In Meredith Whitford's *Shakespeare's Will* (2010), the Dark Lady is only one of Shakespeare's many lovers and is defeated by Shakespeare's wife Anne at the end of the novel, when Shakespeare buys New Place for her as a reward for her long period of suffering. Here the Dark Lady is of ambiguous historical origin, a Scottish woman named Marian/Mara/Maria who is a musician and courtesan. In Andrea Chapin's 2015 novel *The Tutor*, the Dark Lady is a fictional widow named Katharine de L'Isle of Lufanwal Hall, who meets Shakespeare, a tutor for her aristocratic family. Over the course of the novel, this Shakespeare writes *Venus and Adonis* and several sonnets, with Katharine's help. She is determined to win him over regardless of his marital status, and confesses her love for him, awaiting an eventual sexual encounter to fulfil her desires. When this scene finally occurs near the end of the novel, though, he shows little interest in her, and she has to aggressively pursue him. In a subsequent scene a few pages later, Shakespeare violently assaults her, and she soon discovers that he has engaged in numerous dalliances, even impregnating a family maid. In Chapin's novel, Shakespeare is a lustful cad who uses women for artistic inspiration and then drops them. This is an unsympathetic Shakespeare who represents the worst of the male sex, while the fictional heroic Dark Lady triumphs in the end.

This group of Dark Lady novels both resonates with the concerns and tastes of post-millennial female readers and authors, and at times creates a more diverse and multicultural Shakespeare by linking him to a racially 'dark' lady. These Dark Ladies locate Shakespeare in a world of exoticism and sexuality that is likely far from his more normative domestic life. While Dark Ladies provide an alternative personal life for Shakespeare, they can be deeply problematic for what they erase and for what they manipulate, both in terms of Shakespeare's documented family life (a wife and three children) and in terms of the real historical women posited as his fantasy lovers. For writer Aemilia Lanyer in particular, the historical woman most often suggested as the real 'Dark Lady', linking her importance to Shakespeare as opposed to her own literary achievements should give us pause.

The Dark Lady and chick lit

This cluster of post-millennial novels, written by women and geared to a female reading audience, fits Martha Tuck Rozett's description of 'women-centered historical fiction' which 'speak[s] directly to the female experience',[13] but they also combine elements from historical fiction, romance and chick lit. The mixture of history with contemporary literary forms underlines Andrew James Hartley's argument that in the millennium, 'fresh pressures on the cultural mindset are manifesting thematically in the fiction which that culture generates'.[14] Likewise, as Stephanie Harzewski points out in *Chick Lit and Postfeminism*, chick lit was born of social conditions in the 1990s and is 'both a commentary on and a product of the singles market, which expanded in the late 1990s'. She notes that chick lit considers 'the past two decades' upheaval in marriage and education patterns' and 'dramatizes the plight' of women who are frustrated at the limited options for relationships.[15] The protagonist of chick lit is 'typically a single, urban media professional' living in a 'high energy' metropolis. Chick lit 'chronicles heroines' fortunes on the marriage market and assesses contemporary courtship behavior, dress, and social motives', allowing the female reader to 'indulge in perceiving herself as a modern-day version of a classic heroine, her situation cast in the light of a private epic'.[16] The documented historical life of Shakespeare does not fit this paradigm, but creating an imaginary Dark Lady is a way to tailor Shakespeare's life story accordingly. These fictional Dark Ladies are usually bookish, often write, have an income, or are rival authors to Shakespeare. Further, these novels are all set in the 'high energy' environment of theatrical London (not Stratford), where Shakespeare functions as a libertine, and the Dark Lady is a literate, self-sufficient woman who is frustrated with her romantic life. Thus, the Dark Lady paradigm is ideally suited to appeal to readers of chick lit, and provides an opportunity to align a version of Shakespeare's life story with this popular novelistic form aimed at women readers.

In keeping with the typical plot line of chick lit, these various versions of Shakespeare serve as the inadequate male, the Mark Darcy of *Bridget Jones's Diary* (1996), who is too busy with his own career to consider the plight of his love interest. When explaining how she created her Dark Lady novel, Sally O'Reilly describes just such a plot: 'my initial interest in Shakespeare was as an antagonist to Lanyer, and one likely to see her value primarily in terms of her sexual allure, and to privilege his talent and needs as an artist over hers'.[17] Other Dark Lady novels employ a similar storyline. As one reader of Victoria Lamb's *His Dark Lady* bluntly remarked, 'Shakespeare was a bit of a dick'.[18] Similarly, a reader of Sharratt's *Dark Lady's Mask* commented on Shakespeare: 'Not only was he an asshole pretty much the entire book but he was also a whiner, selfish and completely devoid of feeling. He was self-centered and spent so much time feeling bad about himself that I just honestly hated him'. Another reader noted that Sharratt's 'Shakespeare is both likeable in his poetic glory and hateful in his douche bag misogyny'.[19] These Dark Lady novels thus tap into what Stephanie Harzewski calls a 'feminine angst' in chick lit about women's circumstances in society, allowing women writers and readers to 'talk back' to Shakespeare not by remaking his literary texts, but by refashioning his life to cast him in the role of an appealing, charismatic, but always disappointing man who resembles the male targets of chick lit.[20]

The Dark Lady and historical fiction

This array of Dark Lady novels also correlates with historical fiction, relying of course on the historical figure of Shakespeare, but supplementing his story with a fictional Dark Lady, often based on a semi-fictional version of Aemilia Lanyer.[21] As Sally O'Reilly points out, 'whether writing fiction or non-fiction, establishing objective truth is near-impossible', so the best solution for historical novelists is to 'create a proxy for reality'.[22] With one exception, each of these novels includes a note in which the author points out the fictional status of the work, and overtly states the absence of evidence for a relationship between Shakespeare and a Dark Lady. For instance, Mary Sharratt declares that *The Dark Lady's Mask* 'is a work of fiction.

There is no historical evidence to prove that Aemilia Bassano Lanier was the Dark Lady of Shakespeare's sonnets', but she admits that 'as a novelist I could not resist the allure of the Dark Lady mythos'.[23] Likewise, Alexa Schnee observes that while Lanyer 'was a real person', there is 'no proof that she was Shakespeare's mistress, but there is no doubt that they would have known each other'. She confesses that when writing *Shakespeare's Lady*, 'I imagined a romance between the striking Emilia and the passionate William, but all other events in Emilia's life are true'.[24] Similarly, Andrea Chapin's Author's Note states, 'Katharine and the De L'Isle family at Lufanwal Hall in Lancashire are from my imagination', and she admits that she has 'interwoven historical figures with fictional characters' throughout the novel.[25]

Evidence from numerous readers shows a strong proclivity to overlook these disclaimers and to engage with and invest in these Dark Lady characters as if they represented historical truths, rather than what Sally O'Reilly describes as an 'imaginary story built around known historical facts'.[26] Sarah, a UK reader of Victoria Lamb's *His Dark Lady*, noted that 'I feel like I'm learning something as well as having fun with these books'.[27] Another reader, Sandra from Malaysia, noted that Lamb 'weaves fiction with history in such a masterful manner almost making one wonder what is fact and what is fiction'.[28] One reader of Schnee's *Shakespeare's Lady*, notes that she was 'quite captivated by the wealth of history I gleaned from the pages of this book'.[29] Lucinda, a reader of O'Reilly's *Dark Aemilia*, seems to take the events of the novel as fact, describing it as the 'story of the most famous playwright's muse and his one true love'.[30] The power of the narrative structure, combined with the focus on a well-known historical figure (Shakespeare), circulates these stories to a wide readership that does not necessarily separate fact from fiction.

A brief survey of reader responses shows that a striking number of readers attest to making a connection between these novels and their own lives, underlining Diana Wallace's point that 'any historical novel always has as much, or perhaps more, to say about the time in which it is written'.[31] One reader remarked that Schnee's *Shakespeare's Lady* 'gives the reader a very plain view of the human condition' and offers insight 'into a world we don't see often, but one that truly isn't much different from our own today'.[32] A reader of O'Reilly's novel *Dark Aemilia* similarly praised Lanyer because she 'speaks up on behalf of the female sex whenever she can, challenging the views of the men around her. As an intelligent and talented woman, she doesn't have the opportunities that would have been open to her if she had lived today and she finds it very difficult to gain any recognition for her work'.[33] Audra, a '40ish married lesbian with a farmer wife and a bookish kid' also praised O'Reilly's Lanyer for being 'knowing, brash, and unapologetic. She's hungry for her independence, frustrated with her useless husband and her writing, which doesn't match her aspiration. (How I can relate to that!)'.[34] Another reader, Hannah, lauded O'Reilly's Lanyer for her 'love of books and her habit of hiding the few she owns around her house "so they come easily to hand when I have a moment to myself" [which] speaks to any reader with not enough time on their hands, especially those of us who like Aemilia manage households and children'.[35] Reader Sandra Danby noted that 'Aemilia is something of a feminist, in that she struggles against men her whole life for the freedom to live her own life ... She is a fascinating character, a woman of her time or before her time'.[36] Reader Kathleen Kelly also described O'Reilly's Lanyer as 'a little known woman (at least to me) who was ahead of her time'.[37]

Similarly, Mary Sharratt's *The Dark Lady's Mask* elicited numerous responses from women readers who connected Sharratt's story to their own lives. Wanda, a librarian from Alberta, Canada, noted, 'I appreciated the girl power messages throughout, as Amelia struggles to become mistress of her own life and forges important friendships that help her (and her friends) in this regard. And it's true that many a talented woman has had to use the men in her life to get her work out into the world'.[38] New York mystery writer Daniella Bernett extolled Sharratt's novel as 'a vibrant portrait of women during the Renaissance, who were restrained by their sex and yearned for more from life. Their struggles mirror many of the same issues women face today'. She lauded the novel for celebrating 'the perseverance of the human spirit to never give up on one's dreams'.[39] Sharratt's embellishment of Lanyer as the Dark Lady clearly resonated with contemporary women's concerns of girl power and female ambition.

Like chick lit, which according to Heike Mißler 'provides escapism but also gives readers the impression that their own realities are represented', these novels update historical fiction to resonate with modern women's experiences.[40] In one representative example, Meredith Whitford's *Shakespeare's Will* employs a surprisingly contemporary scenario of infidelity. Here, Shakespeare's wife Anne discovers his adultery when she sees strange dark hairs in their bed and lipstick stains on his clothes, and smells a different and exotic laundry scent: 'There was lip-rouge on the hem of a shirt, and long black hairs, too dark to be her own, caught in the lacings. The week after that, his under-linen was torn. And that scent seemed to cling to every garment. Anne stored clean clothes with rosemary, lavender and pepper to keep the fleas and lice at bay. This scent was of chypre and roses and ambergris'.[41] Combining the period detail of historical fiction with the sexual disappointments of chick lit, this Dark Lady novel typifies the bricolage of literary forms and topics geared to its target audience.

The Dark Lady, romance, and #MeToo

An additional resonance with these Dark Lady novels is the form of romance, a genre traditionally linked to women readers.[42] Reader Bonnie Ferrante praised *Dark Aemelia* for being 'a romance at the core', and Sharon Browning criticised *The Tutor* as more 'a sensationalized romance novel than something with worthy literary gristle'.[43] In order to tap into the reading audience for romances, one feature that all of these novels share is an abundance of sex scenes with Shakespeare. As Maya Rodale points out, 'most romance readers enjoy reading stories where the sexual component is a large part of the story and the development of the characters'.[44] However, because Shakespeare is a married man, his relationship with a Dark Lady is technically an adulterous one. Some readers are willing to overlook this fact, in favour of the erotics of romance, but others are bothered and even turned off.

For example, some readers praised *Dark Aemilia* for its 'hot sex scenes', while others critiqued these elements as 'crude, vulgar, and entirely unnecessary', as evidenced by the following example, pointed out by one outraged reader: 'I wonder how many times she's sucked off Inchbald to earn enough to buy such an extravagant gewgaw. Or perhaps he gave it to her in fair exchange, for services rendered. Oh, Lord, now I can see her lips, pulsing away at his groin! And the white crumbs of her face powder, dusting his curly pubes'.[45] Reader J. Lynn Else from Moose Lake, Minnesota panned the book because the characters 'continually jump into bed together and make stupid choices'.[46] Another reader criticised the relationship between Lanyer and Shakespeare as 'a terribly written fanfiction erotica because all it had was a lot of bed scenes and even then there was no room for romance or gestures of that kind'.[47] Likewise, Carla, a reader from Pontypool, UK, objected to Lamb's *Dark Lady* because 'Shakespeare is such a deplorable character, and Lucy is so weak where he's concerned. What they have is not love – he frequently forces himself on her and holds her down until she relents and sleeps with him, yay romance! No. That is not romance, and I'm tired of it pretending that it is'.[48]

Readers of Alexa Schnee's 2012 novel *Shakespeare's Lady*, because it was published by the Christian publisher Guideposts, were especially disapproving of the many adulterous sexual exploits. One reader noted, 'I can't agree with what the main character Emilia did in her affair with William Shakespeare'.[49] Another reader, a home-schooling mother, complained that 'the whole book centers around adultery. Almost everyone in the book is committing adultery in some way or another. That's just not something I approve of, so I generally don't read stories like that. ... I would NOT label it as Christian fiction, though'.[50] Part of the appeal of Dark Lady texts is their potential to enable an alternative sexual life for Shakespeare, one that fuels his imagination and inspires his literary work, but an overly sexualised Shakespeare can at times conflict with the morals of a readership.

Nevertheless, by tapping into the features of romance, these Dark Lady novels circulate to a largely female audience narratives of a particular Shakespeare who is adulterous, lecherous, sexy and domineering. As Susan Strehle and Mary Paniccia Carden argue, 'Love stories are cultural primers, instructing their primarily female readership how to behave, what to fantasize and wish for, and how to interpret the shapes their lives assume. In this sense, romance narratives reproduce and reaffirm the ideas about gender circulating in the culture where they are written and read'.[51] Whether based on historical personages (like Lanyer) or on imaginary women, all of these novels suggest that female sexuality was an empowering force for Shakespeare's art, and that he sought and experienced an artistically inspiring relationship with a woman outside his marriage.

These millennial Dark Lady novels have several implications. First, for Shakespeare, they provide a way to manipulate the outlines and gaps in his life story to suit both the contemporary literary forms and the social issues of concern to women readers. As Julie Sanders points out in *Novel Shakespeares*, twentieth-century women novelists have a long history of engaging in 'the refusal and positive deconstruction of moral and literary absolutes'.[52] For Lanyer, subsuming her life story into a narrative connected to Shakespeare has obvious problems. Kate Chedgzoy has argued that making Lanyer Shakespeare's mistress gives her 'purchase on cultural memory or popular perceptions of the Renaissance beyond the academy' due to her 'capacity as Shakespeare's putative Dark Lady rather than as the author of a significant volume of verse'. She adds that 'the myth of Aemilia Lanyer as Shakespeare's Dark Lady both testifies to our continuing cultural investment in a fantasy of a female Shakespeare, and reveals some of the anxieties about difference that haunt canonical Renaissance literature'.[53]

These seven novels attest to the growing desire for a woman-centred Shakespeare. In light of the recent #MeToo movement, the relationship between Shakespeare and this part-historical, part-imaginary woman updates Shakespeare for contemporary women's issues, but at what cost? The novels featuring Aemilia Lanyer are the most problematic, because they suggest that Lanyer is primarily of interest when she is linked to Shakespeare, as the author of his works (as she is in the play *Emilia*). The resulting updated Shakespeare is one who could love an empowered, literate woman. This is a way to get around the inconvenient truth that all evidence points to the fact that Shakespeare was a married, upwardly mobile, white male.

Conclusion

As works of historical fiction, these novels use gaps in Shakespeare's life to justify imagining a fictional relationship for which there is no documented evidence. As Graham Holderness puts it, 'The documentary facts can be disposed of quickly and simply. There are none. The only certain existence of the Dark Lady is as a fictional character'.[54] Linking Shakespeare to Aemilia Lanyer is compelling, but 'what is missing from the record is one single piece of evidence establishing that there was some personal connection' between the two.[55] While we might be tempted to dismiss the fictional works built on this historical fabrication as innocuous, Andrew Elfenbein notes that 'readers use information that they have learned in fiction to complete later, unrelated tasks, including problem solving and decision making, and they use this information whether or not it is correct'. Misinformation can thus be influential: 'memory seems fragile in the face of fiction's seductions because fiction so easily leads participants to counter what they already know'.[56] Unsurprisingly, therefore, the gap has narrowed between positing a Dark Lady as erotic muse, and proclaiming a Dark Lady as author of the plays by William Shakespeare. The desire to believe that a woman played a role in Shakespeare's creative oeuvre is no more apparent than in Elizabeth Winkler's recent article in *The Atlantic*, boldly entitled 'Was Shakespeare a Woman?'

In this provocative piece, Winkler revisits the authorship conspiracy, arguing that Aemilia Lanyer could be the alternative to the man from Stratford. Describing Lanyer as 'exotic and peripheral', Winkler admits that her 'idea felt like a feminist fantasy about the past – but then, stories about women's lost and obscured achievements so often have a dreamlike quality, unveiling a history different from the one we've learned'. Winkler questions, 'Was I getting carried away, reinventing Shakespeare in the image of our age? Or was I seeing past gendered assumptions to the woman who – like Shakespeare's heroines – had fashioned herself a clever disguise?' Her subsequent questions betray Winkler's real targets – the Shakespeare industry, patriarchy, and the literary canon: 'What would the revelation of a woman's hand at work mean, aside from the loss of a prime tourist attraction in Stratford-upon-Avon? Would the effect be a blow to the cultural patriarchy, or the erosion of the canon's status? Would (male) myths of inexplicable genius take a hit? Would women at last claim their rightful authority as historical and intellectual forces?'[57]

The mysterious vacuity of the Dark Lady offers an ideal niche for cultivating an alternative female 'Shakespeare', but social media backlash against Winkler's assertions has been substantial. Blogger 'Doctor Cleveland', in a piece called 'Shakespeare Wasn't Perfect' (15 May 2019), contends that, 'All we know is that the Dark Lady had dark hair and dark eyes, which doesn't narrow much down. We can't prove that Shakespeare and Lanier ever spoke with one another'.[58] He continues to critique *The Atlantic* for engaging in '"Shakespeare authorship" conspiracy-mongering, this time masquerading as feminism by proposing a female candidate. But the piece doesn't quote even a single line of the real poetry that woman wrote. It can't, of course, because that would give the game away. If the piece let you read Emilia Bassano Lanier's actual poetry it would become dangerously easy to hear that Lanier sounds like herself, not like Shakespeare. So the "feminist" conspiracy theory is dedicated to *silencing the voice of an authentic woman poet*'.[59] Likewise, Dominic Green offers a similar critique in *The Spectator*: 'Since Shakespeare's ascent to divinity in the 19th century, every generation has invented the Shakespeare it needs, even when the Shakespeare it needs is an anti-Shakespeare. Hence this fantasy of an anti-Shakespeare that inverts the pale, male "Stratfordian" truth to invent a female, Jew-ish, black-ish proto-feminist daughter of immigrants'.[60]

Elizabeth Winkler's description of her Shakespeare-as-Aemilia theory, as 'a feminist fantasy about the past' with a 'dreamlike quality', echoes Morgan Lloyd Malcolm's description of her play *Emilia* as 'a memory, a dream, a feeling of her'.[61] Both phrases betray a desire to access an inaccessible, and probably even non-existent, feminist counterpart to Shakespeare. Indeed, reviews and marketing materials for Lloyd Malcolm's play employ even more suggestive language, to link *Emilia* with contemporary women. The Globe website proclaimed, '400 years ago Emilia Bassano wanted her voice to be heard. It wasn't. Her story is still our story. Emilia and her sisters reach out to us across the centuries with passion, fury, laughter and song. Listen to them. Let them inspire and unite us. Times are finally changing. Not fast enough. It's up to you. We are all Emilia. Stand up alongside her and be counted'.[62] This activist agenda was clear to reviewers, even at the expense of historical plausibility.

Paul Taylor, reviewing the play for *The Independent*, notes that, 'Having to fill in the considerable gaps in the evidence, Malcolm takes an attractively robust approach, mounting conjecture upon conjecture, with the odd squirt of wishful thinking', creating 'a passionately considered manifesto rather than a cautious history lesson'.[63] Similarly, Michael Billington, in his aptly subtitled review 'Speculative History of Shakespeare's Lover Brims with Wit and Rage', notes that 'the great virtue of Lloyd Malcolm's speculative history lies in its passion and anger: it ends with a blazing address to the audience that is virtually a call to arms ... in rescuing Emilia from the shades, it gives her dramatic life and polemical potency'.[64] Like the Dark Lady novels that bring together historical fiction and contemporary women's issues, a similar pattern is observed by reviewer J. N. Benjamin in Lloyd Morgan's play, noting that her 'words see each and every woman that came before Emilia, have come since her, and are yet to come ... Emilia is a play that transcends time, and place, to find meaning and relevance in a world far removed from its own'.[65]

At the end of Alexa Schnee's novel *Shakespeare's Lady*, she remarks, 'The Dark Lady, whoever she is, will forever live on'.⁶⁶ This is likely due to the fact that she provides an opportunity to combine Shakespeare's life story with various women's issues and scenarios, not always in a flattering light for Shakespeare, but nevertheless allowing him to speak to contemporary women's issues. Through these Dark Ladies, some based on historical figures and others imaginary, authors have constructed fantasy women to address Shakespeare's perceived sexual and creative needs, and to respond to desires for a more multi-racial and sexually liberated love interest, often far outside the realm of historical evidence.

Katherine Scheil is Professor of English at the University of Minnesota. Her publications include *The Taste of the Town: Shakespearian Comedy and the Early Eighteenth-Century Theater* (Bucknell, 2003), *Shakespeare/Adaptation/Modern Drama* (University of Toronto Press, 2011, co-edited with Randall Martin), *She Hath Been Reading: Women and Shakespeare Clubs in America* (Cornell, 2012), *Imagining Shakespeare's Wife: The Afterlife of Anne Hathaway* (Cambridge, 2018) and *Shakespeare & Stratford* (Berghahn Books, 2019, editor). She is working on a book about the history of women in Stratford-upon-Avon, as well as a book on the afterlife of the Dark Lady of Shakespeare's Sonnets.

Notes

1. The promotional blurb from the Globe is reproduced on the back cover of the play in print. See Morgan Lloyd Malcolm, *Emilia* (London: Oberon Books, 2018). Lanyer's name has been variously spelled as Emilia, Æmilia and Amelia, with either her maiden name of Bassano or married name of Lanyer. On the title page of the first edition of her long religious poem *Salve Deus Rex Judaeorum*, her name is spelled Aemilia Lanyer, and that is the default spelling I am using, unless quoting another source.
2. Michael Billington, '*Emilia* Review: Speculative History of Shakespeare's Lover Brims with Wit and Rage', *The Guardian*, 16 August 2018.
3. 'Review: *Emilia* (Shakespeare's Globe), *WhatsOnStage*, 16 August 2018, www.whatsonstage.com/london-theatre/reviews/emilia-shakespeare-globe-wakefield_47396.html. Accessed 28 March 2021.
4. Recent scholarly work on the Sonnets has challenged the premise that the poems are biographical links to Shakespeare. Paul Hammond, in *Shakespeare's Sonnets:*

An Original-Spelling Text (Oxford: Oxford University Press, 2012) cautions that 'it is a tempting but dangerous assumption that these poems reveal Shakespeare's innermost thoughts and feelings' (93). Likewise, Paul Edmondson and Stanley Wells remark that biographical approaches that connect the Sonnets to Shakespeare's life are 'simplistic and overrid[e] the nuances and complexities of some of the greatest poems ever written in English'. *All the Sonnets of Shakespeare* (Cambridge: Cambridge University Press, 2020), 23.

5. Paul Franssen, *Shakespeare's Literary Lives: The Author as Character in Fiction and Film* (Cambridge: Cambridge University Press, 2016), 108. Stanley Wells notes that the identity of the Dark Lady 'has been endlessly debated but never decided', in 'Arguments Over a Woman', *The Telegraph*, 20 February 1999.
6. Jonathan Bate, *Soul of the Age* (New York: Random House, 2009), 173.
7. Stephen Greenblatt, *Will in the World: How Shakespeare Became Shakespeare* (New York: W. W. Norton, 2004), 255.
8. Anthony Burgess, *Shakespeare* (London: Jonathan Cape, 1970), 145, 146, 148.
9. In her excellent study of the reception history of the Sonnets, Jane Kingsley-Smith observes that the Dark Lady provides 'a means by which women may write back to Shakespeare'. *The Afterlife of Shakespeare's Sonnets* (Cambridge: Cambridge University Press, 2019), 10.
10. As I have argued elsewhere, Shakespeare's wife Anne Hathaway has received similar treatment, in works such as Arliss Ryan's 2010 novel *The Secret Confessions of Anne Shakespeare*, where Anne reveals that she is the real author of the plays by Shakespeare. Katherine West Scheil, *Imagining Shakespeare's Wife: The Afterlife of Anne Hathaway* (Cambridge: Cambridge University Press, 2018), 170–201.
11. O'Reilly's novel was the creative component of her PhD degree at Brunel University: 'Inventing Shakespeare: Re-Imagining a National Icon', *Writing in Practice: The Journal of Creative Writing Research* 5 (2019), unpaginated.
12. This argument is advanced by Duncan Salkeld in *Shakespeare Among the Courtesans: Prostitution, Literature, and Drama, 1500–1650* (Aldershot: Ashgate, 2012).
13. Martha Tuck Rozett, *Constructing a World: Shakespeare's England and the New Historical Fiction* (Albany: State University of New York Press, 2003), 107.
14. Andrew James Hartley, *Shakespeare and Millennial Fiction* (Cambridge: Cambridge University Press, 2018), 4.
15. Stephanie Harzewski, *Chick Lit and Postfeminism* (Charlottesville: University of Virginia Press, 2011), 3.
16. Ibid., 4.
17. O'Reilly, 'Inventing Shakespeare'.
18. www.goodreads.com/book/show/17612518-his-dark-lady. Accessed 28 March 2021. While reader responses are notoriously difficult to find, the site goodreads.com provides extensive reviews of these novels by ordinary readers. Unless otherwise noted, I have relied on this site for reader responses throughout this essay.
19. Both *Dark Lady's Mask* quotes are at www.goodreads.com/book/show/25897736-the-dark-lady-s-mask. Accessed 28 March 2021.
20. Harzewski, *Chick Lit and Postfeminism*, 3.
21. Even though there is a vibrant and growing readership of historical fiction for women, analysis of the topic has not been as positive. As Diana Wallace notes,

'women's historical fiction seems to have attracted particularly virulent criticism'. Wallace observes that one of the 'difficulties in reading women's historical fiction' is the 'persistence of these kinds of knee-jerk populist assumptions – that women's historical fiction is pointless, irrelevant and not just not "proper history," but actively damaging and/or contaminating to "proper history"'. Diana Wallace, 'Difficulties, Discontinuities and Differences: Reading Women's Historical Fiction', in *The Female Figure in Contemporary Historical Fiction*, ed. Katherine Cooper and Emma Short (Basingstoke, UK: Palgrave Macmillan, 2012), 208–210.
22. O'Reilly, 'Inventing Shakespeare'.
23. Mary Sharratt, *The Dark Lady's Mask: A Novel of Shakespeare's Muse* (Boston, MA: Houghton Mifflin Harcourt, 2016), 394. Grace Tiffany includes no author's note or prefatory material in *Paint*.
24. Alexa Schnee, *Shakespeare's Lady* (New York: Guideposts, 2012), 327–328.
25. Andrea Chapin, *The Tutor* (New York: Riverhead Books, 2015), 351.
26. O'Reilly, 'Inventing Shakespeare'.
27. www.goodreads.com/book/show/17612518-his-dark-lady. Accessed 28 March 2021.
28. www.goodreads.com/book/show/17612518-his-dark-lady. Accessed 28 March 2021.
29. www.goodreads.com/book/show/12898548-shakespeare-s-lady#other_reviews. Accessed 28 March 2021.
30. www.amazon.co.uk/gp/customer-reviews/R19XJQK2ABXW31/ref=cm_cr_arp_d_rvw_ttl?ie=UTF8&ASIN=1908434414. Accessed 28 March 2021.
31. Diana Wallace, *The Woman's Historical Novel: British Women Writers, 1900–2000* (Basingstoke, UK: Palgrave Macmillan, 2005), 4.
32. www.goodreads.com/book/show/12898548-shakespeare-s-lady?ac=1&from_search=true. Accessed 28 March 2021.
33. https://shereadsnovels.com/tag/sally-oreilly/. Accessed 28 March 2021.
34. www.unabridgedchick.net/2014/10/dark-aemilia-by-sally-oreilly.html. Accessed 28 March 2021.
35. www.amazon.co.uk/gp/customer-reviews/R1UGZQMNZAGPTA/ref=cm_cr_arp_d_rvw_ttl?ie=UTF8&ASIN=1908434414. Accessed 28 March 2021.
36. www.sandradanby.com/book-review-dark-aemilia/. Accessed 28 March 2021.
37. www.goodreads.com/book/show/18465503-dark-aemilia#other_reviews. Accessed 28 March 2021.
38. www.goodreads.com/book/show/25897736-the-dark-lady-s-mask. Accessed 28 March 2021.
39. www.goodreads.com/book/show/25897736-the-dark-lady-s-mask. Accessed 28 March 2021.
40. Heike Mißler, *The Cultural Politics of Chick Lit: Popular Fiction, Postfeminism, and Representation* (London: Routledge, 2017), 199.
41. Meredith Whitford, *Shakespeare's Will* (Fremantle: Vivid Publishing, 2010), 228.
42. See Janice Radway, *Reading the Romance: Women, Patriarchy, and Popular Literature* (Chapel Hill: University of North Carolina Press, 1984; 1991).
43. https://litstack.com/litstack-review-the-tutor-by-andrea-chapin/. Accessed 28 March 2021.
44. Maya Rodale, *Dangerous Books for Girls: The Bad Reputation of Romance Novels Explained* (Maya Rodale, 2015), 110.

45. Sally O'Reilly, *Dark Aemilia* (Brighton: Myriad Editions, 2014), 305.
46. www.goodreads.com/book/show/18465503-dark-aemilia. Accessed 28 March 2021.
47. www.goodreads.com/book/show/18465503-dark-aemilia. Accessed 28 March 2021.
48. www.goodreads.com/book/show/17612518-his-dark-lady#other_reviews. Accessed 28 March 2021.
49. www.goodreads.com/book/show/12898548-shakespeare-s-lady?ac=1&from_search=true. Accessed 28 March 2021.
50. www.goodreads.com/book/show/12898548-shakespeare-s-lady?from_search=true&from_srp=true&qid=9OIOXYUA3l&rank=1#other_reviews. Accessed 28 March 2021.
51. Susan Strehle and Mary Paniccia Carden, eds, *Doubled Plots: Romance and History* (Jackson: University Press of Mississippi, 2003), xii.
52. Julie Sanders, *Novel Shakespeares* (Manchester: Manchester University Press, 2001), 11.
53. Kate Chedgzoy, 'Remembering Amelia Lanyer', *Journal of the Northern Renaissance* 2 (2010). www.northernrenaissance.org/remembering-aemilia-lanyer/. Accessed 28 March 2021.
54. Graham Holderness, *Nine Lives of William Shakespeare* (London: Continuum, 2011), 141, 143.
55. Ibid., 146.
56. Andrew Elfenbein, *The Gist of Reading* (Stanford, CA: Stanford University Press, 2018), 37.
57. Elizabeth Winkler, 'Was Shakespeare a Woman?', *The Atlantic*, June 2019.
58. https://doctorcleveland.blogspot.com/2019/05/shakespeare-wasnt-perfect.html. Accessed 28 March 2021. 'Doctor Cleveland' is the pseudonym for James J. Marino, Associate Professor of English at Cleveland State University.
59. https://doctorcleveland.blogspot.com/2019/05/shakespeare-wasnt-perfect.html. Accessed 28 March 2021.
60. Dominic Green, 'Was Shakespeare a Woman? Of Course He Was', *The Spectator*, 13 May 2019.
61. Lloyd Malcolm, *Emilia*, vii.
62. www.shakespearesglobe.com/whats-on/emilia-2019/. Accessed 28 March 2021.
63. Paul Taylor, '*Emilia*, Shakespeare's Globe, London, Review', *The Independent*, 16 August 2018.
64. Billington, '*Emilia* Review'.
65. J. N. Benjamin, '*Emilia* Review at Shakespeare's Globe, London', *The Stage*, 16 August 2018.
66. Schnee, *Shakespeare's Lady*, 328.

Chapter 8
Flights of Fancy and the Dissolution of Shakespearean Space-Time in Angela Carter's *Nights at the Circus*

Kate Myers

> Time splits into two trajectories: one virtual the other actual; one that makes the present pass, and the other that preserves itself as past while still part of the present. One forms memory, the other perception; one is oriented toward reminiscence and the past, the other opens out to anticipation and the unknowable future.[1]

In *The Genius to Improve an Invention*, Piero Boitani considers *literary transition* to be transformative, 'a constant reworking of myths ... an intertextual rather than philological echoing through space and time'.[2] It preserves texts but as new creations, hatched into new afterlives but haunted by their origins. Literary transition is a defining feature in the work of both William Shakespeare and Angela Carter.

While much critical attention has been paid to Angela Carter's intertextual appropriation of Shakespeare and her interrogation of the patriarchal ideology at work in his representations of familial strife,

Notes for this section begin on page 135.

critics have focused on Carter's swansong novel, *Wise Children*.³ Indeed, *Wise Children* self-consciously alludes to the Bard and announces its scrutiny and reversal of a father's claim on biological, and Shakespeare's relatively recent claim on cultural, legitimacy. It is easy to see why critics would focus on Shakespeare's influence in *Wise Children* because the novel blatantly borrows from the plots and characters of Shakespeare's plays, as it recounts the story of a convoluted, theatrical family through the perspective of Dora Chance, a 75-year-old showgirl and one of the illegitimate twin daughters of renowned nineteenth-century Shakespearean actor Melchior Hazard. The story begins on 23 April, Melchior's 100th birthday, which, of course, is the presumed birthday of the Bard himself. Flagrant Shakespearean allusions persist throughout the five-act structure of the novel and are numerous. *Wise Children*'s overstated and sometimes tedious use of Shakespearean tropes aside, the intertextual links between Shakespeare and Carter's earlier novel, *Nights at the Circus*, have gone largely unremarked.

Nights at the Circus also builds a bricolage of blatant Shakespearean allusions – from Falstaff's judging 'discretion the better part' to Hamlet's 'what a wonderful piece of work is man!' to a perhaps more appropriate Malvolian surmising via the ever-entrepreneurial, if small-minded circus ringmaster, 'some was born fools, some was made fools, and some make fools of themselves'.⁴ While not all readers of *Nights at the Circus* may notice the references, seasoned readers of Shakespeare likely do notice. Nonetheless, Carter's quoted and adapted Shakespearean language has garnered little critical attention, and the extent to which she explicitly and especially implicitly conjures and disrupts Shakespearean conventions in *Nights at the Circus* has been virtually overlooked. Perhaps a first stab at the over-the-top, self-conscious scrutiny of the Bard in *Wise Children*, *Nights at the Circus* deploys Shakespeare's penchant for the ambiguous and the plausibly deniable to more subtly reconsider the ontological issues of legitimacy by returning to Shakespeare's perennial interest in both time and space, ways of thinking that, I argue, serve to reinforce a legitimisation of masculinity. As it follows the exploits of the ostensibly winged aerialist Sophia Fevvers, *Nights at the Circus* appropriates and ultimately shatters Shakespeare's methods to disrupt both space and time, specifically his disruptions concerning the materiality and disjointedness of time in the *Winter's Tale* and in *Hamlet*. In so doing, Carter reverses time and dismembers space to criticise the systemic problem of the masculine-made-legitimate at the expense of the feminine, a problem that Shakespeare explores and sometimes seems to criticise, but that his temporal and spatial manipulations persistently uphold.

Carter's novel traces the turbulent timeline of Fevvers from her childhood spent as a foundling in a London brothel, to her tenure on display at a Museum of Women Monsters, to her near sacrifice on a Rosicrucian alter to the masculine ego, to her worldwide fame as an aerialist in the circus, to her near demise in an all-male terrorist organisation's attack that explodes the circus train in Siberia. Fevvers gains notoriety in each of these environments in large part because no one knows the answer to what becomes her circus-poster tag line, itself a version of Hamlet's driving ontological question, 'To be or not to be': 'Is she fact or is she fiction?'[5] That is, no one knows whether the wings that seem to grow from Fevvers' shoulder blades are authentic or fabricated, but Jack Walser, a young American reporter, determined to know the truth, intends to debunk Fevvers' story by uncovering lapses that might prove she is, in fact, a fiction. His plan fails as Fevvers draws him further and further into her autobiographical tale until he gives up reporting to join the circus as a clown, just to be near the aerialist with whom he has become infatuated.

Walser's infatuation with Fevvers stems from her bewitching and implausible tale, which she weaves for him in a late-night London interview before they separately – and unknowingly, at first, to her – depart with the circus on a worldwide tour beginning in Russia. It is during this interview that time begins to deteriorate and the space of the material world in Fevvers' dressing room becomes both capacious and suffocating. It is later, during the transcontinental sojourn in Siberia, that the materiality of time finally shatters, spinning off into space as a new and unpredictable beginning. Both of these episodes make use of Shakespeare's ways of thinking about time- and space-disrupted.

Temporal and spatial manipulations appear to be two of Shakespeare's recurrent interests as a writer. Since at least the mid twentieth century, scholars have investigated the ways in which Shakespeare thematises time not only to provide texts across his corpus with structures but also to destabilise those same texts.[6] Though the New Historicist and Cultural Materialist critics turned away from considerations of time in favour of the materiality of local spaces, Sarah Lewis suggests in 'Shakespeare, Time, Theory' that temporality nonetheless has remained as a focal concern for literary theorists.[7] Moreover, space and time themselves have been described as gendered and manipulated to undergird masculine authority. Elizabeth Grosz, following Luce Irigaray, explains:

> in the West time is conceived as masculine (proper to a subject, a being with an interior) and space is associated with femininity (femininity being a form of externality to men). Woman is/provides space for man but occupies none herself. Time is the projection of his interior, and is conceptual, introspective. The interiority of time links with the exteriority of space only through the position of God (or his surrogate, Man) as the point of their mediation and axis of their coordination.[8]

The present study merges the two to highlight how Shakespeare's manipulations of space and time serve a similar purpose: to uphold masculinised systems of legitimacy.

In *The Winter's Tale*, time materialises in the voice of the chorus, when Time takes its turn to speak, and time solidifies to stand still in the living-dead statue of Hermione. A spatial presence, Time, as we know, explains its appearance as a plot device designed to distract and deceive 'slid[ing] o'er sixteen years, and leav[ing] the growth untried of that wide gap, since it is in [Time's] power to o'erthrow law, and in one self-born hour to plant and o'erwhelm custom'.[9] Time overthrows and overwhelms the usual order of things through a series of contradictions: power and the absence of (legal) power, planted and destroyed social order, and the impossibility of self-procreation. Time's language suggests an uneasy, ambivalent transition from the prior acts of the play. With a future-oriented register of fecundity in *growth*, *self-born*, and *plant*, Time smooths over a devastating fictive past that has to be excused so as not to appear criminally destructive. The paradoxical orientation towards time that this scene suggests is not only typical of early modern thinkers on the whole, it is a specific concern of Shakespeare across his corpus.[10] Time's paradox in these opening lines of the speech redoubles the ambivalence that haunts the first three scenes.

Shakespeare manifests Time as a distraction from the atrocities perpetrated by Leontes to uphold his view of masculine social order, atrocities against his family that stem from his suspicion that his wife Hermione has been unfaithful and has given birth to Polixenes' child, atrocities that snowball into the attempted murder of their infant Perdita, the death of their son Mamillius and the purported death of Hermione herself. Rather than maintain his masculine position, Leontes succeeds in destroying his family, alienating his subjects and dissolving himself in a state of perpetual mourning. Yet Leontes is not definitively to blame and Hermione is not definitively exonerated. When the lords of Sicilia return with a sealed oracle from Delphi, the court hears that,

> Hermione is chaste, Polixenes blameless, Camillo a true subject, Leontes a jealous tyrant, his innocent babe truly begotten, and the King shall live without an heir if that which is lost be not found.[11]

Leontes does not believe it until after his son Mamillius dies, leaving him with no heir. Leontes' doubt is not unfounded: the Delphic oracle speaks in often ambiguous riddles. Granted, the ambiguity in the statement may only refer to the King living 'without an heir if that which is lost be not found' because no one yet knows that Mamillius has died nor that the baby, Leontes' remaining heir, will be called Perdita, meaning 'lost'. Moreover, the audience, like the lords of Sicilia, have been primed with sympathy for Hermione to believe the oracle's message and disbelieve Leontes' rantings. Time's interlude distracts from both.

Time's appearance not only translates the audience to Bohemia and the scenes of life, community and love contained therein, it also prevents the audience from lingering over the crimes of the Sicilian king, causing the audience to pivot to consider the crimes Time perpetrates on everyone. In the first line of Time's speech, Time admits to 'try[ing] all' bringing terror ... and bad, that makes and unfolds error', thereby readying the audience to think poorly of Time, not Leontes, despite having just witnessed the King's ferocity.[12] Time leaves the audience with a sinister wish, one that he claims is earnest:

> ... Of this [refusing to explain Perdita's current predicament] allow,
> If ever you have spent time worse ere now;
> If never, yet that Time himself doth say
> He wishes earnestly you never may.[13]

Time asks for forgiveness – 'of this allow' – if the audience deems their time, presumably their time watching the play, badly spent. However, 'ere now' also prompts the audience to consider their bad times in general. Time then wishes that the audience will never experience a bad time – watching the play or, again, otherwise. While these lines seem both contrite and conciliatory, they also turn the audience to contemplate their own bad times, past and future.

In his ambiguous language, Time has primed us to forgive Leontes for his crimes against his family and his kingdom by prompting forgiveness for the universally significant crimes of Time and time itself, and Leontes is all but forgotten as the happier plot unfolds in Bohemia. Thus, Time's material disruption that connects the play's plot lays the groundwork to shore up sympathy for Leontes and therefore maintains his authority as husband, as father and as king, in the final scene. Hermione, who is present at the end as a statue of herself, is the tangible embodiment of the wishful thinking that time can be stopped in its tracks and no longer poses the universal threat that Time hinted at in his soliloquy. Having been presumed dead for the duration of the sixteen-year gap in time, Hermione awakens to a life with, granted, a remorseful husband, but a life that nonetheless re-establishes the status quo of the masculine legitimacy bestowed by the father who now accepts Perdita as his child and releases Hermione from taking responsibility for a plausibly deniable sexual transgression that Leontes vividly imagined but that she did not definitively commit. The two women remain at the mercy of a masculine system of order that neither they nor Time actually 'overwhelm' or 'overthrow'.

While time is captured in an audible voice and frozen into a tangible artefact in *The Winter's Tale*, time in *Hamlet* is dynamic. Time cannot but move, ticking away the hours and months of the prince's inaction and seeming madness. Without the figure of Time making itself visible, Shakespeare more discreetly skips gaps in time in this play, jumping ahead by months between the three, roughly thirty-hour-long episodes by which the play's action is articulated, the spans of its time hinged, or jointed.[14]

However, time is, of course, also 'out of joint', and so is the material reality in Denmark.[15] Time falls out of joint and reality is shaken with the seemingly material appearance of Old Hamlet's ghost. The ghost signifies a kind of disjointed memory. It is a visitation of the past inhabiting the present. Moreover, the ghost manifests a memory of Old Hamlet's demise that disrupts the official, 'given out' memory that he was stung by a serpent.[16] Hamlet and Horatio both read Old Hamlet's ghost as a portent – 'My father's spirit, in arms! All is not well'; 'this bodes some strange eruption to our state'.[17] As an apparition and a portent, the ghost of Old Hamlet becomes a memory of the future, a strange eruption that both interrupts time and suggests a strange turning, a backward movement of time in which predictions for the present's future necessarily exist at once in that future's past and in the present. Time falls out of joint with the appearance of the ghost because the ghost manifests both the past and the future in the present. Time has condensed; it is no longer segmented; it has no joints. The ghost creates the textual equivalent of a skipping record, a temporal loop that neither he nor Young Hamlet can escape. This disruption of time provides the space of the play, in which to confront the murderous Claudius and 'to set [time] right'.[18] The perennial problem is that Hamlet must do both if he is to 'remember' the ghost and establish his legitimacy as the son of the old King, but he never really gets around to doing either and destroys his mother and Ophelia in his attempts.[19] In the drive to achieve this legitimacy, the play itself takes on the shape of a temporal loop, a ring, a chiasmus.

Gilles Deleuze argues that time in *Hamlet* cannot be circular *because* it is unhinged. Deleuze explains that a hinged, revolving door continues revolving in its 'proximity to the Eternal' and disjointed time is a door off of its hinges that enable it to move.[20] I do not disagree: the space of the play is out of joint and is not circular. However, Hamlet's quest that culminates in his death puts time back into joint, as evidenced by the successful revenge perpetrated by Young Fortinbras to reclaim land stolen from his father and uphold his and his father's legitimate right to Elsinore. Moreover, Hamlet's memory takes the form of the ghost as portent: the past exposed in the present establishes Hamlet's future, a future which I suggest is nothing more than a return to the same past. *Hamlet* begins where it ends and ends where the play begins – with the death of a Hamlet. A chiastic structure of return links the two Hamlets throughout. For example, upon the first mention of a Hamlet, Barnardo explains that the ghost arrives 'in the same figure like the King that's dead', and Horatio confirms that 'such was the very armour [the King] had on when he th'ambitious Norway combatted'.[21] At the last mention of Hamlet in the final act, Fortinbras, that is, Young Norway, has Hamlet carried off 'like a soldier to the stage' with 'soldiers' music and the rites of war speak[ing] loudly for him'.[22] The conclusion of the play evokes its beginning, even inaugurates it, as the final lines of the play set the stage for a dead Hamlet to appear as a soldier:

> A figure like your father,
> Armed at point exactly, cap-a-pe,
> Appears before them, and with solemn march
> Goes slow and stately by them...
> And I with them the third night kept the watch;
> Where, as they had deliver'd, both in time,
> Form of the thing, each word made true and good,
> The apparition comes: I knew your father;
> These hands are not more like.[23]

Although Horatio explains the prior appearance of the ghost, the passage also suggests Young Hamlet's dying scene where he, too, appears armed as if a solider, royal and, indeed, stately. Moreover, his dead body is borne off, likely with solemn march. He is himself 'a figure like [his] father' in this final scene that sets a stage similar to the earlier one; like Horatio's hands, these two scenes cannot be more like. This final scene is a beginning that likewise portends the end. That is, the play itself is serpentine, a self-creating ouroboros that devours its tail even as it regenerates. The cyclical violence of upholding the legitimacy of masculine lineage and political power decimates the state of Denmark, yet maintains a masculine status quo in Fortinbras' conquest, yet another son's action to avenge his wronged father.

As Hamlet's appointed witness, Horatio reinforces the link between the ending and the beginning, by which the play appears to take a circular form. In the middle of pronouncing himself dead for the second time in a handful of lines, Hamlet tells Horatio, 'Thou liv'st; report me and my cause aright to the unsatisfied ... If thou didst ever hold me in thy heart, absent thee from felicity awhile, and in this harsh world draw thy breath in pain, to tell my story'.[24] And Horatio complies:

> And let me speak to th' yet unknowing world how these things came about. So shall you hear of carnal, bloody, and unnatural acts, of accidental judgements, casual slaughters, of deaths put on by cunning and forced cause; and, in this upshot, purposes mistook fallen on the inventors' heads. All this can I truly deliver.[25]

Horatio here summarises the plot of the play and pledges to retell the Hamlets' tragedy to Fortinbras and the English Ambassador, who arrive amid the final carnage. Thus, the end of the play directs a return to its own beginning, the recounting of a memory that evokes both Hamlets. Indeed, repeating it in every production of the play,

Horatio never finishes telling their story, its violence like a serpent whose grasp neither Hamlet escapes.

The Hamlets may be trapped in a circle of their own making, eternally seeking means of escape via a paternal line of legitimacy, but Angela Carter's winged protagonist is not. In *Nights at the Circus*, Carter appropriates Shakespeare's tactics of disrupting time and space, but deploys them to different ends. Instead of affirming or at least maintaining a masculinised view of legitimacy, Carter destabilises it. She makes time stand still and spin out of control; she shatters the material world of objects that represent a systemic status quo that excludes or disregards or dehumanises women. These disruptions effectively halt and shatter the temporal and material artefacts that uphold paternal legitimacy. And they find focus in the ambiguity inherent in the hybrid body of Sophie Fevvers.

Fevvers is just as adept an escape artist as she is an aerialist. The novel may be read as a series of serpentine traps in which Fevvers and other women are beholden to the authority and cultural legitimacy of men and from which Fevvers always breaks free. According to the metaphor that governs her being, the 'fully feathered' Fevvers hatches out of many impossibly tight spots, including the allegedly literal egg of her birth: she was found on the steps of a brothel as 'a little babe most lovingly packed up in new straw sweetly sleeping among a litter of broken eggshells', ostensibly a hybrid daughter of Leda and her swan-disguised attacker Zeus.[26] As the presumed product of a sexual assault, Fevvers refuses to be constrained by her origins. Instead, she is reborn into a new life at each escape from a confining situation: that is, each hatching from a series of eggs that confine women in one way or another based on a status quo that benefits men at the expense of women, but out of which women also find the means to gain freedom.[27]

By breaking through the confines of her metaphorical eggs, Fevvers shatters the material reality of her context and circumstances. The brothel where she spent her childhood, then, is a kind of egg in which Fevvers 'was closed up like a shell ... sealed in [an] artificial egg' as the bodies of women were sold for sex and from which she is ejected upon the death of the proprietor Ma Nelson at the demand of Nelson's cleric brother.[28] Fevvers next finds work displaying herself at a museum of female monsters, another egg in which the abnormal or disfigured bodies of a variety of women pose for the pleasure of the male patrons. Fevvers' escape from the museum was more of a kidnapping, having been abducted by the thugs working for a museum patron, Mr Rosencreutz. Rosencreutz creates for Fevvers another sort of egg when his intentions turn out to be sinister and self-serving. 'Versed in esoteric law and magic arts', Rosencreutz planned to sacrifice Fevvers on the altar of his own desire in order to reclaim his youth, his vitality and his virility.[29] Fevvers escapes only to find herself the star of Captain Kearney's Grand Imperial Tour, a circus destined for Russia. The circus train that transports her across the Siberian landscape is also an egg. But it is in the episode with the Russian Duke that Carter appropriates the circular entrapment of masculine legitimacy to which the Hamlets fall victim and uses it to skip both space and time, creating a vector that bypasses its clutches.

The Duke coerces Fevvers into meeting him at his home and bribes her into coming alone, promising a diamond necklace in exchange for an intimate dinner. At great personal risk, Fevvers accepts his invitation. Upon her arrival, the Duke tempts Fevvers with jewel-encrusted egg-shaped boxes and promises her that 'she could have whichever egg she chose just as soon as she took off her shawl and let him see her wings'.[30] Each of the Duke's elaborately jewelled eggs depicts a kind of prison for Fevvers. One egg contains a tiny frame, 'and what should the frame contain but a miniature of the *aerialist* herself'.[31] A second egg contains a tiny tree with a tinier bird that sings 'Only a bird in a gilded cage', which Fevvers finds 'exceedingly troubling' and senses 'imminent and deadly danger'.[32] Another egg, topped with a swan, contains an empty bird cage, which Fevvers takes to be 'a tribute, perhaps, to her putative paternity', suggesting that her avian father was never trapped or at least was able to escape the confines that elude the Hamlets as well as Leontes, offering an image of masculine wishful thinking that would maintain their own authority at the expense of women.[33] As an overt nod to Fevvers' hybrid status as a potential child of Zeus, the result of his rape of Leda, this egg doubles to identify the sexual assault Fevvers suspects she will face. Rather than waiting around for the Duke to rape her, Fevvers escapes using the remaining egg, which contains 'an engine, in black enamel, and one, two, three, four, first-class carriages in tortoiseshell and ebony, all coiled round one another like a snake, with, engraved on the side of each in Cyrillic, the legend *The Trans-Siberian Express*'.[34] In this one image, Carter takes a circular entrapment that appears to threaten strangulation by snake and uses it to create the way out that the Hamlets never had, and does so with the suggestion that the Duke's own impulse towards sexual violence against Fevvers both thwarts him and propels her escape.

> The bitter knowledge she'd been fooled spurred Fevvers into action. She dropped the toy train on the Isfahan runner – mercifully, it landed on its wheels – as, with a grunt and whistle of expelled breath, the Grand Duke ejaculated.
>
> In those few seconds of his lapse of consciousness, Fevvers ran helter-skelter down the platform, opened the door of the first-class compartment and clambered aboard.[35]

Hamlet, for whom there is no escape from the same uncertainty about his own legitimacy that propels the entire plot of his play, will go on seeking his own legitimacy in perpetuity. But Fevvers, who is safely reunited with her maternal surrogate Lizzie, recognises the traps of masculine and paternal authority and – both magically and literally – breaks free from the confines of both space and time, hatching herself out of the material security and cultural legitimacy of powerful male figures who intend to control her, to contain her, to define her or to do her harm.

While in Fevvers' escape Carter appropriates and repurposes elements of Shakespeare's temporal and spatial disruptions that serve to uphold masculine authority, she writes the journalist Walser as a mirror of both Hamlet and Leontes, a mirror that leads Walser through an infantile regression that evokes their faults but leads Walser to a rebirth that shatters any resemblance to his forefathers he once bore. Like Hamlet, Walser is preoccupied with time and questions of legitimacy. Like Leontes, he cannot accept that the woman before him is trustworthy, believable or even real. Time's impact on Walser is palpable and he blames Fevvers and her foster mother Lizzie for bewitching both it and him during his initial interview with the aerialist. He is unnerved by the novel's material representation of Father Time – the mantle clock, rescued by Lizzie from the brothel when it repeatedly and inexplicably strikes midnight over the course of their conversation. Like the circular plot that traps both Hamlets, this Father Time seems to impose an inevitable recurrence. Yet Carter's repetition is made obvious to her characters and obviously makes one of them uncomfortable. It is Walser's discomfort that first denaturalises recurrence – a concept that Carter's novel will explore several times – and it does so by making time itself strange. Space in Fevvers' dressing room also closes in on

Walser as he feels more and more overwhelmed by her larger-than-life presence even as he aims to expose her life as illegitimate, her livelihood a con.

Rather than leave Walser on a tragic trajectory like his Shakespearean forefathers, Carter takes up many tactics of manipulating, stopping, reversing and confusing time, much like those Shakespeare deploys in *The Winter's Tale* and *Hamlet*. The novel formalises this kind of temporal disruption as the narration slips between past and present verb tenses: Walser's Siberian experiences narrated in the past, Fevvers' mostly and conspicuously narrated in the present. The novel thematises temporal disruption through an uncanny recurrence in every vignette across the three-part novel of men who intend to do women harm, each one a mirror of the others with similar, self-interested motivations and similar tactics for manipulating women, each one reliant on magic and wish-fulfilment.

The novel mocks this masculine primacy by developing Walser's character in reverse through a series of increasingly infantile regressions. Walser abandons his adult life and his career as a journalist to run away with the circus as a clown whose performances become ever more infantile, perverse and scatological. The clowns imagine their state to be 'something wonderful, something precious [because they] invent [their] own faces. [They] *make* [themselves]'.[36] It is the lifeless rigidity of the clowns' self-conception – 'the circus permits no copying, no change', yet all of their faces look the same – that subjects them and Walser to regression and the disintegration of space and time.[37] When Fevvers' mantle clock explodes in the train wreck, Walser's time stops altogether.

He does not die. He falls unconscious into a timeless state of infancy, unable to speak, to take care of himself, to remember who he is or even refer to himself as a person. He regains consciousness and a new sense of himself as a mystic in an indigenous and primitive Siberian culture where time also stands still. Like the confused and disjointed sense of time for Hamlet, past, present and future here are one and the same:

> none of them knew in what way the past differed from the present. They weren't too sure what was different at the future, either.[38]

As Wylie Sypher defines the different measures of time that emerge in Shakespeare's plays, 'archaic time sense is closely associated with fertility rituals, and behind these rituals is an abiding faith in renewal – the past will recur as the future'.[39] It seems, then, that Carter's manipulations of time, mockery of fertility rituals, misgivings about recurrence, and metamorphosised renewals unravel the temporal sense that Sypher identifies in both *Hamlet* and *The Winter's Tale*.

Because Walser's regressive metamorphosis culminates in undifferentiated, eternally present time but a present that is grammatically marked as past, Carter can formally and thematically highlight the troubling perpetuation of masculine authority. Walser's new community might have disabused him of the traditional patriarchal structures since it was unconcerned with the legitimacy of one's ancestry and unfamiliar with the either-or logic that Walser had at one time wanted to use to expose Fevvers. Indeed, it 'made no categorical distinction between seeing and believing', and in this culture 'there existed no distinction between fact and fiction; instead a sort of magical realism'.[40] Walser did not find this kind of renewal, just a nascent recurrence of the same status quo and traditional patriarchal structures. For instance, this culture used its mystical beliefs surrounding childbirth to devalue women. The practices echo the traumas women face at the hands of men in this novel and the trauma Hermione faces at the hands of her husband, and Perdita's supposed illegitimacy. To wit, at the expense of pregnant women, the tribe legitimised children and ensured that they would not be stolen by evil entities who would spirit them away to modern culture. The women were banished from the confines of the village to give birth in makeshift shelters, alone and in mortal danger.

Juxtaposing the moments of Walser's rebirth with this practice, the novel confirms Walser's inclusion in the tribe and acquiescence to misogyny when he calls to mind the control of women's bodies in his prior existence, unprompted and unexpectedly singing in English 'Only a bird in a gilded cage!' before 'a door slammed shut on his memory, and for the time being, he lived as a tribal child'.[41] When Fevvers finds him in the Siberian wilderness, Walser does not know her, but he has pulled from the memory of his former life 'some kind of chant, some kind of dirge, some kind of Siberian invocation of the spectral inhabitants of the other world which coexists with this one, and Fevvers knew in her bones his song was meant to do her harm' because she recognised it: 'Only a bird in a gilded cage–'.[42]

Although 'anxious as to whom this reconstructed Walser might turn out to be', Fevvers emerges to assert her facticity and fast-forward time to the dawn of the new century.[43] As in *The Winter's Tale*, Carter's novel thwarts the ravages of time and those who were lost have been found. Like *Hamlet*, the three-part novel returns to its narrative beginnings with Walser questioning Fevvers about her identity. Fevvers confirms the textual reboot: 'Now that's the way to start an interview! ... Get out your pencil and we'll begin'.[44] Carter's ostensible bird-woman Fevvers and her newly hatched partner give themselves over to the never-settled questions of who is fact and who is fiction.

Unlike both Shakespearean plays, time at the end of Carter's novel is propelled by women and by Fevvers' hope of an egalitarian future with Walser, who finds his way out of his haze, a new creation.[45] Leaving both Walser and Fevvers undefined, Carter's novel anticipates Elizabeth Grosz's refusal 'to seek answers' in favour of 'pos[ing] questions as aporias, as paradoxes – that is to insist that questions have no readily available solutions' in order not to foment revolution but

> endless negotiation, the equation of one's life with struggle, a wearying ideal but one perhaps that can make us less invested in any one struggle and more capable of bearing up to continuous effort.[46]

Grosz invites us to bear up 'to continuous effort to go against the relentless forces of sameness, [to be] more inventive in the kinds of subversion we seek, and more joyous in the kinds of struggle we choose to be called to,' and, in Fevvers, so does Carter.[47] Fevvers, laughing with delight, never definitively proves whether or not she is 'the only fully-feathered intacta in the history of the world', and leaves Walser wondering, good-humouredly, if 'he might be the butt of the joke'.[48] If not Walser, then perhaps for Carter the Hamlets and Leontes are.

Kate Myers is Assistant Professor and Director of the Writing Program at The University of Olivet. Her research investigates unacknowledged Semitic underpinnings of early modern English rhetorical and literary conventions of writing, including formalised affect and temporality in Shakespeare's plays. Her other research and teaching interests include the afterlives of Shakespeare and his contemporaries in nineteenth- and twentieth-century American and British literature, as well as critical and antiracist pedagogies.

Notes

I thank A. Samuel Kimball, Jillian Smith and Alex Menocal for their comments on the early stages of my investigations of Angela Carter's novels. I am also grateful for the participants of the Shakespeare and the Modern Novel seminar at the 2018 Conference of Shakespeare Association of America, especially Katherine Scheil for her observations and questions as the primary respondent to a condensed version of the present project.

1. Elizabeth Grosz, 'Time Out of Joint', in *Time and History in Deleuze and Serres*, ed. Bernd Herzogenrath (New York: Continuum, 2012), 147–151, here 149.
2. Piero Boitani, 'Preface to the American Edition', in *The Genius to Improve an Invention: Literary Transitions* (Notre Dame, IN: Notre Dame University Press, 2002), ix–xiv, here xii.
3. Angela Carter, *Wise Children* (New York: Penguin Books, 1993).
4. Angela Carter, *Nights at the Circus* (New York: Penguin Books, 1984), 151, 70, 102; cf. William Shakespeare, *Henry IV, Part I*, ed. David Bevington (Oxford: Oxford University Press, 2008), 5.4.118; William Shakespeare, *Hamlet*, ed. G. R. Hibbard (Oxford: Oxford University Press, 2008), 2.2.301; William Shakespeare, *Twelfth Night, or What You Will*, ed. Roger Warren and Stanley Wells (Oxford: Oxford University Press, 2008), 2.5.135–137.
5. Carter, *Nights at the Circus*, 7 (*Hamlet*, 3.1.57).
6. Shakespeare's interest in *time* is evident in the number of instances in which the concept appears across his plays and poems: 1,373 discrete occurrences.
7. Sarah Lewis, 'Shakespeare, Time, Theory', *Literature Compass* 11, no. 4 (2014), 246–257, here 247.
8. Elizabeth Grosz, 'Space, Time, and Bodies', in *Space, Time, and Perversion: Essays on the Politics of Bodies* (New York: Routledge, 1995), 83–101, here 99.
9. *The Winter's Tale*, 4.1.5–9.
10. Cf. Ricardo Quinones, *The Renaissance Discovery of Time* (Cambridge, MA: Harvard University Press, 1972); and John Spencer Hill, 'Time in Shakespeare', in *Infinity, Faith, and Time: Christian Humanism and Renaissance Literature* (Montreal: McGill-Queen's University Press, 1997).
11. *The Winter's Tale*, 3.2.130–134.
12. *The Winter's Tale*, 4.1.1–2.
13. *The Winter's Tale*, 4.1.29–32.
14. The first act constitutes one episode. The break in action must account for Ophelia's confirmation that Old Hamlet has been dead for four months by the second scene of act three, but the flow of action beginning in act two, scene one remains unbroken until at least the start of act three. The next gap in time is less clear, but time must elapse to account for Polonius's burial, Ophelia's descent into madness, Laertes' return from Paris, and Hamlet's departure for England. The events of the end of the play are continuous. Cf. G. R. Hibbard, 'General Introduction' in *Hamlet*, 1–66, here 35–36.
15. *Hamlet*, 1.5.196.
16. *Hamlet*, 1.5.36.
17. *Hamlet*, 1.2.257, 1.1.69.
18. *Hamlet*, 1.5.197.
19. *Hamlet*, 1.5.91, and passim.

20. Gilles Deleuze, 'On Four Poetic Formulas that Might Summarize the Kantian Philosophy', in *Essays Critical and Clinical*, trans. Daniel W. Smith and Michael A. Greco (Minneapolis: University of Minnesota Press, 1997), 27–35, here 27–28.
21. *Hamlet*, 1.1.41, 60–61.
22. *Hamlet*, 5.2.349–353.
23. *Hamlet*, 1.2.199–203, 208–212.
24. *Hamlet*, 5.2.291–292, 299–302.
25. *Hamlet*, 5.2.332–338.
26. Carter, *Nights at the Circus*, 12.
27. There are many more instances of women being confined for the benefit of men but breaking free as a result of a feminine intervention, including one character's escape from an abusive relationship with a man to find a mutually fulfilling relationship with another woman and the women who escaped from a panoptical prison for women accused of murdering their husbands.
28. Carter, *Nights at the Circus*, 39.
29. Ibid., 79.
30. Ibid., 189.
31. Ibid., 189.
32. Ibid., 190.
33. Ibid., 192.
34. Ibid., 191.
35. Ibid., 192.
36. Ibid., 121 (italics original).
37. Ibid.
38. Ibid., 258.
39. Wylie Sypher, 'The Measures of Time: Four Time Schemes', in *The Ethic of Time: Structures of Experience in Shakespeare* (New York: Seabury, 1976), 1–22, here 1.
40. Carter, *Nights at the Circus*, 260.
41. Ibid., 266.
42. Ibid., 289.
43. Ibid., 291.
44. Ibid., 291.
45. Ibid., 291.
46. Elizabeth Grosz, 'Introduction', in *Space, Time, and Perversion*, 1–6, here 6.
47. Ibid., 6.
48. Carter, *Nights at the Circus*, 294, 295.

Chapter 9

Hamlet's Displacement as a Recurrent Case in Cather's *A Lost Lady* and Al Halaby's *Once in a Promised Land*

Tareq Zuhair

Psychology and psychoanalytic critical analysis are two different disciplines, yet they are interrelated as both fields of knowledge entice readers to reflect on the inner human psyche through exposure to intense feelings and desires. However, the former addresses real people, while the latter sheds light on fictional characters that mirror true human cases. In her article, 'Some Reflections on the Links between Psychoanalysis and Literature', Eileen McConnell argues that both disciplines can reflect our own inner world and how inaccessible unconscious feelings and desires control our reaction to the outer physical world:

> The psychoanalytic process and the reading of a literary text touch at frequent points: both are ways of finding out about oneself, about one's inner and outer worlds, and how they interact. They enable us to 'read' our experiences. They have, therefore, a certain congruence

Notes for this section begin on page 154.

of direction towards self-knowledge. They search for a particular kind of understanding. In exploring the literary text, one is discovering oneself gaining insight into the complexities of the multifarious self.[1]

Freudian psychoanalysis, through neurosis and displacement, examines how the mind reacts to human failure and probes the unconscious motives that prompt characters to be careless, miserable, disappointed, depressed and mad. Experience in life in general goes through the cycle of gain and loss, whether sexual, emotional, social, materialistic and so on. Loss and its prime consequence, the suppression of the feeling of victory, create a sort of anguish and suffering. In his seminal book, *Studies of Histeria* (1895), Freud attributes the causes of anguish to the absence of fulfilling certain desires that are beyond the person's ability. Most of these desires are absorbed by the unconscious mind. He notes, 'If the chains of ideas in neurotic and particularly in hysterical patients produce a different impression, if in them the relative intensity of different ideas seems inexplicable by psychological determinants alone, we have already found out the reason for this and can attribute it to the existence of hidden unconscious motives'.[2]

Freud contends that being in a restless emotional or mental state stems from the feeling that certain desires or goals will never be achieved. This has a detrimental effect on the neurotic person, who either consciously or unconsciously realises this fact. Unachievable ambitions drive the mind to behave in irrational ways and instigate disturbing feelings. Neurosis has become a prime psychological disorder in the twenty-first century. The Freudian interpretation of this psychological reaction and how it influenced the lives of people across centuries has generated a heated discussion among literary critics who have adopted the Freudian definition of neurosis and analysed Hamlet's psyche from this prism. Shakespeare introduced Hamlet as a repugnant neurotic character in the sixteenth century. Hamlet's personality plays a crucial role in creating his restless mind. Literary critics believe that Hamlet's neurosis stems mainly from different suppressed combined desires: the inability to defy his uncle, his failure to attain love from his mother, and his loss of the throne after his father's murder. In critical essays, one element is selected and analysed as the main factor that drives Hamlet to behave repugnantly and put blames on people who are not the source of his trouble.

As Terry Eagleton succinctly states in his well-known book, *Literary Theory: An Introduction*, 'Neurosis is defined in psychoanalysis as a mild psychiatric disorder characterised by anxiety, depression, or hypochondria. It is associated with suppressed beliefs and desires that have no proper outlet'.[3] According to critics, Hamlet serves as a backdrop example of the neurotic character, which makes him mad, evil and lost. Such a character has been repeated in modern and postmodern literature in different contexts. Edith Kurzweil in *Literature and Psychoanalysis* notes that 'Hamlet has been interpreted as evil or good, as lunatic or feminine, as murdering his love for Ophelia or being too close to his mother'.[4] The different views of Hamlet as aggressive, malevolent and so on are interrelated as they reflect Hamlet's reaction to his dissatisfying situation. Analysing his behaviour with a psychoanalytic view can reveal how his reactions are intertwined.

Some critics consider Hamlet as a character who loses his ability to think rationally because he unwillingly relinquishes both the throne and his mother to his uncle. These critics' primary argument is that Hamlet's irrational rage causes his unreasonably long delay in exacting his vow of revenge. One view is that Hamlet is a man paralysed by his own intelligence and introverted nature. In 'Intentional Meaning in Hamlet: An Evolutionary Perspective', Joseph Carrol argues that Hamlet could have listened to the ghost of his father and killed his uncle from the beginning but instead chooses to think more deeply about this action because he has a broader perception of his situation. He notes, 'Achieving a specific practical goal is clearly not adequate to account for Hamlet's motivation'.[5] In 'Something in Me Dangerous: Hamlet Melancholy, and the Early Modern Scholar', Emily Anglin takes another view. She believes that Hamlet shrewdly exploits his melancholy to create the privacy that helps him eliminate his uncle.[6] R.S. White shares her views in 'Smiles that Reveal, Smiles that Conceal', arguing that smiles are psychological reactions that either show or conceal something.[7]

Despite these different views and opinions, Hamlet's delay in killing his uncle is attributed to his neurotic behaviour, which can be interpreted as madness or smartness. The title hero character is fully aware of his actions but lacks the courage to accept the fact that neither the death of his father nor his mother's marriage to his uncle causes his neurosis. It is his inability to defy the source of all his troubles, his uncle. As a result, he wrongly transfers his hatred of his uncle onto less threatening female characters, such as his mother, Gertrude, and fiancée, Ophelia. The mind of Hamlet uses displacement as a pathological defence to overcome painful experiences. Such a psychological reaction creates a feeling of hostility, madness and indecisiveness. Displaced people are judged as mad or mentally unstable since their behaviour is irrelevant to the situation, and this leads to more loss and defeat. According to Freud in his book *Interpretations of Dreams* (1899), 'In the Psychoanalysis of neuroses the fullest use is made of these two theorems – that, when conscious purposive ideas are abandoned, concealed purposive ideas assume control of the current ideas, and that superficial associations are only substitutes by displacement for suppressed deeper ones'.[8] Frustration can be transferred to humans, animals and objects. It can also include irrelevant actions and reactions to certain situations. In this article, male characters attribute failure to their female partners, whether they are mothers, friends, sisters or daughters. This phenomenon has become apparent in twentieth- and twenty-first-century literature, especially in Cather's *A Lost Lady* (1923)[9] and Al Halaby's *Once in a Promised Land* (2007).[10] In both literary works, the main protagonist fails to accept failure and instead moves frustration onto weaker female characters instead of choosing the proper action. This article suggests that neurosis and displacement have multivalent connotations depending on the situation and stem from one cause: the fear of facing failure, which keeps characters from achieving their goals and drives them to go astray.

Despite this gloomy fact about family life, literature also offers a positive image about family. In *The Zoo Story* by Edward Albee,[11] Jerry, whose parents deserted him when he was a boy, is shocked to meet Peter, who enjoys his family life, in Central Park in New York. As the conversation between the two develops, Jerry learns that Peter shares genuine mutual love with his wife and two daughters. Despite the turbulent economic situation in the US, Peter never lets external pressures influence his psyche and he prefers to enjoy and maintain an ideal family life. In *Great Expectations*, by Charles Dickens,[12] Scrooge decides to break up with his fiancée, Belle, for the sake of wealth. Belle will play a pivotal role in the life of Scrooge later when the Ghost of the Past allows Scrooge to see how happy she is with her considerate husband and lovely children. Seeing this makes him realise that his ex-fiancée has decided to avoid being influenced by the negative feelings of greed and hatred that this lonely old man has due to his past. The death of Scrooge's mother while giving birth to him and his bad relationship with his unloving father, who considers Scrooge a financial burden, has made him run after money to compensate for the loss of his family life. This article suggests that Hamlet can provide a template for the analysis of contentious family relationships in 'family' literature, particularly when it comes to neurosis and displacement and their negative or even deadly influence on members of the family.

Displacement of intense feelings of hostility towards powerless women in *Hamlet* as a means of avoiding the truth

Hamlet's plot implies that a character can react to sudden changes by behaving irrationally. The plotline of the play shows that Hamlet's uncle, Claudius, stealthily kills his king brother, Old Hamlet, succeeds to the throne, marries his dead brother's wife, Gertrude, and prevents his nephew, Hamlet, from becoming king. The ghost of Old Hamlet appears and tells Hamlet that he suffered an unnatural death, being murdered by his brother, Claudius. He urges Hamlet to seek justice and look for his lost right. Unable to accept his father's death and confront his uncle, Hamlet unconsciously transfers his detestation for his uncle onto his mother, Gertrude, the weakest person in the play. Hamlet's disappointment at his mother's ignorance of him and at her hasty marriage after the death of his father is a mask that hides the true cause of his frustration, his weakness to defy his uncle. As a result, he becomes furious not against his uncle but against all women because of his mother's fast decision to remarry. Hamlet considers Gertrude's deed a legal act of lust: 'She married – O, most wicked speed, to post / with such dexterity to incestuous sheets / It is not, nor it cannot come to good / But break my heart, for I must hold my tongue'.[13] By steering his anger towards his mother instead of his uncle, Hamlet becomes a partner in his father's murder. He focuses on taking revenge on those who love and protect him, instead of on Claudius. Such perplexity has caused the hero's own destruction.

Hamlet's paradoxical tendency to feel happy in unhappy situations is another clear sign of intentional displacement. Instead of feeling sad, in the scene in the graveyard with Horatio he rejoices about life. Although the scene is melancholic and set alongside dead people and scattered skulls, Hamlet smiles while logically talking to Horatio about the concept of death. As Stuart Schneiderman in

'The Saying of Hamlet' says, 'No one wants to know the truth; what he does want is for the truth to remain unsaid. For this reason he suspends his saying during the period of the search'.[14] Hamlet's displacement helps him evade the sordid truth, his weakness to accept his defeat. His avoidance of the fact that his uncle, not his mother, deserves punishment makes him appear mad and indecisive. If Hamlet's mother refused to marry Claudius, would Hamlet be free from neurosis? I suggest that if Gertrude, Hamlet's mother, rejected his uncle's marriage proposal, Hamlet would continue to accuse her of being disloyal to his father because she could not defend the throne. Hamlet would continue to be cruel to his mother, whose defencelessness encourages him to blame her for everything that happens. Hamlet's following words, addressed to his mother, reveal his far-fetched reactions:

> Infects unseen. Confess yourself to heaven,
> Repent what's past; avoid what is to come;
> And do not spread the compost on the weeds
> To make them ranker. Forgive me this my virtue
> For in the fatness of these pursy times
> Virtue itself of vice must pardon beg,
> Yea, courb and woo for leave to do him good.[15]

Hamlet asks his mother to repent and stop committing sins. Ironically, Hamlet is the sinful one, as he steers his frustration towards his mother – who is a victim of Claudius – instead of protecting her. Hamlet's anger also extends to Ophelia, his fiancée. In her essay 'The Psychology of Hamlet', Eileen Cameron notes, 'It is as though Hamlet's own feelings of despair, frustration, and self-loathing are mystically transferred to Ophelia. This transference of negative energy results in her own death rather than the death of Hamlet'.[16] Hamlet expresses his anger and dissatisfaction about the notions of marriage and love to Ophelia, and advises her to enter a nunnery so that she can avoid breeding sinners. He says: 'Get thee to a nunnery. Why wouldst thou be a breeder of sinners? I am myself indifferent honest, but yet I accuse me of such things, that it were better my mother had not borne me'.[17] By telling Ophelia to follow this suggestion, Hamlet probably unconsciously alleviates his neurotic state by imagining his mother entering a nunnery after her husband's death. His inability to change his situation drives him to be cruel to Ophelia. The displacement of hatred from Claudius to Gertrude and from Gertrude to Ophelia is achieved. Hamlet again describes the hideous face and soul of his uncle indirectly through Ophelia's face. He says:

> I have heard of your paintings too, well enough. God has given you one face and you make yourselves another. You jig, you amble, and you lisp, your nickname God's creatures, and make your wantonness your ignorance. Go to, I no more on't; it hath made me mad. I say we will have no more marriages. Those that are married already – all but one – shall live; the rest shall keep as they are.[18]

Hamlet insists on using displacement to protect himself from facing his uncle. The ghost of Old Hamlet tells Hamlet that Gertrude is innocent and helpless to defend herself, clarifying that his brother has deceived her and that Hamlet's anger must be directed towards Claudius. Despite this clarification, Hamlet's meetings with his mother and Ophelia are always merciless, whereas his encounters with his uncle are timid. When Hamlet has the opportunity to kill his uncle when praying in isolation, he does nothing and justifies his action by saying: 'And now I'll do't – and so 'a goes to heaven'.[19] As the quotation clarifies, Hamlet avoids killing his uncle even though he seizes the right opportunity. Again, he puts blame on a religious belief that if someone is killed while praying, he or she will go to paradise instead of hell. Hamlet allays his anxiety by justifying the cause behind his avoidance of encountering his uncle with the truth. After that, instead of facing his uncle with the truth that keeps teasing him, he asserts it to his mother instead:

> A murderer and a villain;
> A slave that is not twentieth part the tithe
> Of your precedent lord; a vice of kings;
> A cutpurse of the empire and the rule,
> That from a shelf the precious diadem stole
> And put it in his pocket![20]

In this scene, but before saying these words, Hamlet attempts to kill his uncle indirectly. Believing that Claudius is hiding behind the curtains while he talks cruelly to his mother, he mercilessly stabs him. In discovering that he has killed Polonius, not Claudius, his rage and anger flare; as the king's chief counsellor, Polonius has been ordered to hide behind the curtains and eavesdrop on Hamlet's conversation with his mother. This incident is followed by Ophelia's death later in the play, which shows how Hamlet's erroneous behaviour has devastating effects on his loved ones. When Hamlet sees Ophelia dead, he realises that his irrational behaviour has hurt those closest to him.

For Hamlet, regret is no longer useful, and all he can do is eliminate the true cause of his frustration: his uncle. Despite this realisation, Hamlet is still indecisive and unable to envision the solution to his dilemma. He discloses the true cause of his suffering to Horatio as follows:

> Does it not, think thee, stand me now upon
> He that hath killed my king, and whored my mother,
> Popped in between th'election and my hopes;
> Thrown out his angle for my proper life,
> And with such cozenage – is't not perfect conscience
> To quit him with this arm? And is't not to be damned
> To let this canker of our nature come
> In further evil?[21]

Towards the end of the play, Hamlet admits that Ophelia and his mother are victims of his fear of confronting his uncle; however, the cause of his state remains outside his sphere of influence. In the final scene of the play, Hamlet again avoids his uncle and fights Laertes instead. Hamlet's rage impacted only his mother, Polonius, Ophelia and Laertes. Hamlet finally decides to kill his uncle after watching his mother die from drinking poisoned wine that Claudius had intended for Hamlet. Prior to the fatal duel, Hamlet, who will himself die from a wound inflicted by a poisoned blade, says to Horatio:

> Sir, in my heart, there was a kind of fighting
> That would not let me sleep. Methought I lay
> Worse than the mutinies in the bilboes. Rashly
> And praised be rashness for it, let us know
> Our indiscretion sometime serves us well
> When our deep plots do pall; and that should teach us
> There's a divinity that shapes our ends
> Rough-hew them how we will.[22]

Hamlet's case represents an individual who is imprisoned by his own fears of facing a challenge or changing his situation. Niel Herbert in *A Lost Lady* (1923) and Jassim Haddad in *Once in a Promised Land* (2007) are other two characters who steer their anger towards weaker female characters whom they love and ultimately lose. Niel Herbert directs his anger and frustration towards the woman he loves, Mrs Marian Forrester, since she is less threatening than the man he hates and fears, Ivy Peter, who represents the filthy age of industrialism, and loses her love. Jassim, a hydrologist, steers his hatred of his situation towards his wife Salwa since he cannot defy the true cause of his devastation: the political repercussions against Arabs after the events of 11 September 2001. Both regret their repugnant behaviour after they lose everything.

Hamlet's incarnation as Niel Herbert in *A Lost Lady*

Hamlet's displacement acquires new contextual meaning after rereading the play from a psychoanalytic viewpoint, taking into consideration the circumstances that govern Hamlet's emotions and his misuse of his reactions. Similarly, in Cather's novella, Niel Herbert, whose family life is not a happy one, finds himself attached to Mrs Marian Forrester, a beautiful young lady married to a farmer, Captain Daniel Forrester, an owner of a large farm plantation in the Midwest prairie. Niel finds a father and a mother in this childless couple. In the novel, life was ideal and devoid of problems at the time when Captain Forrester was young. When he got old, he lost his health and money and he was about to die. This has a devastating influence on his wife, Mrs Marian Forrester. In addition, the arrival of Ivy Peter to the area has made the situation worse since he has come only to buy the farm after the death of Captain Forrester to start his business there. His presence is not welcomed by Niel, who realises that this man will ruin his ideal image of family that he finds in Mr and Mrs Forrester. The intrusion of Ivy Peter, a man who represents filthy industrialism and avarice, poses a threat to Niel's dreams of keeping the Forrester family as his own family. Similar to Claudius who steals the throne from his brother, Ivy does his best to take over Captain Forrester's plantation. In *The Voyage Perilous: Willa Cather's Romanticism*, Susan Rosowski summarises the novel, saying, 'One can argue, for example, that characters and settings symbolise ideas in a social allegory of the decline of the west: the pioneer order and virtues in Captain Forrester, the vulnerable beauty of the pioneer dream in the fragile march and the young wife, corrupting materialism by Ivy Peter'.[23] For Niel, the Forrester family is an ideal family. The narrator of the novel depicts this relationship: 'Curiously enough, it was as Captain Forrester's wife that she most interested Niel, and it was in her relation to her husband that he most admired her'.[24] Like Gertrude, Mrs Forrester finds herself weak and unable to live on her own. Her husband is old, weak and ill, and the local residents anticipate his death. 'Captain Forrester, the last vestige of a noble and dying pioneer race, succumbs to the likes of Ivy Peter, the decedent representatives of a new race of men who are intent upon materializing the frontiers.'[25] After her husband's death, Mrs Forrester realises that she has no choice but to sell the farm to Ivy Peter, remarry and leave the area.

Unlike Hamlet, Niel is not portrayed as a hero. Neither the circumstances nor the sequence of events call for such characteristics or complexity of the plot. Like Hamlet, after the death of the Captain, Niel views Mrs Forrester as disloyal to her dead husband. During the period shortly before his death and the period after, he discovers that she drinks too much and has love affairs with Frank Ellinger and Ivy Peter. Her affairs are devoid of emotions, but she chooses this life to escape from the sordid truth of her weakness. In her article 'Finding Marian Forrester: A Restorative Reading of Cather's *A Lost Lady*', Anneliese H. Smith finds that this novella is similar in plot to Hamlet but within a twentieth-century context.

> As epigraph to *A Lost Lady* Cather chose lines from *Hamlet*, Act IV, scene 5, Ophelia's 'Come, my coach! Good night, ladies; good night, sweet ladies, good night, good night'. Cather knew *Hamlet* well. In her student essay 'Shakespeare and Hamlet'(1891,8) her sympathies are with the young prince, 'He was very sensitive, he felt intensely, and he suffered more than other people'; but she also describes him as 'but a boy'. 'Frailty, thy name is woman' is 'a boy's first glimpse of a thing that he shudders at. It is not light matter to him that women are fickle: his mother is a woman, and Ophelia is one'. Parallels with Niel Herbert come easily to mind, as do others. Certainly, in *A Lost Lady*, 'the time is out of joint' and there is 'something rotten' in the land. Moreover, in *A Lost Lady*, as in *Hamlet*, women are victims of masculine heroics, self interest, and ignorance.[26]

Like Gertrude, Mrs Forrester is unable to face life alone after the death of her husband. Willa Cather describes her as follows: 'She was older. In the brilliant sun of the afternoon one saw that her skin was no longer like white lilacs, it had the ivory tint of gardenias that have just begun to fade'.[27] The ghost of Old Hamlet has told Hamlet that Gertrude is innocent, weak, defeated and unable to change her situation by herself. The narrator in *A Lost Lady* shares this view with the ghost, saying:

It was Mrs. Forrester herself who had changed. Since her husband's death, she seemed to have become another woman. For years, Niel and his uncle, the Dazells and all her friends, had thought of the captain as a drag upon his wife. A care that drained her and dimmed her and kept her from being all that she might be. But without him, she was like a ship without ballast, driven hither and thither by every wind.[28]

Similar to Hamlet, Niel understands that Mrs Forrester is too weak to face the change; nevertheless, he does not help her. The narrator says: 'Niel knew that she faced the winter with terror, but he had never seen her more in command of herself – or more the mistress of herown house than now, when she was preparing to become the servant of it. He had the feeling, which he never used to have, that her lightness cost her something'.[29] Mrs Forrester is lost like Gertrude after the death of her husband. As compensation, she seeks to establish a new relationship with another man. She is later successful when she gets married to a millionaire and leaves Sweet Water. Niel has been shocked twice by Mrs Forrester's behaviour: the first time when he discovers her secret affair with Ellinger and the second when he finds that she allowed Ivy Peter to touch her. Like Hamlet, despite his full awareness of her fragility, he puts all the blame on her for being disloyal to her husband during his last years of life and after his death. He continues to be cruel to her and accuses her of being sinful. When he overhears her in the bedroom talking about love with Ellinger, he becomes mad. As Susan J. Rosowski puts it in 'Willa Cather's *A Lost Lady*: Art Versus the Closing Frontier', 'He assumes that Mrs. Forrester puts away her exquisiteness when she is with her lover and that, after having given herself up to sexuality, she "recovers herself", putting aside sexuality and resuming her former nature'.[30]

Niel is also severely shocked when he overhears Mrs Forrester's telephone call with Ellinger. Niel rejects her character by cutting the telephone wires while she is talking to Ellinger after marrying Odgen. 'He dumped the Lilies he bought for Mrs. Forrester saying: Lilies that fester smells worse than weeds.'[31] He finds that her haste to engage in illegitimate love makes her rotten. As Morris Dickstein in *A Mirror in the Roadway: Literature and the Real World* says, 'Niel mutters to himself echoing the disillusionment of Shakespeare's ninety-fourth sonnet with its lament: sweetest things turn sourest by their deeds'.[32] The emergence of Ivy Peter has a devastating effect on Niel's life. After the death of Captain Forrester, Peter buys the farm. Despite his awareness of the danger that Ivy presents to the region, Niel refuses to face him and reprimands Mrs Forrester instead of protecting her from him or from other similar men who want her as a whore. Hamlet's displaced depiction of the hideous face of Claudius in Ophelia's face is repeated in Niel's view of Ivy's face. The narrator's description of the face of Ivy Peter in the novel shows how detestable his face is: the face of modernism, capitalism and industrialism. He says:

> Niel noticed among the passengers a young man in a grey flannel suit, with silk shirt of one shade of blue and a necktie of another... Niel looked up and saw the red, bee stung face with its two permanent dimples, smiling down at him in a contemptuous jocularity.[33]

Similar to Hamlet's view of his mother, Niel is always angry about the way Mrs Forrester allows Ivy to treat her, asif she were inferior to him. He has no respect for her. Once Mrs Forrester carries a heavy pail, and Ivy does not bother to help her. 'She bent a little with the Pail's weight but Ivy made no offer to carry it for her. He let her trip away with it asif she were a kitchen maid.'[34] Niel sadly resists such hideous truths but he is powerless to change it. Like Hamlet who hates his uncle, he does not like or respect Ivy. Cather describes the nature of the relationship between them as follows: 'He and Ivy had disliked each other from childhood, blindly, instinctively, recognizing each other through anticipation, as hostile insects do'.[35] This relationship shows the struggle between the new stream of thinking and the old one. Niel does not like Ivy's selfish attitude towards people and nature; every time he meets him, he feels agitated and uncomfortable with him but fears refusing him. This attitude allows Ivy to win in the end, gaining the farm and compelling Marian Forrester to remarry and leave the area. The narrator summarises this situation as follows:

> It was what he most held against Mrs. Forrester; that she was not willing to immolate herself, like the widow of all these great men, and die with the pioneer period to which she belonged; that she preferred life on any terms. In the end, Niel went away without bidding her goodbye. He went away with weary contempt for her heart.[36]

Unlike Hamlet, who dies at the end of the play and regrets his repugnant behaviour towards his mother, Niel chooses to bury the past and lead a different life. Convinced that his battle with Ivy is lost, 'he came to be very glad that he had known her, and that she had had a hand in breaking him in to life. He has known pretty women and clever ones since then – but never one like her'.[37] Like Hamlet who lost everything in the end, Niel has realised that he has lost the plantation, Marian Forrester and the ideal life that he envisions in his mind. Similar to Niel, Jassim Haddad in *Once in A Promised Land* (2007) establishes the same relationship between Niel and Mrs Forrester with his wife. His inability to be a responsible husband and a man who can cope with change and challenge has made him lose the dream of being a successful engineer and enjoying an ideal family life.

Events after 11 September and losing the dream in *Once in a Promised Land*

Twenty-first-century literary works by Arab writers in the diaspora mainly reveal the tensions between the East and the West and the world chaos created by terrorism and the accusations that Arabs are the source of destruction. Laila Al Halaby's novel offers instructive insights into the struggles facing Arab Americans in post– September 11 America. The clash between the West and the East is based largely on false stereotypes. Jassim Haddad, the main protagonist, arrives in America dreaming of becoming a renowned hydrologist by making water accessible to all people worldwide. This dream is dissipated by the tenuous life he leads in exile with his wife, Salwa Haddad, who also feels isolated and alienated from American society despite her efforts to integrate into the new environment. Consistent accusations of being a terrorist by the FBI agent anger him, and he steers his frustration towards his wife, who starts a foolish love affair with Jake, an American clerk, to compensate for her emotional loss. Marta Bosch-Vilarrubias notes in her book *Post-9/11 Representation of Arab Men by Arab American Women Writers* that men suffer from the new reality. She says, 'the Arab American men represented in these novels living right after 9/11 suffer life changing identity crisis. Their traumatic experience is twofold. On the one hand, they share the national trauma resultant from the collapse of the Twin Towers, while, on the other, they experience a personal trauma, being perceived as monster-terrorists'.[38] Salwa blames Jassim for making her leave Jordan for the US, preventing her from becoming pregnant and sharing no real love with her. Because of his situation and his negative attitude towards himself and his wife, Jassim also begins an unrequited love affair with Penny.

Both characters are too weak to challenge the hostile atmosphere against Arabs that emerged at that time due to the events of 11 September. Instead of facing this sordid truth and defending their situation, they begin to blame each other for what happens to them. This reaction devastates their family relationships and makes Jassim, like Hamlet, regret his repugnant behaviour against the woman who loves him. In his article 'Uses and Abuses of Trauma in Post-9/11 Fiction and Contemporary Culture', Ulrike Tancke proposes that the trauma Salwa and Jassim endure has little to do with 9/11, but he neglects to consider the state-sponsored racism that directly resulted from the attacks and its effect on their lives.

> It is not the repercussions from 9/11 as such that cause Salwa and Jassim's life to disintegrate. The traumatizing events in the novel are the result of coincidence and only vaguely connected events, and of the propensity of human beings to ... inflict pain on each other. Hence, *Once in a Promised Land* critically and self-consciously explores the contemporary fascination with trauma: we tend to sweepingly apply ubiquitous and simplistic categories such as '9/11', while the traumatizing potential of violence and guilt inherent in human relationships are impossible to predict.[39]

Prior to the 11 September attacks, Al Halaby's protagonists, Jassim and Salwa Haddad, led a good life in Tucson, Arizona. After the attacks, Jassim becomes the focus of an FBI investigation and Salwa begins to experience longing for her homeland. Similar to Niel Herbert, Jassim loves Salwa, but he consistently takes out his frustration on her. As the narrator says: 'He loved Salwa because in her, he saw home, which made her both more precious and a source of resentment'.[40] Despite his love for her, he follows Hamlet's advice for Ophelia about the need to avoid giving birth to sinners by becoming a nun, but in a different context. He compels his wife to take birth control pills. Although it is unclear why he wants this, it could be that he is afraid that children would be a burden since his life in the US is not easy and his situation after 11 September has become critical.

After the events of 11 September, Jassim feels chained by the suspicions against him wherever he goes. 'September 11, 2001, made all those who looked Arab, Muslim, or Middle Eastern, especially men, more visible in the United States, and consequently more easy victims of anti-Arab racism. As a result, Arab American women writers have been writing as well about Arab men's reactions to 9/11.'⁴¹ Feeling that he is on the brink of losing his job and his reputation, he isolates himself from Salwa. 'Salwa has nothing to do but to watch TV and find a way to pass time. Years of grief and nightmare television had taught her to watch closely, to recognize mental illnesses and peculiar conditions, so when that man had walked in and panicked, she knew, she felt his fear, his nausea.'⁴² Like Hamlet, he feels that he has lost the throne of becoming a renowned hydrologist. In addition, he realises that he is weak and cannot defy the rumours against Arabs after 11 September. He says: 'Just because I am an Arab, because I was raised a Muslim, you want to believe that I am capable of doing evil. Is it something best to look within before casting a broad net.' 'The words get ahead of him, and he was not sure what he had just said'.⁴³ Like Hamlet who avoids confrontation with his uncle, he does not dare to face the FBI and prove that they are wrong. Tancke justifies Jassim and Salwa's choice of new friends after 11 September as a way of ameliorating the destructive impact of the event. She says: 'caught in an increasingly tangled web of half-truths, omissions, silence and fateful coincidence, both start seemingly random affairs with people that they have met by chance'.⁴⁴

Jassim's ignorance of Salwa's needs and his view of her as a burden – especially if she were to give birth to a child –diverts his frustration and anger with his situation towards her. Like Hamlet, his repugnant behaviour kills her – not physically, but emotionally and spiritually. Her failure to become pregnant after stopping the birth control pill secretly ruins her life and her love for her husband. 'A miscarriage can be a traumatic event in a woman's life. You do not have children.'⁴⁵ Salim Al-Ibia in 'Islam and Terrorism in Post 9/11 Literature' notes: 'the Haddads' happiness quickly turns into misery soon after the terrorist attacks of 9/11, which leaves them physically and spiritually broken and estranged from each other'.⁴⁶ Nevertheless, Jassim is cruel to his wife, first by continuously ignoring her, then by blaming her for what happens to him, and then preventing her from becoming pregnant. As a result, Salwa finds herself alienated twice: first from her home, Jordan, and second from her life with her husband. As a result, she finds in Jack some sort of compensation for her losses. Finding that Jack has deceived her and made her look treacherous to her husband, she finally decides to leave the US and goes back to Jordan emotionally and spiritually dead. Jassim's affair with Penny is also not successful. Frustrated and agitated with his situation, Jassim extends his frustration from his wife to Penny, who finds Jassim unstable in their relationship. Unable to be happy with her, he decides to return to Salwa. Before Jassim and Penny's last meeting in a parking lot, the narrator says: 'He had married Salwa because he had wished to protect and nurture her. Because he needed her. Quite possibly, she had married him for need as well. Jassim lacks the depth of love with Penny'.[47] This depth of love that the couple misses is revealed by Randa, Salwa's closest friend, who says:

> Am I happy? Am I happy with my children? They are healthy and good, thank gods. I am happy to have the opportunity to be at home with them. I am happy my life is safe and predictable. I am happy that my husband is a good man and respects me as his wife and as an independent person.[48]

At the end of the novel, like Hamlet, Jassim realises that he has devastated the people he loves. As the narrator says, 'the brain, when it is in a state of danger, has odd ways of dissecting and processing the information around it'.[49] Losing his job and his love affair with Penny makes him realise that his reaction to his situation is improper, and eventually he regrets his deeds. He says to Salwa: ' Salwa, Habibti, I am sorry that I have kept you from having a family. I am ready now. Whether we are here or somewhere else, I am ready for a family. If that is still what you want'.[50] Both characters have suffered from the consequences of the political situation in the United States after the events of 11 September and become detached from each other. 'September 11 assumes a type of primacy in this context; Al Halaby illustrates how the events of that day did not evoke complete unity but in many ways created division and distrust. The division and distrust end up playing themselves out on the bodies of Jassim and Salwa. Both characters become disconnected from one another in roughly the same proportion that they become disconnected from their society.'[51] Hamlet, Niel and Jassim have lost the company of the women they love and respect.

Conclusion

Freud states in his book *Civilization and Its Discontents*(1930) that, 'What we call happiness in the strictest sense comes from the (preferably sudden) satisfaction of needs which have been dammed up to a high degree'.[52] Based upon this saying, neurosis and displacement are two psychiatric disorders that bring more misery and failure. Hamlet, Niel and Jassim fail to react in a proper way to the dilemmas they face. They consciously and unconsciously believe that their lives are ruined by surrounding circumstances. Thomas MacCary comments on the situation of Hamlet, 'In Hamlet, we only learn of its existence from its inhabiting consequences. Hamlet is able to do anything except take vengeance on the man who did away with his father and took his father's place with his mother, the man who shows him the repressed wishes of his own childhood'.[53] It becomes obvious upon analysing Hamlet's lines about his mother and Claudius that Hamlet experiences the pain of losing his father, being alienated from his mother because of displacement, and unable to blame the man responsible for all of this. Hamlet lets his dilemma stifle him and make him incapable of doing anything. Hamlet is aware of his actions but unable to act properly. Hamlet's famous soliloquy summarises the whole concept of neurosis and its consequences:

> To be or not to be, that is the question.
> Whether 'tis nobler in the mind to suffer
> The slings and arrows of outrageous fortune
> Or to take arms against a sea of troubles
> And by opposing end them, To die – to sleep.[54]

In accordance with the discussion in this article, the excerpt above clarifies and summarises the psychological state of many literary characters. Hamlet, Niel Herbert and Jassim Haddad choose not to be and thus to face the consequences of this decision, especially psychological pain and failure. Regardless of their social position, cultural background and time period, the three characters choose to avoid encountering the true cause of their suffering, and instead they inflict emotional and spiritual pain on the people they love, thereby causing their own destruction and disillusionment. Steven Salaita has clarified that Laila Al Halaby's novel does not only address Arab problems in the US during the events of 11 September; it has to do with human weakness and failure to change certain situations: 'Although *Once in a Promised Land* will certainly be known as a novel that captures the anxieties of a particular moment in American history, it also entails a universal character study of the desires and flaws of humankind'.[55]

Tareq Zuhair is an assistant professor at the University of Petra, where he teaches literature and literary theory. His research focuses on the nexus between literature and real life. His field of research includes psychoanalysis, modernism, postmodernism, hybridity and multiculturalism. He has published a book entitled *The Disintegration of the American Dream and the Decay of Family Connections*. Noor Publishing (2016) E-mail: tzuhair@uop.edu.jo

Notes

1. Eileen McConnell, 'Some Reflections on the Links between Psychoanalysis and Literature', *Psychodynamic Counselling* 1, no. 4 (1995), 591, https://doi.org/10.1080/13533339508404156.
2. Ivan Smith, ed., *Freud Complete Works* (EPUB, 2011), 258.
3. Terry Eagleton, *Literary Theory: An Introduction* (London: Blackwell, 1996), 152.
4. Edith Kurzweil, *Literature and Psychoanalysis* (New York: Columbia University Press, 1983), 20.
5. Joseph Carrol, 'Intentional Meaning in Hamlet: An Evolutionary Perspective', *Style* 44, no. 1/2 (2010), 239, https://www.jstor.org/stable/10.5325/style.44.1-2.230.
6. Emily Anglin, 'Something in Me Dangerous: Hamlet Melancholy, and the Early Modern Scholar', *Shakespeare* 13, no. 1 (2014), 15–29, https://doi.org/10.1080/17450918.2013.877963.
7. R. S. White, 'Smiles that Reveal, Smiles that Conceal', *Shakespeare* 12, no. 2 (2016), 134–147, https://doi.org/10.1080/17450918.2015.1026930.
8. Smith, *Freud Complete Works*, 964.
9. Willa Cather, *A Lost Lady* (Lincoln: University of Nebraska Press, 1997)
10. Laila Al Halaby, *Once in a Promised Land* (Boston, MA: Beacon Press, 2007)
11. Albee, Edward, the Zoo Story (Samuel French, 1959)
12. Charles Dickens, *A Christmas Carol* (London: Chapman & Hall, 1843)
13. William Shakespeare, *Hamlet* (Saint Paul, MN: EMC/Paradigm Publishing, 1998), 1.2.156–158.
14. Stuart Schneiderman, 'The Saying of Hamlet', *Substance* 3, no. 8 (1973), 78, doi:10.2307/3684281.
15. *Hamlet* 3.4.149–155.
16. Eileen Cameron, 'The Psychology of Hamlet', *International Journal of Language and Literature* 2, no. 3 (2014), 169, doi:10.15640/ijll.v2n3a11.
17. *Hamlet* 3.1.120–123.
18. *Hamlet* 3.1.141–148.
19. *Hamlet* 3.3.74.
20. *Hamlet* 3.4.97–101.
21. *Hamlet* 5.2.62–69.
22. *Hamlet* 5.2.4–9.

23. Susan Rosowski, *The Voyage Perilous: Willa Cather's Romanticism* (Lincoln: University of Nebraska Press, 1986), 116.
24. Cather, *A Lost Lady*, 43.
25. Conrad Eugene Oswalt, *After Eden: The Secularization of American Space in the Fiction of Willa Cather and Theodore Dresier* (Lewisburg, PA: Bucknell University Press, 1990), 54.
26. Anneliese H. Smith, 'Finding Marian Forrester: A Restorative Reading of Cather's *A Lost Lady*', *Colby Quarterly* 14, no. 4 (1978), 221–225, https://digitalcommons.colby.edu/cq/vol14/iss4/7.
27. Cather, *A Lost Lady*, 26.
28. Ibid., 62.
29. Ibid., 145.
30. Susan J. Rosowski, 'Willa Cather's *A Lost Lady*: Art Versus the Closing Frontier', *Great Plains Quarterly* 2, no. 4 (1982), 241, http://digitalcommons.unl.edu/greatplainsquarterly/1635/.
31. Cather, *A Lost Lady*, 47.
32. Morris Dickstein, *A Mirror in the Roadway: Literature and the Real World* (Princeton, NJ: Princeton University Press, 2005), 64.
33. Cather, *A Lost Lady*, 57.
34. Ibid., 67.
35. Ibid., 58.
36. Ibid., 95.
37. Ibid., 96.
38. Marta Bosch-Vilarrubias, *Post-9/11Representations of Arab Men by Arab American Women Writers* (New York: Peter Lang Publishing, 2016), 119.
39. Ulrike Tancke, 'Uses and Abuses of Trauma in Post-9/11 Fiction and Contemporary Culture', in *From Solidarity to Schisms: 9/11 and after in Fiction and Film from Outside the US*, ed. Cara Cilano (Amsterdam: Rodopi, 2009), 85.
40. Halaby, *Once in a Promised Land*, 325.
41. Bosch-Vilarrubias, *Post-9/11 Representations*, 136.
42. Halaby, *Once in a Promised Land*, 293.
43. Ibid., 232.
44. Tancke, 'Uses and Abuses', 77.
45. Halaby, *Once in aPromised Land*, 310.
46. Salim Al-Ibia, 'Islam and Terrorism in Post 9/11 Literature', *Studies in Literature and Language* 10, no. 2 (2015), 22, doi:10.3968/6196.
47. Halaby, *Once in aPromised Land*, 325.
48. Ibid., 283.
49. Ibid., 321.
50. Ibid., 302.
51. Steven Salaita, *Modern Arabic Fiction* (Syracuse, NY: Syracuse University Press, 2011), 90.
52. Smith, *Freud Complete Works*, 4475.
53. Thomas MacCary, *Hamlet: A Guide to the Play* (Westport, CT: Greenwood Press, 1998), 105.
54. *Hamlet* 3.1.57–60.
55. Salaita, *Modern Arabic Fiction*, 94.

Chapter 10
Susan Abulhawa's Appropriation of Shakespeare's *Romeo and Juliet*

Yousef Abu Amrieh

> A village of villages surrounded by gardens and olive groves and bordered to the north by a lake, in the thirteenth century Beit Daras was on the mail route from Cairo to Damascus ... Once a station for the powerful, history had broken it down into ruin, and what remained stood tenderly, holding all of time now, where children played and where young couples went to escape watchful eyes. (Susan Abulhawa, *The Blue between Sky and Water*, 7)

> CHORUS: Two households, both alike in dignity,
> In fair Verona, where we lay our scene,
> ...
> A pair of star-cross'd lovers take their life,
> Whose misadventured piteous overthrows
> Do with their death bury their parents' strife.
> (Shakespeare, *Romeo and Juliet*, The Prologue)

Notes for this section begin on page 174.

Susan Abulhawa's Appropriation of Shakespeare's Romeo and Juliet   157

The purpose of this article is to examine how Palestinian American novelist Susan Abulhawa appropriates in her novel *The Blue between Sky and Water* (2015) themes, tropes and motifs that Shakespeare employs in his love tragedy *Romeo and Juliet* (c. 1596). The article shows how Abulhawa depicts four Palestinian love stories/marriages that collapse due to violence. Yet, while Romeo and Juliet's love story is undercut by an 'ancient grudge' between the two lovers' Veronese families, the love stories/marriages in Abulhawa's novel are wrecked by wars and conflicts. As the above two epigraphs show, the two literary works narrate stories of cities and villages that once nurtured love stories, but unfortunately, love stories faded away due to ongoing feuds and conflicts. Just as Shakespeare's prologue informs the audience that the play is about a love story set in 'fair Verona', the first few lines of Chapter 1 of Abulhawa's novel highlight how idyllic Beit Daras, the village from which the Baraka family immigrated to Gaza, was a favourite place for lovers' rendezvous. While the epigraphs celebrate Verona and Beit Daras as lovers' safe havens, the two places, unluckily, are also sites of tragic events. As Naomi Conn Liebler argues, Shakespeare's 'Verona is a failed *civitas*, and by the end of the play, a dying *urbs*, its entire younger generation gone'.[1] Similarly, because of wars and conflicts, Beit Daras is deserted by its inhabitants who flee to Gaza.

The novel relates the stories of four generations of the Palestinian Baraka family who, prior to the 1948 war and the creation of the State of Israel, lived in the village of Beit Daras. As the family is forced to leave the idyllic village, the family's mystical matriarch Um Mamdouh is killed, her son Mamdouh is shot in his leg and permanently maimed, her oldest daughter Nazmiyeh, recently married to Atiyeh, is raped and Um Mamdouh's youngest daughter, Mariam, is killed by Israeli soldiers. The survivors flee to Gaza where they live as refugees. Nazmiyeh gives birth to eleven boys before she finally delivers baby girl Alwan. Between daily labour and yearning for lost lands, Atiyeh passes away far from his native Beit Daras. On the other hand, Mamdouh marries Yasmine and leaves Gaza for Egypt and Kuwait before he finally settles in the USA. Widowed in exile and traumatised by the death of his only son in an accident, Mamdouh decides to return to Gaza along with his granddaughter, Nur. Unfortunately, Mamdouh's untimely death precludes Nur's reunion with her Palestinian family. In the meantime, Alwan marries fisherman Abdel Qader and after a series of abortions she gives birth to Khaled and Rhet Shel, named after American peace activist Rachel Corrie who was killed by the Israeli army in 2003 in the Gaza Strip.

On Khaled's tenth birthday in 2008, Abdel Qader is killed in a bombardment. Khaled himself enters a rare kind of coma until his death a few years later. Alwan is diagnosed with cancer, and in the absence of proper medical treatment, she relies on herbs for medication. In the meantime, Nur finishes her studies in the USA and works as a psychotherapist. One day she meets Dr Jamal Musmar, who was invited to the USA to talk about the humanitarian crisis in the Gaza Strip. Nur and Jamal are at once attracted to one another, and Nur follows Jamal to Gaza as a volunteer in a relief mission where she witnesses the conditions under which Palestinians live. Later, Nur discovers her lost identity, and she is reconnected with her family. Unfortunately, the Nur-Jamal love story vanishes into thin air due to adverse social, cultural and political circumstances.

Abulhawa's novel, like Shakespeare's love tragedy, depicts love stories/marriages that are ruined by violent events. In addition, Abulhawa employs some of the themes, tropes and motifs that Shakespeare employs in his play, including love at first sight, the (negative) impact of families on these love stories, exile/banishment, use of herbs/traditional medicine, humour and parties that practically turn ominous and fateful. Abulhawa's employment of these themes, tropes and motifs reinforces the relationship between the two texts in a way that draws the reader's attention to the possibility that Abulhawa is appropriating Shakespeare's play. As René Weis puts it, the storyline of *Romeo and Juliet* has 'almost universal appeal ... that several of the best-known recent adaptations of the play do not contain a single word by Shakespeare'.[2] The storyline, Weis continues, has inspired an unparalleled 'range of adaptations in different genres ... across language and cultural barriers'.[3] Certainly, Abulhawa is portraying different socioeconomic, political, historical and cultural contexts. Yet the love stories/marriages she portrays are, like Romeo and Juliet's, entangled in violence, conflicts and feuds. At the same time, Abulhawa's novel depicts an ongoing human crisis in Gaza due to wars and conflicts.

The story of Shakespeare's two young lovers is reproduced, albeit differently, in Abulhawa's novel. *The Blue between Sky and Water* portrays at least four love stories/marriages that, due to wars and conflicts in Gaza, end tragically. The first love story is that of Nazmiyeh and Atiyeh who are banished from their native village of Beit Daras to Gaza. Their love story/marriage survives harsh conditions, including rape, siege and displacement. Yet this love story/marriage, ends with Atiyeh's premature death away from Beit Daras. The second love story/marriage is that of Mamdouh and Yasmine. The two lovers flee Gaza and emigrate to the USA. In exile, they lose their son in an accident, and Yasmine dies of cancer. This, in turn, reflects negatively on their granddaughter Nur, who grows up as a rootless child. The third love story/marriage that Abulhawa depicts is that of Alwan and Abdel Qader, and it reflects the hard socioeconomic, political and cultural conditions that Palestinians in Gaza endure. Just like the previous two love stories/marriages that end tragically, this love story/marriage unfortunately also ends tragically when Abdel Qader is killed in a bombardment and their son, Khaled, enters a rare kind of coma. The final love story that the novel depicts is that of Nur and Jamal. This relationship is not ruined directly by war, but Jamal chooses to leave Gaza for a better life in Canada.

Appropriating Shakespeare

Julie Sanders argues that 'in appropriations the intertextual relationship may be less explicit [and] more embedded' than it is in adaptations.[4] Sanders' argument implies that a reader may convincingly argue that one text is appropriating another without directly and explicitly citing allusion and references. She further explains that appropriation 'affects a more decisive journey away from the informing source into a wholly new cultural product and domain'.[5] Hence, one may argue that the meaning of a certain text is only complete when it is read within the web of other texts 'from a new or revised political and cultural position ... to highlight troubling gaps, absences, and silences within the canonical texts to which they refer'.[6] Here, one may cite Jonathan Culler's words that a text is in 'a dialogue with other texts, an act of absorption, parody, and criticism'.[7] Culler insists texts are embroiled in a wider net that 'include[s] the anonymous discursive practices, codes whose origins are lost, which are the conditions of possibility of later texts'.[8] Culler maintains that any text is 'comprehensible only in terms of other texts which it prolongs, completes, transforms, and sublimates'.[9]

In this context, Christy Desmet argues that 'appropriation ... may be seen as a dialogical phenomenon – not simply a conversation or collaboration between appropriating and source texts, but an exchange that involves both sharing and contested ownership'.[10] In other words, the relationship between the two works is not unilateral but rather both texts influence each other since the latter text sheds light on issues that have not been viewed previously in this new manner. Therefore, Desmet insists that 'fidelity and infidelity ... exist only in dialogic relation to each other, creating multiple permutations of faithfulness and unfaithfulness within appropriations'.[11] Seen from this perspective, one may look at appropriations as reproducing a text by necessarily introducing changes and deviations from the original text in a way that opens new horizons and spaces for interpreting both texts. Still, Desmet argues that if we reconsider appropriation as 'reception rather than as production', we can make connections between texts across times and space and establish contingent moments of recognition and insight to put these texts into a different perspective.[12] Desmet, therefore, highlights the fact that appropriations are valued precisely for 'showing us a different connection, a previously unacknowledged resemblance, between two texts or persons'.[13] Similarly, Douglas Lanier proposes 'a rhizomatic conception of Shakespeare' which situates Shakespeare's cultural authority 'in the accrued power of ... the multiple, changing lines of force ... that have been created by and which respond to historical contingencies'.[14] This rhizomatic conception of Shakespeare, Lanier maintains, 'stresses the power of those ever-differentiating particulars ... to transform and restructure the aggregated Shakespearean field into something forever new'.[15]

Arab writers in diaspora: writing across cultures

To fully understand the significance of Abulhawa's appropriation of Shakespeare, one needs to take into account Abulhawa's position as a Palestinian American writer. As an Arab writer in diaspora, Abulhawa 'straddle[s] two cultures' and skilfully uses English to relay the experiences of Arab characters in the Arab world and in diaspora.[16] With a contrapuntal vision, Arab writers in diaspora try to bridge the gaps between cultures and to open corridors of dialogue between the East and the West.[17] Several studies have examined how Arab authors in diaspora appropriate Shakespeare's works for aesthetic and thematic ends. For instance, Yousef Awad investigates how Arab

American novelist Rabih Alameddine draws on Shakespeare's representation of traumatic events in *King Lear* and *Macbeth* to depict the repercussions of Lebanon's civil war on his characters in *I, The Divine* and *An Unnecessary Woman*, respectively.[18] In addition, Awad and Mahmoud Al-Shetawi argue that Arab British novelist Jamal Mahjoub's historical novel *The Carrier* (1998) rewrites, by appropriating some tropes, motifs and episodes, Shakespeare's *Othello* in a way that enables Mahjoub to comment on Shakespeare's representation of the Moor in his masterpiece.[19] More recently, Awad and Barkuzar Dubbati have examined Arab British novelist Robin Yassin-Kassab's appropriation of Shakespeare's *Hamlet* in his post-9/11 novel, *The Road from Damascus* and 'identif[ied] parallel techniques and crucial plot developments that help Yassin-Kassab problematize the ideological representation of the Arab Muslim in diaspora'.[20]

This article builds on the findings of the above papers and shows how Abulhawa, as an Arab American novelist, draws on Shakespeare's *Romeo and Juliet* to represent contemporary love stories/ marriages in Gaza, and in the process, portray how wars and conflicts affect people's daily experiences in Gaza. Abulhawa fuses in her writings contemporary Arab issues with Western canonical narratives 'in order to resist stereotypes and misconceptions about Arabs in US culture'.[21] Yet Geoffrey Nash plays down the claim that Arab diaspora literary works 'possess the potential' to undermine the stereotyping of Arabs and Muslims.[22] Nash asserts that the notion that Arab writers in diaspora 'are more effective' in resisting such stereotyping 'is not conclusively borne out by the evidence'.[23] Nevertheless, one may convincingly argue that there has been a remarkable increase in Arabic literature in diaspora in the aftermath of 9/11. As Claire Gallien puts it, the literary production of Arab writers, addressing a global audience in English, can be interpreted 'as a form of response or "writing back" ... to legacies of colonialism in the not-yet-postcolonial present ..., to the politics of war ..., and to mounting racism and Islamophobia in the West'.[24] For Gallien, Arabic literature in diaspora 'belong[s] to ecotonal zones where language and literary traditions and inspirations, East and West, enmesh and produce rhizomatic structures of indistinguishable roots and stems'.[25] Seen from this perspective, one may argue that Abulhawa appropriates Shakespeare's love tragedy to narrate Palestinian stories of woes and anguish in war zones.

Romeo and Juliet in Arabic and Palestinian literature

In his article '*The Martyrs of Love* and the Emergence of the Arab Cultural Consumer', Mark Bayer points out that *Romeo and Juliet* is the first Shakespeare play translated into Arabic and staged at a public theatre in Cairo around 1890 by Iskander Farah's theatrical company.[26] According to Bayer, the play, which was translated by Najib al-Haddad, is 'an eclectic ensemble of individuals and foreign and vernacular cultural elements' including lavish costuming, schmaltzy Arabic pop songs, representations of tribal feuds and conflicts and elements of Sufi mysticism.[27] Bayer also argues that the popularity of the play for over twenty years among 'less learned – and less pretentious – audiences' was precisely because of the liberties taken by the translator and the players.[28] Bayer concludes that Haddad 'discovered in *Romeo and Juliet* striking affinities with various Arabic cultural traditions that he was able to amplify to further appease local audiences'.[29] Bayer's conclusion becomes even more convincing when one reads Abdulla Al-Dabbagh's article 'The Oriental Framework of *Romeo and Juliet*'. Al-Dabbagh argues that 'the Islamic Sufi conception of the unity of existence (*wahdat alwujud*) and the explanation of evil that it provides ... provide the most suitable framework for understanding a play like *Romeo and Juliet*'.[30] For Al-Dabbagh, the Sufi framework of the play resolves 'the seeming contradiction ... between "fate" and "free will" which has often troubled critics of this play'.[31]

In fact, the play has been adapted by several Arab writers, playwrights and directors. Yvette K. Khoury examines Oussama al-Rahbani's adaptation of *Romeo and Juliet* under the title of *Akhir Yom (The Last Day)*, first produced in 2004. It reconstructs aspects of the 2003 national basketball finals between al-Hikmeh and al-Riyadi, where a riot broke out between the two clubs' fans.[32] In the play, Shakespeare's lovers are caught up in a political power struggle between two rival families, Ra'i and Matar, and the corresponding territories defined by their basketball teams.[33] Another recent Arab adaptation of Shakespeare's play is *Romeo and Juliet in Baghdad* that was performed on the stage of Shakespeare's Globe as an event in 'Globe to Globe', part of the World Shakespeare Festival in 2012.[34] The play was directed by Monadhil Daood with surtitling and other assistance from the RSC's Deborah Shaw.[35] The heads of the two feuding families are two brothers. The older Montague represented the Shia, while the younger Capulet represented the Sunni.[36] In this adaptation, Romeo and Juliet were cousins kept apart since childhood by sectarian prejudice and sibling jealousy.[37] The play, according to Margaret Litvin, Saffron Walkling and Raphael Cormack, was primarily about Iraq and Iraqis with only a trivial role for an Anglo-American soldier, pushing the IV machine on which the old, sick Montague depends.[38]

The play has also been adapted to reflect factional Palestinian rivalries and the Palestinian-Israeli conflict. For instance, *Romeo and Juliet* has inspired director Ali Abu Yassin and novelist Atef Abu Saif to come up with a play about two Palestinian lovers whose parents are members of the two rival Palestinian movements, Fatah and Hamas.[39] In addition, Sahar Kayyal's short story 'Shakespeare in the Gaza Strip' is an attempt by the writer to describe the perils of teaching and performing *Romeo and Juliet* by a group of Palestinian schoolgirls under the supervision of their American teacher, Miss James.[40] At the same time, the short story shows, through Kayyal's representation of the character of Muna, the hardships that Palestinians in Gaza endure under Israeli occupation.[41]

In her article '"Dreamers Often Lie": On "Compromise", the Subversive Documentation of an Israeli-Palestinian Political Adaptation of Shakespeare's *Romeo and Juliet*', Yael Munk examines how Anat Even's 1996 documentary 'Compromise' highlights the hardships of carrying a joint Palestinian-Israeli theatrical production.[42] In particular, Munk argues that although the 1994 production of *Romeo and Juliet* by two theatre directors, the Israeli Eran Baniel and the Palestinian Fuad Awad, at the Jerusalem Khan Theatre was an attempt 'to reproduce on stage an illusion of co-existence', Even's 'Compromise' reveals that this attempt 'was, however, doomed to fail; for political conflicts, even when resolved on stage, tended to penetrate the walls of the rehearsal room'.[43] Munk concludes that Even's 'Compromise' 'does not comply with this compromise and even undermines it [... by] reveal[ing] all that the play's directors intended to camouflage'.[44]

The play has also acquired a special position among professors of English language and literature who spend time at Palestinian schools and universities. For instance, in 'From Verona to Ramallah: Living in a State of Emergency', Monica Brady reflects on her experience of teaching *Romeo and Juliet* to Palestinian students in a school in Ramallah.[45] Brady shows how students' interpretations and interactions with the text were heavily influenced by the socioeconomic, political and cultural context in which these students live. For instance, Brady argues that students' comments on the scene where Lord and Lady Capulet meet with Paris and suggest that he and Juliet be married that very week highlight the significance of the impact of the death of a key leader, like Tybalt, on the parents' decision. Brady argues that this scene is read by the students as a manifestation of 'the anger and the anxiety of replacing lost leaders' since these students 'have grown up with targeted assassinations carried out by the Israeli government'.[46]

Similarly, in *Romeo and Juliet in Palestine: Teaching under Occupation*, Tom Sperlinger looks back at his experience of teaching Shakespeare's play to Palestinian students at the Abu Dis campus of Al-Quds University. In response to Sperlinger's question of 'how the play might be adapted as a film in Palestine', students come up with various scenarios that reflect the socioeconomic, political, historical and cultural circumstances in Palestine.[47] One student suggested that the play should be set in the present time because 'the Palestinians are at the peak of their troubles'; another student suggested that the play should be set in the late 1940s or '50s 'when there was a famous dispute between two families in Jerusalem'; a third student pointed out that the violent context qualifies the play to be set at any time in Palestine.[48] Students have also commented on banishment and some suggested that Verona ought to be Jerusalem and Romeo might be banished to Ramallah or Gaza. Some students thought that Juliet might be from Jerusalem and Romeo from the West Bank, and because they have different ID cards (according to the stipulations of the Oslo Accords of 1993), they would be in perpetual separation from each other.[49] Some other students pointed out that Juliet should be a Christian Palestinian and Romeo a Muslim, or Romeo could be Israeli and Juliet a Palestinian.[50]

Themes, tropes and motifs

What the above section shows is that Shakespeare's *Romeo and Juliet* has been incorporated into Arab and Palestinian cultural capital. Hence, it is unsurprising that Palestinian American novelist Susan Abulhawa draws on themes, tropes and motifs that Shakespeare employs in his love tragedy, including love at first sight, the (negative) impact of families on these love stories, exile/banishment, use of herbs/traditional medicine, humour and parties that practically turn ominous and fateful. To start with, Romeo is immediately attracted to Juliet when he sees her at the party: 'What lady's that which doth enrich the hand / Of yonder knight?' (1.5.41–42).[51] Romeo then sings the praises of Juliet's beauty (1.5.43–52). Juliet responds to Romeo's advances, and the two touch each other's hand and kiss (1.5.92–108). Romeo's words begin a sonnet, divided between the two of them 'in parallel units of almost equal length and almost equal frankness'.[52] Romeo's love at first sight is 'breathtaking' and so is the reaction of Juliet, who welcomes Romeo's move and accepts the kiss with which the sonnet concludes.[53]

Similarly, in Abulhawa's novel, at least two love stories can be described as love at first sight. The first love story/marriage is that of Nazmiyeh and Atiyeh. Fifteen-year-old Atiyeh has just insulted Nazmiyeh's mother. The narrator informs us that 'Nazmiyeh bore into him with a stare ... that he stopped for a moment, more unsure of the world than he had ever been' (18).[54] Atiyeh is startled and 'his ribs pressed down on his heart with embarrassment and, he was sure, with love' (19). The narrator elaborates: 'No one could have perceived that fleeting glance, though it lasted an eternity between the two of them' (19). In the coming months, the two begin to secretly meet and 'communicat[e] only with their eyes' (25). They begin to meet on the first Thursday of every month and they actually 'agreed that it not *sinful to hold hands*, and ... their *hands* created an amorous language that spoke of complicity and promise' (26, emphasis added). One may argue that Abulhawa's choice of words reminds the reader of the party scene where Romeo and Juliet associate holding hands and kisses with sin, which Romeo insists on taking back: '*Sin* from thy lips? O trespass sweetly urged! / Give me my *sin* again' (1.5.92–108, emphasis added). When Atiyeh and Nazmiyeh marry, they, like Romeo and Juliet, have not had 'a wedding celebration' due to the unstable political situation in the country and the recurrent 'atrocities committed by Zionist gangs' (26).

Similarly, love at first sight characterises Nur and Jamal's story. The first time Nur sees Jamal is at a fundraiser for Palestine held in the USA. Although Nur does not recognise Jamal, he catches her eye because he 'create[s] a gravity where he sit[s]. His presence tug[s] at Nur' (165). The narrator describes how Nur feels when she touches Jamal's hand: 'Touching his skin thrilled her, however briefly their hands met. The words were lost and the silence between them grew awkward' (166). In a way, this echoes Romeo and Juliet's love at first sight which, according to Janette Dillon, amounts to 'astounding boldness' since it starts even before they exchange words.[55] When Nur moves to Gaza, she is secretly reunited with her lover in a scene reminiscent of Romeo and Juliet's rendezvous in Juliet's room prior to Romeo's banishment to Mantua. Juliet tries to dissuade Romeo from leaving her by convincing him that the day has not broken yet: 'Wilt thou be gone? it is not yet near day. / It was the nightingale, and not the lark, / That pierced the fearful hollow of thine ear' (3.5.1–3). Just as Romeo and Juliet's lovemaking ends by daylight, in Abulhawa's novel, Nur meets Jamal in darkness and returns home '*barely before the sun*' (221, italics in original). Khaled, who inexplicably knows all, informs the reader that Jamal '*wanted to wake up next to her* [Nur]*, but they never slept and he left while the moon still reigned over a dark sky*' (232, italics in original).

The second theme/trope/motif that the two novels share is the (negative) impact of families on love stories/marriages. In *Romeo and Juliet*, the Capulets and Montagues are embroiled in an 'ancient grudge' (Prologue, 1–4). As the play opens, we hear the citizens of Verona denouncing the two feuding families: 'Down with the Capulets, down with Montagues!' (1.1.72). When Romeo discovers that Juliet is a Capulet, he knows that this relationship is doomed to fail: 'My life is my foe's debt' (1.5.117–118). Similarly, Juliet is distraught to know that Romeo is a Montague (1.5.137–150). She suggests that she and Romeo should renounce their families and acquire new identities: 'Deny thy father and refuse thy name, / Or, if thou wilt not, be but sworn my love, / And I'll no longer be a Capulet' (2.2.33–36). She insists that familial affiliations are pretentious (2.2.38–48). Romeo responds affirmatively to Juliet's plea: 'I take thee at thy word. / Call me but love, and I'll be new baptized. / Henceforth I never will be Romeo' (2.2.49–51). Friar Laurence agrees to marry Romeo and Juliet with the hope that their marriage will result in reconciling the two families (2.4.85–88), but unfortunately his plan fails. When Mercutio is slain by Tybalt, he curses both families: 'A plague a' both houses! I am sped' (3.1.92, 3.1.102 and 3.1.108). Eventually, as David Bevington succinctly puts it, the death of the two lovers 'must pay the price of their families' irrational hatred'.[56]

Abulhawa's novel begins by highlighting the histories of Beit Daras's main families: 'There were five major family clans in Beit Daras, and each had its neighborhood' (11). The Baraka family, the narrator informs us, had arrived from Egypt five centuries earlier and changed their family names 'because they had escaped the wrath of a tribal feud or had perhaps dishonored their families in some way and had had to leave' (11). In Abulhawa's novel, 'the family' also plays a key role in defining love stories/marriages. For instance, Atiyeh 'fight[s] his own family to defend' Nazmiyeh since his parents have never accepted her (52). Moreover, the Nur-Jamal love story is thwarted by family interventions. Comatose Khaled comments on how Alwan views Nur's love affair with Jamal: '*Mama thought Nur selfish, because she hadn't stopped to think of the repercussions her actions could have on the rest of the family. On Rhet Shel. Their home would be dubbed a house of whores*' (222, italics in original). Like Alwan, Nazmiyeh, who becomes Nur's de facto nurse/guardian, draws Nur's attention to the fact that she is dishonouring and disgracing her family by having an affair with Jamal: '"What you do affects your entire family. And protecting the family must come before your individual fancy"' (242). These words affect Nur deeply and she reflects on her position as a girl who 'descended from a family grounded in ancient earth who was accountable to and fortified by the love and loyalty of family' (243). Finally, Jamal's message to Nur reveals that he too is under pressure from his family: '"I am trying to hold on to my family"' (243).

The third theme/trope/motif that the two literary texts share is exile/banishment. In Shakespeare's play, Romeo is banished because he kills Tybalt (3.1.189–198). Juliet is immediately devastated by the news of her lover's banishment (3.2.112, 3.2.124 and 3.2.131–133). Friar Laurence tries to calm Romeo down, arguing that banishment is far better than death (3.3.11). However, Romeo equates banishment with death:

> Hence banished is banished from the world,
> And world's exile is death: then 'banished'
> Is death mistermed: calling death 'banished',
> Thou cutt'st my head off with a golden axe,
> And smilest upon the stroke that murders me. (3.3.19–23)

In Abulhawa's novel, exile/banishment is a central theme/trope/ motif. The Baraka family is forced along with other Palestinians to leave their native village of Beit Daras for Gaza, where they live as refugees. Exile/banishment is more pertinent to Mamdouh and his granddaughter Nur whose lives are shaped and determined by exile and banishment. Abulhawa devotes chapters 19, 20, 21 and

22 to describing the hardships Mamdouh and his granddaughter undergo in exile. Mamdouh tells Nur about Beit Daras and how his family was banished from it (71). At the start of Chapter 25, Khaled highlights how exile/banishment has played a major role in shaping Nur's identity:

> *But with Nur, life hurled her so far that nothing around her resembled anything Palestinian, not even the dislocated lives of exiles. So it was ironic that her life reflected the most basic truth of what it means to be Palestinian, dispossessed, disinherited, and exiled.* (89, italics in original)

Nazmiyeh urges her brother Mamdouh to return to Gaza since '"there is no dignity in life or death away from your home and family"' (118). Her words echo Edward Said's description of exile as 'a condition legislated to deny dignity – to deny an identity to people'.[57] Thus, in both narratives, exile/banishment occupies a central space. However, while in Shakespeare's plays exile/banishment influences only the two lovers, in Abulhawa's novel a whole nation is exiled/banished.

The fourth common theme/trope/motif between the two literary texts is the use of herbs/traditional medicine to solve urgent problems and cure people. In *Romeo and Juliet*, it is Friar Laurence who celebrates the remedial power of herbs. The first time that Friar Laurence appears on the stage, he sings the praises of herbs:

> Within the infant rind of this small flower
> Poison hath residence and medicine power,
> For this, being smelt, with that part cheers each part,
> Being tasted, slays all senses with the heart.
> Two such opposed kings encamp them still
> In man as well as herbs, grace and rude will,
> And where the worser is predominant
> Full soon the canker death eats up that plant. (2.2.19–26)

Al-Dabbagh argues that Friar Laurence's speech is 'a perfect expression of the Sufi idea of the unity of existence and of the seemingly paradoxical co-existence of conflicting elements'.[58] He maintains that this soliloquy epitomises the 'philosophic core' of Shakespeare's play since it depicts the story of a young couple whose love is 'born in the midst of the feuding hatred of their families, and of how only the lovers' death can bring about a new life of peace and unity'.[59] True to his words, Friar Laurence tries to help Juliet by preparing a sleeping potion (5.3.244) from his herbs to avert her marriage to

Paris (4.1.93–101). Unfortunately, his plan collapses, and Juliet eventually commits suicide.

In Abulhawa's novel, the beekeeper's widow is a herb specialist whose role, to some extent, resembles that of Friar Laurence. Once the beekeeper's widow is forced to leave Beit Daras and settle in Gaza as a refugee, she makes the habit of 'making herbal remedies' (47). When Alwan is diagnosed with a malignant tumour, the beekeeper's widow insists that 'Arab medicine' can play a key role in curing her (244). Just like Friar Laurence, she keeps a secret garden to which she sends Nur to pick specific plants (244). Nur is 'stunned to find rows and rows of various plants ... Among the various herbs and vegetables grew marijuana plants' (244–245). Indeed, the beekeeper's wife prepares an infusion for Alwan (245–247). At one point, the beekeeper's widow reveals to Nazmiyeh that the plants from which she makes the medicine are hashish leaves. Yet, she maintains: '"Allah made this plant for all who inhabit His earth. He did not forbid us to use it"' (250). The beekeeper's widow also defends her use of hashish in her remedies when Alwan objects: '"He [Allah] created this stuff just like He created you. And He put it in your life to heal your body"' (254). In the absence of proper medical treatment, Alwan accepts the old widow's formula. In fact, the concoction helps heal Alwan (251). The physician informs Alwan that she '"rarely see[s] tumors shrink to this extent"' (252).

One may argue that the beekeeper's widow uses almost the same discourse that Friar Laurence uses when describing how herbs and weeds can be poisonous and curative. However, one may add that in Abulhawa's novel, Alwan accepts the beekeeper's assistance. In an article titled 'This Brutal Siege of Gaza Can Only Breed Violence', Karen Koning AbuZayed shows how in Gaza 'medication is in short supply, and hospitals are paralyzed by power failures and the shortage of fuel generators'.[60] She asserts that due to the siege, patients are unable to travel outside Gaza for treatment, 'worsening their medical conditions and causing preventable deaths'.[61] When comparing the two 'herb/traditional medicine' episodes in Shakespeare's play and Abulhawa's novel, one may argue that they are not identical; one may even describe the relationship between them as 'shadowy', to use Julie Sanders' words on the interplay between appropriations and their sources.[62] Yet Abulhawa's depiction of how herbs are employed in her text 'carries a physical palimpsest', inviting the reader to make a link between the two texts.[63]

Although the two literary works depict tragic events, a sense of humour permeates the two texts as chatterer mother figures/ nurses repeatedly use sexually-imbued language. Bevington argues that *Romeo and Juliet* 'has the odd distinction of being the funniest of Shakespeare's tragedies'.[64] As Dillon puts it, 'the Nurse has the dominant comic role' in the play.[65] For instance, she uses more than thirty lines to give Juliet's exact age (1.3.17–48). In addition, after listening to Mercutio's bawdy words, the Nurse, on a mission to bring news from Romeo to Juliet, uses the sexual connotation of the word 'ropery' to inquire about Mercutio's identity (2.4.140). She chatters on and uses words with sexual innuendoes:

> An 'a speak anything against me, I'll take him down, an 'a were lustier than he is, and twenty such jacks, and if I cannot, I'll find those that shall. Scurvy knave! I am none of his flirt-gills, I am none of his skains-mates. And thou must stand by too, and suffer every knave to use me at his pleasure? (2.4.144–150)

Moreover, she uses bawdy language when she reports to Juliet that Friar Laurence has agreed to marry her to Romeo and that Romeo will come to her room later that night: "I am the drudge and toil in your delight, / *But you shall bear the burden soon at night* (2.5.69–76, emphasis added). The Nurse insinuates that Juliet will bear the weight of Romeo when they retire to bed later that night.

In Abulhawa's novel, Nazmiyeh, who plays the role of Nur's de facto nurse in Gaza, is the one who frequently uses bawdy language. For instance, when she surveys the young wives on board the bus that is taking them to see their jailed male relatives, she unabashedly comments, '"May Allah curse all the Jews for denying your poor husband the juices of those ripe apples." She picked up her own breasts. "Mine used to stand at attention, too. But my hungry husband and babies sucked them dry"' (113). Addressing her daughter-in-law, she inquires if her son '"know[s] what he's doing in bed? If he doesn't, you shouldn't be afraid to teach him"' (127). Furthermore, mocking Jamal's westernised wife, Maisa, Nazmiyeh sarcastically asks Nur and Alwan: '"Do you think Maisa yells in French and English when el doktor [Jamal] fucks her?"' (189). Nazmiyeh's obscene language gives the novel a sense of hilarity and merriment that lessens the weight of the tragic events. Towards the end of the novel, when Nur travels to Egypt, Nazmiyeh, comically, asks Nur to get her '"some sexy bed clothes. Just in case Allah sends me a husband"' (261).

The final common theme/trope/motif that the two literary texts share is that in both works, parties and celebrations practically turn ominous and fateful. To start with, Romeo accidentally learns about Capulet's party when an illiterate servant asks Romeo to read for him the names of the people invited: 'but I am sent to find those persons whose names are here writ, and can never find what names the writing person hath here writ. I must to the learned' (1.2.40–43). Romeo, disguised, goes to the party, but he is identified by Tybalt who, were it not for Capulet's restraint, would have slit Romeo's throat (1.5.88–91). The next day, Tybalt challenges Romeo to a duel (3.1.65–66) in which Mercutio is killed (3.1.118). Romeo slays Tybalt, who dies immediately (3.1.133). The second party in the play is the one held to celebrate Paris and Juliet's wedding. Juliet, who has taken a sleeping potion prescribed by Friar Laurence, is thought dead (4.5.23–29). Capulet sums up the situation by saying that this celebration has turned into a funeral: 'All things that we ordained festival / Turn from their office to black funeral' (4.5.84–85).

Similarly, in Abulhawa's novel, parties are ominous and portentous. The first party is held on the beach to celebrate Alwan's first birthday. It is at a time of growing militant resistance to the Israeli occupation in which Mazen, Atiyeh and Nazmiyeh's eldest son, is actively involved. During the party, a group of undercover Israeli agents arrest Mazen (61–62). He is due to spend thirty years or more in prison until Hamas successfully exchanges thousands of Palestinian prisoners for the Israeli soldier Gilead Shalit. The second party is held on 27 December 2008 to mark Khaled's tenth birthday, and it is exactly on that date that a fight between Israel and Hamas breaks out (149). The third party, which is held upon an assumed request by long-dead Mariam, resembles in some of its details Capulet's party. Khaled, who is in a coma, scribbles a few words on paper (230). Since Nazmiyeh is illiterate, she recruits a fifth-grade boy to read: '"It says, Mariam would like you to have a party. She ... she, she said she never left and she ... she is in Beit Daras"' (231). Ominously, Khaled dies the next morning (236). People comment: '*"That poor family. It is what happens when someone dares to just have a party for no reason? Can't we just be joyful without punishment following?" said another*' (239, italics in original).

Love and violence in Gaza

Having discussed how Abulhawa appropriates some of the themes/tropes/motifs that Shakespeare employs in *Romeo and Juliet*, I would like now to concentrate on how love stories/marriages in Abulhawa's novel collapse due to wars and conflicts. In the two literary works, love and violence entwine. Shakespeare's play 'begin[s] and end[s] with violence'.[66] Indeed, the two lovers are separated, and they eventually die due to the ongoing conflict between their families. Prince Escalus's policy of zero-tolerance against violence reflects Shakespeare's deep concern with 'the factionalism that had torn England apart during much of the sixteenth century'.[67] In Abulhawa's novel, several love stories/marriages are under duress chiefly because of ongoing wars and conflicts.

The novel represents the repercussions of these violent confrontations through portraying the ups and downs of the Alwan-Abdel Qader love story/marriage. More than the other three love stories/marriages in the novel, the Alwan-Abdel Qader relation reflects the harsh conditions that Palestinian people endure in Gaza. Alwan and Abdel Qader marry for love: 'She wanted to live out a story of seduction and romance that grows from a glance to a gaze to breathless longing, and maybe to a forbidden dance of the hands' (109). Alwan's idea of love recalls Romeo and Juliet's love at first glance. Although Alwan fails to deliver a baby, Abdel Qader remains patient, and his love for his wife increases: '"We get in life only what Allah wills, habibti. Let's just put this in His hands for now," Abdel Qader said' (121). As the siege on Gaza tightens, their marriage undergoes grave and critical tests. Abdel Qader, a fisherman by trade, is deprived of his source of income when his boat is sunk and one of his mates is killed (132). As head of the family, he begins to experience the humiliation of obtaining humanitarian aid from the UN and charities: 'He wanted to walk out of his skin, out of his anger and his impotence. There was no job to go to' (136). Alwan tries to relieve her husband's pain: '"I'm sorry, Abdel Qader. Hit me if you want. I can take it. But please don't turn away from me"' (137). Her words move him; he kisses her forehead and squeezes her close: '"It's not your fault, Alwan. By Allah's will and mercy, we will get through this"' (137).

Abdel Qader feels that he is stripped of his masculinity as he finds himself unemployed. According to Aitemad Muhanna, wars and conflicts in Gaza have 'affected the structural and historical basis of livelihood management based on male domination and patriarchy within households and local community based organizations'.[68] Muhanna explains that this dislocation has been exemplified by men losing their economic capacity as providers for their families, being unable to provide security for their family members and losing their influence in kin and community institutions.[69] In the novel, Abdel Qader has become disgruntled and violent, but Alwan has managed to contain her husband's anger. According to Muhanna, women in Gaza at times of crises feel that they 'are obliged to bear the material and psychological consequences of the crisis of male bread-winners'.[70] They stand beside their jobless husbands during these hard conditions.[71] Muhanna summarises the situation in the following words:

> In the situation of a crisis of masculinity, the reciprocity of exchanges of power is understood by both genders as one in which a woman enhances the sense of masculinity of her man in public, while he provides her with the love and respect to maintain her social status in the family and the wider society.[72]

Thus, while Alwan-Abdel Qader's love story/marriage surpasses the severe conditions brought about by harsh socioeconomic circumstances, it is brought to an end with Abdel Qader's death on the day they were planning to celebrate Khaled's tenth birthday. Abdel Qader is killed, Alwan is widowed and Khaled enters a coma.

Conclusion

In her article on Shakespeare and the ethics of appropriation, Desmet argues that 'in Shakespeare sightings of all kinds, what matters is less what the author intended than how a connection to Shakespeare is recognized'.[73] This article has shown how Palestinian American novelist Susan Abulhawa appropriates in her novel *The Blue between Sky and Water* themes, tropes and motifs that Shakespeare employs in his love tragedy *Romeo and Juliet*, including love at first sight, the (negative) impact of families on love stories, exile/banishment, use of herbs/traditional medicine, humour and parties that practically turn ominous and fateful. In the novel, Abulhawa depicts four Palestinian love stories/marriages that are embroiled in perpetual violence. Yet, while Romeo and Juliet's love story is undercut by an 'ancient grudge' between the two lovers' Veronese families, the love stories/marriages in Abulhawa's novel are destroyed by wars and conflicts.

Abulhawa's appropriation of Shakespeare's play, to use Desmet's words on appropriations, 'operates not simply according to a technical standard of formal fidelity, but also according to the ethical achievement of fealty, an acceptance of responsibility for the bond that binds disparate narratives conceptually and emotionally in the face of their manifest differences'.[74] Desmet centralises the importance of reception over reproduction, and hence she lays the groundwork for the reader to link seemingly disparate texts. Drawing on Desmet's paradigm, one may argue that appropriations are creative and inventive pieces that instigate careful examinations of connections between texts that are separated temporally and spatially. Seen from this perspective, Abulhawa's *The Blue between Sky and Water* can be viewed as an appropriation of Shakespeare's *Romeo and Juliet* since the two literary works share similar themes, tropes and motifs and depict love stories/marriages akin to that of Shakespeare's 'star-cross'd lovers', which end tragically due to ongoing violence.

Yousef Abu Amrieh is a Professor at the University of Jordan. His first monograph, *The Arab Atlantic: Resistance, Diaspora, and Transcultural Dialogue in the Works of Arab British and Arab American Women Writers* (Lambert Academic Publishing, 2012), is based on his 2011 PhD thesis at the University of Manchester. Since then, he has published a number of articles exploring such themes as cultural translation, identity and multiculturalism in the works of Arab writers in diaspora.

Notes

This article was written during a sabbatical leave granted by the University of Jordan to the researcher.

1. Naomi Conn Liebler, '"There is no world without Verona walls": The City in *Romeo and Juliet*', in *A Companion to Shakespeare's Works: The Tragedies*, vol. 1, ed. Richard Dutton and Jean E. Howard (Malden, MA: Blackwell Publishing, 2003), 303–318, here 306.
2. René Weis, 'Introduction', in *Romeo and Juliet*, The Arden Shakespeare (London: Bloomsbury, 2012), 1–116, here 1–2.
3. Ibid., 52.
4. Julie Sanders, *Adaptation and Appropriation* (London: Routledge, 2006), 2.
5. Ibid., 26.
6. Ibid., 98.

7. Jonathan Culler, 'Presupposition and Intertextuality', *Comparative Literature* 91, no. 6 (1976), 1380–1396, here 1383.
8. Ibid., 1383.
9. Ibid., 1387.
10. Christy Desmet, 'Recognizing Shakespeare, Rethinking Fidelity: A Rhetoric and Ethics of Appropriation', in *Shakespeare and the Ethics of Appropriation*, ed. Alexa Huang and Elizabeth Rivlin (New York: Palgrave, 2014), 41–57, here 42.
11. Ibid., 43.
12. Ibid., 55.
13. Ibid., 55.
14. Douglas Lanier, 'Shakespearean Rhizomatics: Adaptations, Ethics, Value', in Huang and Rivlin, *Shakespeare and the Ethics of Appropriation*, 21–40, here 29.
15. Ibid., 31.
16. Yousef Awad, *The Arab Atlantic: Resistance, Diaspora, and Trans-cultural Dialogue in the Works of Arab British and Arab American Women Writers* (Saarbrücken: LAP Lambert Academic Publishing, 2012), 12.
17. Ibid., 12.
18. Yousef Awad, 'Bringing Lebanon's Civil War Home to Anglophone Literature: Alameddine's Appropriation of Shakespeare's Tragedies', *Critical Survey* 28, no. 3 (2016), 86–101, here 87, https://doi.org/10.3167/cs.2016.280306.
19. Yousef Awad and Mahmoud F. Al-Shetawi, 'Jamal Mahjoub's *The Carrier* as a Re-writing of Shakespeare's *Othello*', *International Journal of Applied Linguistics and English Literature* 6, no. 5 (2017), 173–181, here 174, http://dx.doi.org/10.7575/aiac.ijalel.v.6n.5p.173.
20. Yousef Awad and Barkuzar Dubbati, 'Hamlet's Road from Damascus: Potent Fathers, Slain Ghosts and Rejuvenated Sons', *Borrowers and Lenders: The Journal of Shakespeare and Appropriation* 11, no. 2 (2018), 1–20, here 1.
21. Awad, *The Arab Atlantic*, 41.
22. Geoffrey Nash, 'Arab Voices in Western Writing: The Politics of the Arabic Novel in English and the Anglophone Arab Novel', *Commonwealth Essays and Studies* 39, no. 2 (2017), 27–38, here 36.
23. Ibid., 36.
24. Claire Gallien, 'Anglo-Arab Literatures: Enmeshing Forms, Subverting Assignation, Minorizing Language', *Commonwealth Essays and Studies* 39, no. 2 (2017), 5–10, here 8.
25. Ibid., 10.
26. Mark Bayer, '*The Martyrs of Love* and the Emergence of the Arab Cultural Consumer', *Critical Survey* 19 (2007), 6–26, here 6, https://doi.org/10.3167/cs.2007.190302.
27. Ibid., 7.
28. Ibid., 11.
29. Ibid., 22.
30. Abdulla Al-Dabbagh, 'The Oriental Framework of *Romeo and Juliet*', *The Comparatist* 24 (2000), 64–82, here 73, https://doi.org/10.1353/com.2000.0014.
31. Ibid., 77.
32. Yvette K. Khoury, '*Akhir Yom (The Last Day)*: A Localized Arabic Adaptation of Shakespeare's *Romeo and Juliet*', *Theatre Research International* 33 (2008), 52–69, here 54, https://doi.org/10.1017/S0307883307003392.

33. Ibid., 57.
34. Margaret Litvin, Saffron Walkling and Raphael Cormack, 'Full of Noises: When "World Shakespeare" Met the "Arab Spring"', *Shakespeare* (2015), 1–12, here 2, https://doi.org/10.1080/17450918.2015.1066842.
35. Ibid., 5.
36. Ibid., 5.
37. Ibid., 6.
38. Ibid., 6.
39. Saud Abu Ramadan, 'Feature: Gazan "Romeo and Juliet" Reflects Palestinian Political Deadlock', *New China*, 28 April 2016, http://www.xinhuanet.com/english/2016-04/28/c_135321161.htm.
40. Sahar Kayyal, 'Shakespeare in the Gaza Strip', in *Dinarzad's Children: An Anthology of Contemporary Arab American Fiction*, ed. Pauline Kaldas and Khaled Mattawa (Fayetteville: University of Arkansas Press, 2004), 197–206, here 202–203.
41. Ibid., 204.
42. Yael Munk, '"Dreamers Often Lie": On "Compromise", the Subversive Documentation of an Israeli-Palestinian Political Adaptation of Shakespeare's *Romeo and Juliet*', *Altre Modernità: Rivista di studi letterari e culturali* 3 (2010), 174–181, here 176.
43. Ibid., 177.
44. Ibid., 180–181.
45. Monica Brady, 'From Verona to Ramallah: Living in a State of Emergency', *Changing English* 22, no. 4 (2015), 365–377, here 365, https://doi.org/10.1080/1358684X.2015.1109832.
46. Ibid., 370.
47. Tom Sperlinger, *Romeo and Juliet in Palestine: Teaching under Occupation* (Winchester, UK: Zero Books, 2015), 2.
48. Ibid., 2.
49. Ibid., 2.
50. Ibid., 2–3.
51. Line references come from the following edition of Shakespeare's play: *Romeo and Juliet*, The Arden Shakespeare, 3rd series, ed. René Weis (London: Bloomsbury, 2012).
52. Janette Dillon, *The Cambridge Introduction to Shakespeare's Tragedies* (Cambridge: Cambridge University Press, 2007), 49.
53. Ibid., 49.
54. Page references from Abulhawa's novel are given in parentheses in the text, and refer to the following edition: *The Blue between Sky and Water* (London: Bloomsbury Library, 2015).
55. Dillon, *The Cambridge Introduction*, 49.
56. David Bevington, *How to Read a Shakespeare Play* (Malden, MA: Blackwell Publishing, 2006), 53.
57. Edward W. Said, *Reflections on Exile and Other Literary and Cultural Essays* (London: Granta Books, 2000), 175.
58. Al-Dabbagh, 'The Oriental Framework of *Romeo and Juliet*', 73.
59. Ibid., 74.

60. Karen Koning AbuZayed, 'This Brutal Siege of Gaza Can Only Breed Violence', in *On Palestine*, ed. Noam Chomsky and Ilan Pappé (London: Penguin, 2015), 47–49, here 48.
61. Ibid., 48.
62. Sanders, 32.
63. Anston Bosman, 'Shakespeare and Globalization', in *The New Cambridge Companion to Shakespeare*, ed. Margreta de Grazia and Stanley Wells (Cambridge: Cambridge University Press, 2010), 285–301, here 295.
64. Bevington, *How to Read a Shakespeare Play*, 37.
65. Dillon, *The Cambridge Introduction*, 45.
66. Bevington, *How to Read a Shakespeare Play*, 50.
67. Ibid., 40.
68. Aitemad Muhanna, *Agency and Gender in Gaza: Masculinity, Femininity and Family during the Second Intifada* (London: Routledge, 2013), 165.
69. Ibid., 165.
70. Ibid., 166.
71. Ibid.
72. Ibid., 173.
73. Desmet, 'Recognizing Shakespeare, Rethinking Fidelity', 55.
74. Ibid., 55.

Index

#MeToo, 45, 106, 112, 114

abjection, 12, 25
adaptation, 6, 20–22, 24, 26, 40–41, 48, 53, 55, 58–59, 61, 66, 68–71, 74–75, 77–80, 87, 89, 91, 96, 98, 117, 162–163, 174–176
affective communities, 98
ambiguity, 5, 125, 129
anime, 74
apocalyptic, v, 3, 6–17, 19, 21–25, 63
appropriation, vi, 21, 24, 28, 40–41, 98–99, 121, 156–157, 159–161, 163, 165, 167, 169, 171, 173–175, 177
autobiography, 123
authenticity, 20–21

biography, ii, 59, 66, 72–73, 105–106

canon, v, 29, 68–71, 73, 75, 77, 79, 81, 83, 85, 115
canonical, 89, 114, 159, 161
chick lit., 108
circulation, 6, 9, 23, 77
civilization, 11–13, 25, 64, 152
classics, 28
classification, 60, 65, 92

comedy, 4, 44, 47, 56, 77–78, 92, 97, 102, 117
communities, 3–4, 9, 88, 98–99
creative, ii, 2, 21, 70, 80, 115, 117–118, 174
critical, iv, 3, 6, 20–22, 25, 41, 44–45, 47, 70, 91, 101–102, 121–122, 134, 136–138, 150, 172, 175
cultural capital, 4, 6, 9, 24, 68–69, 74, 81–82, 164

deconstruction, 114
derivative genre, 2, 58, 59, 61
derivatives, 58, 61
displacement, vi, 5, 137–143, 145, 147, 149, 151–153, 155, 159
disruption, 25, 126–127, 132
dissemination, 87
domestic abuse, 45–47
domination, 46, 172

empathy, 54, 88, 95–96, 98
eschatology, 8, 24

fandom, 99, 103
fantasy, 2–3, 72, 96, 105, 108, 114–117
feminist, 30, 45, 47, 89, 93, 95, 102, 104–105, 111, 115–116

fiction, 1–4, 7, 10, 14–15, 24–25, 34–35, 42, 47, 56, 59–61, 66, 69–77, 79–83, 86–88, 91–93, 96, 98–99, 101–102, 108–116, 118–119, 123, 133–134, 150, 155, 176
  crime fiction, 2, 79
  detective fiction, 71–72
  dystopian fiction, 3, 7, 13
  gothic fiction, 2
  horror fiction, 59, 71–72
  mystery fiction, 60, 72, 111,
  science fiction, 10, 15, 24, 70, 72
  supernatural fiction, 1, 3
  utopian fiction, 2
futuristic, 7, 79

gender, 31, 36, 40, 45, 47–50, 52, 55, 77, 87, 90–92, 96, 100–101, 113, 177
  gender politics, 31, 45, 47–48, 50, 55, 87, 96, 100
genre, 4, 29, 59–60, 62–63, 69, 71–73, 77–81, 88, 92, 112
girlhood studies, 48
graphic novel, 14, 59, 66

highbrow, 1, 91
historical fiction, 2, 72, 77, 108–109, 111–112, 114, 118–119
history, 2, 4, 8, 29, 31–32, 46, 49, 58, 66, 75, 87, 98, 100, 104–105, 108, 110, 114–120, 134–135, 153, 156
homoeroticism, 77
humanity, 11–12

identity, 4, 12, 31, 50, 53, 91, 118, 134, 149, 158, 168, 170, 174
ideology, 36, 46, 121
imagination, 25, 33, 39, 110, 113
incest, 31

legitimacy, 5, 122, 124, 126–131, 133
literariness, 48, 56, 69, 81–82, 102

literary transition, 121

masculinity, 37, 54–55, 96, 122, 172–173, 177
materiality, 122–123
metafiction, 2
middlebrow, 4, 88, 91–93, 96–99, 101–102
millennial, vi, 4, 47, 56, 82, 102, 104–105, 107–109, 111, 113, 115, 117–119
misogyny, v, 3, 44–49, 51, 53, 55, 57, 93, 109, 133
modernization, 44
Modernity, 2, 12, 29
Multicultural, 107

narrative, 1–2, 7, 17, 31, 39, 42, 47–48, 55–56, 59, 61, 64, 70–72, 74, 77–78, 80–81, 88, 90, 93, 101, 110, 114, 134
neurosis, 5, 138–142, 152–153
novel, i–iii, v, 1–5, 10–20, 22–23, 25, 28–29, 31, 33, 36, 41, 43–45, 48, 50–52, 54–55, 59–64, 66, 68–69, 71, 73–77, 79–80, 82–84, 88, 90–102, 105–107, 109–113, 117–120, 122–123, 129, 131–135, 145, 148–150, 152–153, 157–159, 161, 165–173, 175–176
novella, 2, 145–146

oppression, 46, 50, 54

patriarchy, 45, 56–57, 94, 102, 115, 119
performance, 10, 13, 17, 20, 26, 40, 48, 51–52, 57, 59, 76, 82
politics, 31–32, 45, 47–48, 50, 55, 87, 91, 96, 100, 119, 135, 161, 175
popular culture, 6, 15, 23, 68, 78, 82
pornography, 41

post-apocalyptic, v, 3, 6–11, 13–17, 19, 21, 23–25, 63
post-feminist, 45
post-millennial, 107–108
postmodern, 2, 139
progressive, 35, 47, 105
psychoanalysis, 29, 31, 137–140, 154

readership, 2, 80, 87, 92, 98, 102, 110, 113, 118
realism, 1, 79, 97, 133
reception, 20, 40, 52, 87, 91, 95, 118, 160, 174
recontextualization, 60
resistance, 48, 90, 102, 171, 174–175
rewriting, 3, 28–29, 33, 39, 46, 56, 82, 89
rhizomatics, 6, 20–21, 24, 26, 175
romance, 1–4, 50, 55, 62, 73, 77, 83, 108, 110, 112–113, 119–120, 172

sexism, 44, 46–47
sexual abuse, 34
sexual violence, 35, 131
space, vi, 3, 5, 14, 29, 54, 72, 95–96, 121–125, 127, 129–133, 135–136, 155, 160, 168

space-time, vi, 121, 123, 125, 127, 129, 131, 133, 135
subordination, 45–46, 56–57
survival, 3, 10–11, 13–19, 24–25, 63–64, 86, 98–99

text, 6, 13, 21–24, 26, 30, 39, 61, 91, 98, 100, 102, 118, 137–138, 159–160, 163, 169, 176
time, vi, 2, 5, 7–8, 13, 15, 19–20, 22–24, 27, 30–31, 33–35, 38, 41–42, 47, 50–51, 54–55, 61, 63–65, 69–72, 75, 80, 82, 89–90, 95, 97, 100, 104, 106, 109–111, 115–116, 121–136, 145–148, 150–151, 153, 156, 158, 163–165, 168, 171
tragedy, 4–5, 74, 128, 158, 161, 164, 173
tragicomedy, 4, 62
trauma, 8–9, 11–12, 15–16, 23, 133, 149–150, 155

women readers, 106, 109, 111–113

Young Adult fiction, 83

www.ingramcontent.com/pod-product-compliance
Lightning Source LLC
Chambersburg PA
CBHW071345080526
44587CB00017B/2970